PENGUIN REFERENCE BOOKS

The Penguin Dictionary of Geography

W. G. Moore was educated at Burton-on-Trent Grammar School, where a film review brought him his first pen-money, and later took his B.Sc. at London University. He has spent most of his working life teaching, tutoring, lecturing, and writing, and has contributed to a variety of journals, from daily newspapers to quarterly reviews. In 1938 he published *The Geography of Capitalism* and then wrote the geographical section of Odhams' *Complete Self-Educator*. At the start of the Second World War he was commissioned in the meteorological branch of the RAF, spent some years in Iraq, Persia, and the Middle East, organized the meteorological service for Persia, and completed his RAF career by lecturing on Meteorology and Climatology. He has since written, in addition to this volume, *The Penguin Encyclopedia of Places*, and *The World's Wealth* which the *Economist* described as 'a brilliantly carried out survey of the resources – animal, vegetable and mineral – from which man gets his living', *The Soil We Live On*, and a number of series of books including *Essential Geography*, *Adventures in Geography*, *New Visual Geography* and *Man and His World*, and contributed to the Larousse *Géographie Universelle* (English edition). He has also edited a large number of geographical filmstrips.

D1461210

W. G. MOORE

THE PENGUIN DICTIONARY OF

GEOGRAPHY

SEVENTH EDITION

DEFINITIONS AND
EXPLANATIONS OF TERMS
USED IN
PHYSICAL GEOGRAPHY

PENGUIN BOOKS

PENGUIN BOOKS

Published by the Penguin Group
27 Wrights Lane, London W8 5TZ, England
Viking Penguin Inc., 40 West 23rd Street, New York, New York 10010, USA
Penguin Books Australia Ltd, Ringwood, Victoria, Australia
Penguin Books Canada Ltd, 2801 John Street, Markham, Ontario, Canada L3R 1B4
Penguin Books (NZ) Ltd, 182–190 Wairau Road, Auckland 10, New Zealand

Penguin Books Ltd, Registered Offices: Harmondsworth, Middlesex, England

Published in Penguin Books 1949
Second edition 1952
Reprinted with revisions 1958
Reprinted with revisions 1962
Third edition 1963
Fourth edition 1968
Reprinted with revisions 1973, 1974
Fifth edition 1974
Sixth edition 1981
Seventh edition 1988

Printed and bound in Great Britain by
Richard Clay Ltd, Bungay, Suffolk
Filmset in Monophoto Times

ACKNOWLEDGEMENTS

The author's thanks are due to the following for the use of photographs:

Agent General for Queensland, for Plate 5.
British Airways, for Plate 28.
Canadian Pacific Railway, for Plates 19 and 21.
J. Allan Cash, for Plates 7, 13, 29 and 30.
Cox's Cave, Cheddar, for Plate 17.
French National Tourist Office, for Plates 12 and 32.
High Commissioner for New Zealand, for Plates 27 and 31.
K PM Line, for Plate 18.
Mats Wibe Lund, Reykjavik, for Plate 8.
Werner Lüthy, for Plate 16.
Netherlands and N I Information Bureau, for Plate 20.
Royal Norwegian Embassy, London, for Plate 10.
Shell Photographic Service, for Plates 24 and 25.
State Highway Commission, Oregon, USA, for Plate 2.
State Highway Commission, South Dakota, USA, for Plate 1.
Swiss National Tourist Office, for Plates 4, 11 and 23.
Trans World Airlines, for Plate 9.
United States Information Service, London, for Plates 3, 6, 14, 15, 22 and 26.

AUTHOR'S NOTE

When this book was started, it was intended to embrace the entire field of Geography, but very soon it became evident that such a volume could not be compressed within the covers of a Penguin without making some of the definitions and descriptions so brief as to be virtually useless. It was thought preferable, therefore, to limit the volume, broadly speaking, to Physical Geography, including, of course, a generous sprinkling of Climatological and Meteorological terms, and a number of unclassified terms which might conceivably be met during a study of Physical Geography.

For the student who consults the book purely as a dictionary, the individual definitions and descriptions should prove adequate. There may be readers, however, who are interested enough in a particular branch of the subject to seek more information than is included in a single item. For them, the headings which are suggested for further reading are indicated in the text by the use of *italics*. A reference to **abyssal deposits**, for example, would suggest for further reading the items on *abyssal* and *oozes*.

The asterisk inserted after certain headwords indicates that a relevant illustration appears in the plates.

A

aa. The Hawaiian term, pronounced ah-ah, which is sometimes used for *block lava*.

ablation. The process of carrying away or removing, now generally restricted to the loss of ice by a glacier, mainly by surface melting and evaporation and the *calving* of icebergs.

aborigines. The people who are believed to have been the original inhabitants of a region, i.e. those who were found living in the region when it was first discovered by Europeans. The term is often applied especially to Australian aborigines, who are known colloquially as 'abos'.

abrasion. The wearing away of part of the earth's surface by the action of wind, water, or ice, utilizing moving debris, e.g. sand, as an abrasive material.

absolute drought. In the British Isles, a period of at least fifteen consecutive days, none of which has received as much as 0.2 mm of rain; the definition has not been internationally accepted. See *drought*.

absolute humidity. The amount of water vapour present in unit volume of air, usually expressed in grams per cubic metre; the term is sometimes wrongly applied to the pressure of the water vapour in the air. See *humidity*, *relative humidity*.

absolute or **Kelvin scale.** The temperature scale named after Lord Kelvin (1824–1907) and based on his work on thermodynamics. The lower 'fixed point' is approximately equivalent to $-273°$ on the *Celsius scale*. To convert a temperature on the *Celsius scale* to one on the absolute or Kelvin scale, 273 must be added to the former: $K = C + 273$. An advantage is that temperature readings are positive even at the extremely low values reached in the upper *atmosphere*.

abyssal. The term usually means 'belonging to the lowest depths of the *oceans*'. It is assumed that in general the abyssal region has a depth greater than about 4,000 m – but its limits cannot be thus defined with precision. As sunlight does not penetrate to these depths, there is no plant life. There are, however, species of animal life, whose nature varies with the depth owing to differences in temperature and in supplies of food and oxygen. Much of their food consists of organic matter which sinks from the waters above. Conditions on the ocean floor at these great depths are extremely uniform – perpetually dark, cold, and covered with a barren expanse of ooze or clay, principally *red clay*. See *deep*, *deep-sea plain*.

abyssal deposits. The solid matter which covers the floor of the *abyssal* region of the oceans. See *oozes*.

abyssal plain. See *deep-sea plain*.

abyssal rocks. See *plutonic rocks*.

accumulated temperature. The sum over a certain period, e.g. a month, of the products of time (in days) and the excess of the mean daily temperature (in degrees) above a given value, measured in day-degrees, affording a useful measure of the effectiveness of temperature in promoting plant growth. In Britain 42°F (5.5°C) is usually taken as the basic temperature, all temperatures above this value being considered favourable to plant growth in a European climate.

accumulation, mountain of. A term, now little used, for a mountain formed by the collection of material on the earth's surface, the best-known example being that of a volcano, or a mountain produced by the ejection of material from a volcano. Mountains of accumulation are frequently of great height and symmetrical in shape, and tend to occur as isolated peaks.

acid lava. See *lava*.

acid rain. Rain which has been acidified during its descent from the clouds by picking up pollutants from the atmosphere. Probably the most noxious pollutants are oxides of sulphur and nitrogen, which in water form acids; they are emitted in quantity from power stations, vehicle exhausts, etc. These pollutants are spread by the prevailing winds, and thus have caused considerable damage to the environment, especially on the lee side of their sources.

In NE Canada, for instance, many lakes and rivers have suffered loss of fish and vegetation and restriction of the growth of timber, attributed to acid rain coming from industrial plants discharging into the atmosphere to the south, in the USA, including the Tennessee Valley area. In Europe, the Scandinavian countries, particularly Norway and Sweden, have been the principal victims. Here the damage to the forests has been widespread and is of concern to the valuable industries which draw their raw materials therefrom: Britain, to the south-west, is blamed for allowing pollutants from its power stations and vehicles to destroy Scandinavian forest and lake resources, while Poland and East Germany are also regarded as culprits. In southern Poland lime was distributed from aircraft to neutralize the acid rain in the soil – a practice that was also followed over the lakes of New York State, USA. Elsewhere in Europe, large numbers of trees, for example in the Black Forest, West Germany, have succumbed to the attacks of acid rain, and the effects have been felt as far north as the Arctic regions. According to Sweden, Britain is responsible for over 15 per cent of the pollutants derived from sulphur and nitrogen.

adiabatic. A term applied to the changes taking place in the pressure and temperature of a gas, e.g. air, when heat is neither added to nor taken from it. See *lapse rate*.

adit. A passage driven horizontally, or approximately so, into a hill slope in order to extract a mineral, such as coal, or possibly to effect drainage. See also *drift mining*.

adobe (Spanish). A clay or loess deposit, probably wind-blown, found in the arid parts of the S W United States and Mexico; originally applied to the sun-dried bricks into which the material is made.

adret (French). A mountain slope which faces more or less equatorwards, and, being largely exposed to the sun's rays, receives considerable light and warmth during the day. The term is principally used of the Alps. The equivalent Italian term is adretto, the German Sonnenseite. See *ubac*.

adretto (Italian). See *adret*.

advection. Transmission by horizontal movement: usually applied to the transfer of heat by horizontal movement of the air – in distinction from *convection*, in which the movement is vertical. The most familiar example is the transfer of heat by the movement of tropical air from low to high latitudes.

advection fog. A *fog* which is formed when air moves horizontally over a cool surface and is thereby cooled below the *dew point*. It may occur over land or sea. In Britain it is often caused by warm moist air, e.g. in a *warm sector*, moving over the land after a cold spell. The frequent advection fogs of the Grand Banks off Newfoundland are formed when warm moist air over the Gulf Stream, moving northwards, passes over the cold Labrador current.

aeolian. Relating to, or caused by, the wind. Aeolian deposits are materials which have been transported and laid down on the earth's surface by the wind, and include *loess*, and the sand of deserts and dunes.

aerography. The subject which seeks to describe the properties, dimensions etc., of the atmosphere: now rarely used.

aerology. The science which treats of the atmosphere.

affluent. A *tributary*; a stream flowing into a larger stream.

afforestation. The process of transforming an area into forest, usually when trees have not previously grown there. See *reforestation*.

African tornado. See *tornado* (1).

after-glow. The radiance or glow occasionally seen in the sky in mountainous regions after sunset, commencing when the sun is about 3° or 4° below the horizon.

agglomerate. A mass of coarse rock fragments or blocks of *lava* produced by volcanic eruptions. Usually the fragments are angular, and the agglomerate differs from a *volcanic ash* by reason of their greater size. See *breccia*, *conglomerate*.

aggradation. A process which tends to build up the land surface by deposition of solid material in its lower areas; the term is usually applied to a river, in which case it involves the laying down of sediment on the river bed. When, along a certain stretch, the river is unable to carry all its solid loose material, for instance, the surplus is deposited at the head of the stretch, and so increases the slope of the bed. See *degradation*.

agonic line. A line on a map joining places of zero magnetic declination, i.e. places where the magnetic compass points true north as well as magnetic north. In general, declination increases with increasing distance from the agonic line. See *declination, magnetic*.

agriculture. The practice of cultivating the soil in order to produce crops. In its most primitive form, as, for instance, in tropical regions like the Amazon valley and Central Africa, it simply consists in setting the plants in forest clearings; in its more advanced form, however, it demands great knowledge and skill. The type of agriculture practised in a region depends to a great extent on climatic factors, such as rainfall and temperatures, and on the kind of soil. The term is sometimes loosely used to include *pastoral farming* as well as the cultivation of crops.

agronomy. The branch of agriculture which deals with the scientific cultivation of crops, including such problems as the yield, control of diseases, development of special varieties, etc., and also soil management – conservation, fertility, etc.

aiguille (French). A sharply pointed rock pinnacle, or 'needle-like' *peak*, especially in the Alps: e.g. the Aiguille du Midi, in the Mont Blanc massif.

air gap. See *wind gap*.

air mass. A mass of air more or less homogeneous in character, covering a considerable area of the earth's surface, and bounded by frontal surfaces (see *front*). Air masses are usually classified according to the regions where they originated, e.g. tropical or polar, and according to whether they are of maritime or continental type. An air mass may thus be classified, for example, as tropical maritime, or polar continental.

airport. An aerodrome situated on a recognized air route.

Aitoff's projection. An equal-area or *homolographic projection*, in which the whole of the earth's surface is represented on an ellipse. Land masses near to the centre of the map have a fairly accurate shape, but those near to the eastern and western margins are badly distorted; it is superior to *Mollweide's projection*, which it resembles, however, in that the angles of intersection of the meridians and parallels are not so greatly altered towards the margins.

albedo. The proportion of solar radiation falling on a non-luminous body which the latter reflects, usually expressed as a decimal. The albedo of the earth is approximately 0.4, i.e. about 40 per cent of the solar radiation is reflected back into space; the value is much higher, of course, for a snow-covered surface, lower for dark soil, etc.

alidade. A simple sight-rule used in surveying with the *plane table* for observing distant objects and taking angular measurements; also the more elaborate instrument equipped with a telescope and used for the same purpose.

alkali flat. An alkaline, level area in an arid region into which one or more desert streams may lead. In the dry season, after evaporation of water, it becomes a barren area of hard mud covered with alkaline salts; after heavy rainfall it becomes a shallow, muddy lake. See *playa*.

alluvial cone. An *alluvial fan* in which the deposit is deep and its surface is steeply inclined, owing to the rapid sinking and evaporation of the water of the stream and the consequent dropping of the entire load.

alluvial fan. The deposit of sediment laid down by a swift-flowing stream as it enters a plain or an open valley, so called on account of its shape. It is in dry regions that the alluvial fan is commonest, for there the alternate drying up and flooding of the mountain streams favour its formation. The alluvial fan sometimes grows till it is many km (miles) across, and several fans made by neighbouring streams often unite to form a continuous plain, known as a *piedmont alluvial plain*; under these conditions the depth of alluvial material may be hundreds of metres. Much of the water of a stream is absorbed by the loose material of its fan, and the soil formed by the fan is often of great agricultural value. Some geographers regard *alluvial fan* and *alluvial cone* as being synonymous.

alluvial plain. A level tract bordering a river on which *alluvium* is deposited; it may be situated on a *flood-plain*, on a *delta*, or on an *alluvial fan*.

alluvium. The surplus rock material consisting mainly of sand and silt, which a river has carried in suspension, and which it has been forced to deposit. Some of the most fertile land in the world consists of alluvium deposited in the valleys and deltas of the great rivers.

Alpine. Belonging to the Alps, or, alternatively, to the higher regions of a mountain system: applied in reference to the typical climate, relief (glacial features), flora, etc., of the regions (e.g. the Alpine climate). See *mountain climate*.

Alps.* Term applied, chiefly in the European mountain system known as the Alps, to the Alpine pastures of relatively gentle slope which lie above a U-shaped valley and are often used in summer for grazing livestock. See *transhumance*.

altimeter. A type of aneroid *barometer*, used principally in aircraft, which is graduated to show the approximate height above the ground or above mean sea level, instead of the atmospheric pressure.

altiplano. In the Andes of S. America a region of elevated plateaux or intermont basins between the Western and Eastern Cordilleras at an altitude of about 3,500 m, mainly in W Bolivia but extending N into Peru and S into Argentina. It contains Lakes Titicaca and Poopó. Climate, vegetation, and economy are those of the *puna*.

altitude. (1) Vertical distance above *mean sea level*, usually measured in feet or metres.

(2) Angular distance above the horizon measured in a vertical plane, e.g. of a heavenly body.

altocumulus. A type of medium *cloud* which in general consists of a mass of small, relatively thin, globular patches, sometimes so close together that their edges join.

altocumulus castellanus. A variety of *altocumulus* cloud, in which many of the cloudlets have developed turreted tops. It indicates upper air instability and thundery conditions.

altostratus. A type of medium *cloud* in the form of a continuous sheet or veil, which is sometimes thin, sometimes so thick as completely to obscure the sun or moon. Normally the sun or moon shines through it indistinctly, with a gleam. It resembles thick *cirrostratus* cloud, but does not give a halo with sun or moon. Being often associated with the approach of a *depression*, it usually presages a period of rain.

anabatic wind. A local wind caused by the flow of air during the day up valleys and mountain slopes; the slopes become heated by the sun, the air above rises in a *convection* current, and the air of the anabatic wind moves in to take its place. An anabatic wind thus often alternates with the night-time *katabatic wind*. See *valley wind*.

anemogram. The continuous record of wind speed and often also of direction made by an *anemograph*; both traces show rapid fluctuations caused by eddies due to obstacles in the path of the wind at the surface.

anemograph. A self-recording *anemometer* which gives a continuous trace of the speed and often also the direction of the surface wind. One of the best-known types is the Dines tube anemograph, in which the wind pressure acts upon the opening of a tube which is arranged as a vane always to face the wind; the pressure is transmitted via the tube to a float carrying a pen, and the height of the latter above the zero position of the *anemogram* – which is fixed to a rotating drum – indicates the wind speed.

anemometer. An instrument by which the velocity and often also the direction of the wind is measured, usually in miles per hour or metres per second. The commonest type is that in which a system of cups is employed. One type, for instance, shows the rate of rotation of the cups, so that the wind velocity can be obtained, by means of a speed indicator. A very open exposure is required, in order to reduce the effects of eddies and gusts.

aneroid barometer. See *barometer*.

aneroidograph. A self-recording aneroid *barometer*. See *barograph*.

annular eclipse. See *eclipse, solar.*

anomaly. A departure from the normal in an element or feature. See *gravity anomaly, temperature anomaly.*

Antarctic Circle. The parallel or line of latitude at 66° 32′ S, commonly assumed to be 66° 30′ S. Owing to the inclination of the earth's *axis*, the sun does not set here on one day of the year, about 22 December, the southern midsummer; similarly, the sun does not rise about 21 June, the southern midwinter. Within the Antarctic Circle, the number of such days increases with nearness to the Pole. At any particular time of the year, conditions are the converse of those at the *Arctic Circle.*

antecedent drainage. A river system in which the original direction of flow has been maintained across land where uplift has taken place. See *antecedent river.*

antecedent river. A river which has cut through land that has risen in its path, and so has maintained its course: so called because it is antecedent to the present topography. One of the best-known examples is afforded by the Colorado R, USA, in its creation of the Grand Canyon.

anthracite. The hard, shiny black coal which is the coal of highest rank, i.e. containing the lowest proportion of water and volatile matter and the highest fixed carbon content; it is usually considered to represent the final product in the transformation of vegetable matter through *peat, lignite,* and *bituminous coal.*

anthropogeography. The study of the distribution of human communities on the earth in relation to their geographical environment; it thus bears the same relation to Anthropology as *biogeography* does to Biology, and as *zoogeography* does to Zoology, etc. Some geographers assume it to be synonymous with Human Geography.

anticline. The arch or crest of a *fold* in rock strata. See *syncline.*

anticlinorium. A huge arch, in form resembling an *anticline,* each limb of which consists of a number of small *folds.*

anticyclone. A region in which the atmospheric pressure is high compared with that of adjacent areas, and which shows at least one closed *isobar*; generally there is a series of concentric closed isobars, approximately circular or oval in shape, the highest pressure being at the centre. In the northern hemisphere the general wind circulation is clockwise round the anticyclone, in the southern hemisphere anti-clockwise. Near the centre the winds are usually light and variable, often calm, but increase in strength somewhat towards the edge of the anticyclone.

In the temporary anticyclones of temperate latitudes, quiet, settled weather conditions are characteristic, in contrast to the weather of *depressions* or cyclones; in summer, skies are often cloudless, and temperatures relatively high, but in winter there is so much radiation

7

Arrangement of isobars and surface winds in an anticyclone (N Hemisphere).

that the lower layers of air become excessively cooled, and often fog also results. Such anticyclonic conditions may persist for a considerable period, for anticyclones move very slowly, and often remain almost stationary for several days.

In addition to these temporary anticyclones, there are two great belts of permanent anticyclones, situated mainly over the oceans at about 30° N and 30° S, which move slightly northwards and southwards and also extend and diminish, with the seasons. See *horse latitudes*. Seasonal anticyclones form, too, over the great land masses in winter, the most noteworthy example being the Siberian anticyclone.

antipodes. Two places situated on opposite sides of the earth, so that a straight line drawn through the earth from one to the other passes through the centre. London, England, and Antipodes Island, southeast of New Zealand, for example, are approximately antipodes to each other; the island is actually opposite to a point just north-west of Barfleur, on the coast of Normandy. To be exact antipodes, two places must be distant from each other by 180° of longitude, and one must be as many degrees N latitude as the other is S latitude. At antipodes, both the seasons and day and night are thus opposite: e.g. winter at one is simultaneous with summer at the other, and noon at one is simultaneous with midnight at the other. The term is often extended to include the whole region on the opposite side of the world from a given place; in Britain, for example, Australia and New Zealand are sometimes referred to as the Antipodes.

anti-trades or **counter-trades.** The winds of the upper air experienced in the regions of the *trade winds*, and blowing in the reverse direction to those on the surface; e.g. in the region of the NE trade winds (i.e. NE at the surface), the upper wind, the anti-trade, is SW. The anti-trades are believed to be return currents, carrying the air brought equatorwards by the trade winds back to higher latitudes. The term has been wrongly used to denote surface winds which are opposite in direction to the trade winds; e.g. the SW surface winds of the North Atlantic region, opposite in direction to the NE trade winds.

aphelion. The position of the earth in its *orbit* when it is at its greatest distance from the sun, i.e. about 4.8 million km (3 million miles) farther away than when it is at *perihelion*. It reaches this position during the northern *summer*; the northern hemisphere then receives the direct rays of the sun, the days are of maximum length, and the increased insolation more than counterbalances the greater distance from the sun. The term is also used for the position of any other planet or a comet when it is at its greatest distance from the sun.

apogee. The position in the orbit of the *moon* or of any *planet* when it is at its greatest distance from the earth.

apparent time. Solar time, or time as indicated by the apparent motion of the sun, and registered, for instance, by a sundial. Apparent noon at any point on the earth's surface, then, is the instant when the sun reaches the highest point of its apparent diurnal path – or when the shadow of a vertical object is shortest. Apparent time is synonymous with *local time*.

aquiclude. A rock stratum which, being relatively impermeable, obstructs the passage of ground water; the term is used chiefly by American geologists.

aquifer or **aquafer.** A layer of rock which holds water and allows water to percolate through it.

arable land. Land which is suitable for ploughing, as distinguished from permanent pasture and woodland. Sometimes, however, the term is applied specifically to land which is actually ploughed and on which crops are cultivated.

Archaean era. See *pre-Cambrian*.

archipelago. (1) A sea studded with islands, originally applied to the sea known as the Aegean Sea (see Fig. p. 10).

The group of islands, or archipelago, of the Aegean Sea.

(2) A group of islands. This is now the only meaning in general use. Besides the classic example of the islands of the Aegean Sea, specifically named groups include the Tuamotu or Low Archipelago in the S Pacific and the Archipiélago de las Perlas (Pearl Islands) in the Gulf of Panama.

Arctic Circle. The parallel or line of latitude at 66° 32′ N, commonly assumed to be at 66° 30′ N. Owing to the inclination of the earth's *axis*, the sun does not set here on one day of the year, about 21 June, the northern midsummer; about 22 December, the northern midwinter, the sun does not rise. Within the Arctic Circle, the number of such days increases with nearness to the Pole. At any particular time of the year, conditions are the converse of those at the *Antarctic Circle.*

Arctic smoke. A shallow fog formed chiefly in inlets of the Arctic Ocean when extremely cold air from the land moves out over the warmer sea and causes condensation of water vapour.

arcuate delta. See *delta.*

arenaceous. A term applied to sedimentary rocks, either loose or cemented, which contain sand, e.g. sandstone.

arête (French).* A sharp mountain ridge, often formed by the erosion of two adjoining *cirques*. On many mountain masses, cirque erosion has taken place on several sides, leaving a series of arêtes radiating from the summit; examples may be seen on the Matterhorn, Snowdon. See *horn.*

A type of artesian well: B is a permeable layer, A and C impermeable layers, W is the well.

argillaceous. A term applied to sedimentary rocks containing a substantial proportion of clay minerals, e.g. shale.

argon. An inert gas present in the atmosphere to the extent of rather less than 1 per cent of dry air.

arid.* Deficient in *rainfall*: usually applied to a climate or a region in which the rainfall is barely sufficient to support vegetation, sometimes – quite arbitrarily – to one in which the average annual rainfall is less than 250 mm (10 inches).

arroyo (Spanish). A stream bed, situated in a desert area, which is normally dry, but is transformed into a temporary watercourse, even a torrent, after heavy rain; when the rain has ceased, the water soon subsides, and the bed dries up again. The term is mainly used in North and South America. See *wadi, nullah.*

artesian well. A type of *well* which normally gives a continuous flow, the water being forced upwards by the hydrostatic pressure; this pressure is due to the outlet of the well being some depth below the level of the source of the water. It is often found where a basin-shaped, permeable layer of rock, such as chalk, is sandwiched between two impermeable layers, such as clay, so that rain falling on the *outcrop* of the permeable layer will filter through and collect underground. As the water cannot escape below, the permeable layer becomes saturated to the rim of the basin, and if a well is sunk through the upper impermeable layer into it, the water flows into the well. Should the *water table* at the outcrop, i.e. the source of the water, be sufficiently high, the water in the well will gush out above the ground, possibly as a fountain, without the necessity of pumping. An artesian well may also be formed, for instance, on a coastal plain, where water passes downwards through a porous layer of rock, lying between two impervious layers, towards the sea. The depth of artesian wells varies considerably; some are only a few metres deep, others hundreds of metres. Many small towns and villages rely on them for their supply of water. They are specially valuable for irrigation in semi-arid regions, such as the Great Plains of the United States and parts of Australia. The name is derived from Artois, the French province where some of the earliest artesian wells were constructed.

ås (pl. **åsar**) (Swedish). In Scandinavia, an *esker*.

ash, volcanic. See *volcanic ash*.

ash cone or **cinder cone.** The conical hill or mountain built up with the ejected material from a *volcano*. The slopes of a *cinder cone* are usually steeper than those of an *ash cone*, for its material, being coarser, has a greater angle of repose.

asteroid or **planetoid.** A minor *planet*, of which there are many, revolving round the sun between the orbits of Mars and Jupiter. The largest is about 700 km in diameter, the smallest probably less than 30 km in diameter.

asthenosphere. The soft, heated rock layer immediately below the rigid *lithosphere*, allowing the lithospheric plates to move slowly about the earth's surface. See *mid-oceanic ridge*.

Atlantic coast. See *discordant coast*.

atlas. A collection of maps bound into a volume. The figure of Atlas supporting the heavens was used as a frontispiece in certain early collections of maps, e.g. in Mercator's Atlas (1595) and the term came to be used for the collection itself.

atmosphere. The envelope of air which surrounds the earth, consisting principally of a mixture of gases – mainly *oxygen* (21 per cent), *nitrogen* (78 per cent), *carbon dioxide* (0.03 per cent), *argon* (nearly 1 per cent), *helium* and other rare gases (0.01 per cent) in dry air, and a variable quantity of water vapour. The nitrogen, a chemically inactive gas, serves merely to dilute the more important oxygen. With increasing height above the earth's surface, the atmosphere becomes more and more rare, but within the layers through which adequate investigations have been carried out, the relative proportions of the gases (excluding water vapour) remain almost constant. From the viewpoint of climate and general weather conditions, the amount of water vapour present in the atmosphere, usually expressed as *relative humidity*, is of paramount significance; the *temperature* of the atmosphere and the *atmospheric pressure* are also important. The atmosphere is divided into the *troposphere*, the lowest portion, the *stratosphere*, the *mesosphere* and the *thermosphere*. See also *ionosphere*, *ozonosphere*.

atmospheric pressure. The pressure at a point due to the weight of the column of air above that point. At the earth's surface (sea level) this pressure equals about 14.7 lb per square inch, or 1,033 gm per sq. cm, and with increasing height above the surface, the overlying column of air being shortened, the pressure decreases. The atmospheric pressure is measured by a *barometer*, and is normally registered in *millibars*.

atoll. A *coral reef* in the shape of a ring or horseshoe, enclosing a *lagoon*. According to Darwin's theory, an atoll began as a fringing reef round an island, then the island became submerged owing to subsidence, leaving only the ring-shaped reef enclosing a lagoon. According to Murray's theory, an atoll was formed on the top of a plateau or hill

A typical atoll in the Pacific Ocean.

which rose from the ocean bed to a depth at which the reef-building corals live; the outer corals of a number of colonies grew most readily and reached the surface first, thus forming an atoll enclosing a lagoon. Neither theory, however, is entirely satisfactory, for atolls are formed in both these and probably in other ways.

attrition. The mutual wearing down of rock particles during transport by wind, water, or ice, so that they become reduced in size, smoothed and rounded: not to be confused with *abrasion*.

aureole, metamorphic. See *metamorphic aureole*.

aurora australis or **southern lights.** The light phenomenon seen in the southern hemisphere, corresponding to the *aurora borealis* of the northern hemisphere, being most often visible in latitudes higher than about 65° S. Like *aurora borealis*, it takes place in the *ionosphere*.

aurora borealis or **northern lights.** The light phenomenon seen in the sky at night in the northern hemisphere, mainly in the higher latitudes. Aurora comprises an electrical discharge, and when observed as far south as in England it is almost always accompanied by a *magnetic storm* – but not when it is limited to higher latitudes. It assumes a variety of forms: the most stable form is the quiet arc of light, which sometimes persists with little visible change for many hours; an arc with streamers, on the other hand, is constantly changing shape. Like *aurora australis*, it takes place in the *ionosphere*.

Aurora is very rarely seen in southern Europe, is uncommon in the United States and southern England, but its frequency increases rapidly northwards; it is common, for instance, in the Orkneys and Shetlands, and a belt of maximum frequency running north of Norway and south of Greenland encircles the *north magnetic pole*. Its actual frequency is uncertain for it is obscured by daylight and by cloudy skies, and, when weak, by moonlight or twilight.

autumn. For middle latitudes, the season following the *summer*, and known in the United States as the *fall*, reckoned astronomically to last in the northern hemisphere from the autumnal *equinox* (about 22 September) to the winter *solstice* (about 22 December); in the southern hemisphere the dates correspond to the northern *spring*. See *seasons*.

autumnal equinox. See *equinox*.

avalanche. A vast mass of snow and ice at high altitude which has accumulated to such an extent that its own weight causes it to slide rapidly down the mountain slope, often carrying with it thousands of tons of rock. An avalanche may thus work immense havoc, destroying villages, roads, forests in its path. The term is sometimes used for a fall of purely rock materials, but this phenomenon is better described as a *landslide*.

avalanche cone. The mass of material deposited where an avalanche has fallen, including snow, ice, rock, and all other objects which have been carried away by it.

avalanche wind. The high wind produced by an *avalanche*, which sometimes causes destruction at a considerable distance from the avalanche itself.

aven (French). A term applied in France, mainly in the *Causses* region, to a *sinkhole*. See also *ponor*.

axis, earth's. The imaginary line, joining the North Pole and the South Pole through the centre of the earth, on which the earth rotates once in every 24 hours. It has an inclination of approx. $66\frac{1}{2}°$ to the plane of the earth's *orbit*, and its position at any time of the year is thus parallel to its position at any other time. See *precession of the equinoxes*.

azimuth. The horizontal angular distance between the vertical plane passing through the observer and the Poles of the earth and the vertical plane passing through the observer and the given object; it may be measured in degrees (0°–180°) eastward or westward from the Pole, as in nautical astronomy, or in degrees (0°–360°) clockwise from true north, as in meteorology.

azimuthal projection. See *zenithal projection*.

azonal soil. A soil which has not been sufficiently subject to soil-forming processes for the development of a mature profile and so is little changed from the parent rock material. Examples are soils forming on screes, on recently deposited alluvium, and on sand dunes.

B

backing. The anti-clockwise change of direction of a wind, e.g. from E through N E to N. It is the opposite change to *veering*.

backwash. The receding movement of sea water down a beach after the breaking of a wave. See *swash*.

bad lands, badlands. * An elevated, arid region which is seamed and lined with deep gullies by the occasional heavy rain, normal precipitation being insufficient to support an adequate protective covering of grass or other vegetation. It is thus almost valueless for agriculture or pasture land. Unequal resistance of the rocks often leaves tall columns and platforms standing out above the surrounding land. Such a region is named after the so-called Bad Lands of the western USA, where they occur particularly in western South Dakota.

baguio. The *tropical cyclone* experienced in the Philippine Islands: a number of the tropical cyclones or *typhoons* of the western Pacific pass over the islands.

bahada, bajada (Spanish). A *piedmont alluvial plain*, formed by the co-alescence of several *alluvial fans*.

bai-u. See *plum rains*.

bajada (Spanish). See *bahada*.

balance of trade. The difference between the value of the *exports* and the *imports* of a country. If the exports are the greater, the balance is regarded as favourable; if the imports are the greater, the balance is usually regarded as adverse. Invisible exports and imports may be included in the calculations.

ballon sonde or **sounding balloon.** A balloon with a meteorograph attached, formerly used for taking 'soundings' of the upper air. After being inflated with hydrogen, it is set free, and rises through the atmosphere to a height of several kilometres; the self-recording instruments of the meteorograph register the pressure, temperature, and humidity at various heights. Finally, the balloon bursts, the meteorograph falls to earth, being protected from injury by a light bamboo framework, and the meteorological records are obtained. The *ballon sonde* has been superseded by the *radiosonde*. See also *pilot balloon*.

bank. (1) A portion of the sea bed raised above its surroundings, but covered with enough water to permit navigation, e.g. the Dogger Bank in the North Sea. See *sandbank*.

*Sand bars along the coast of Texas, with bays and
lagoons on the landward side.*

(2) The sloping ground along the edge of a river, stream, or lake.

banket (Afrikaans). The conglomerate rock which forms the rich gold
reef of the Witwatersrand area in the Transvaal, South Africa, so named
after a type of cake made by the Boers, which it is supposed to resemble.

banner-cloud. A cloud which forms on the lee side of a mountain or hill
summit. The enforced rise of air due to the obstruction of the mountain
causes the water vapour in the air to condense and form the cloud;
some distance down wind there is a descent of air, causing a re-heating
and evaporation of the water drops, and there the banner-cloud disappears. Thus, although there is a constant stream of new air
through the banner-cloud, the cloud itself remains stationary. Two
well-known examples of a banner-cloud are the Table Cloth over Table
Mountain, near Cape Town, and the cloud which forms over the
Matterhorn.

bar. (1) The unit of atmospheric pressure, equal to one million dynes per
square centimetre, and equivalent to 750.1 mm or 29.53 in. of mercury
at 0°C in latitude 45°; for actual measurement of atmospheric pressure,
the *millibar* is in more general use.

(2) A ridge of sand and shingle formed in the sea across the mouth of

Dominant Wind

A typical barkhan.

a river or the entrance to a bay or harbour and lying approximately parallel to the coast: often called an *offshore bar*. To distinguish between the bar which is submerged, even if only at high tide, and the bar which is exposed, the latter is sometimes termed a *barrier beach* or *barrier island*. See *tombolo*, *spit*, *nehrung*.

barkhan, barchan, barchane, or **crescent dune.** A crescent-shaped sand *dune*, with the horns of the crescent projecting down wind, caused by the sand being blown round the edges as well as over the top of the heap, forming in a region where the wind direction is virtually constant; the windward slope is gentle, the leeward slope relatively steep. It is common in the desert areas of Turkestan. Sometimes several of the barkhans join together, and so lose their individual crescent shape.

barogram. The continuous record of atmospheric pressure made by a *barograph*.

barograph. A self-recording *barometer*, in which a continuous trace of the atmospheric pressure is made on a *barogram* fixed to a rotating drum actuated by clockwork. One type records the variations of pressure shown by a mercury barometer, but the type in commonest use is a modified aneroid barometer, sometimes called an *aneroidograph*. The barograph is more useful for indicating the rise and fall of atmospheric pressure than for giving the actual pressure at any particular time.

barometer. The instrument used for measuring the *atmospheric pressure*. In its simplest form, known as the mercury barometer, a column of mercury is held in a closed glass tube inverted over a bath of mercury; this column of mercury is thus balanced against the weight of the atmosphere, and its length affords a measure of that weight, i.e. of the atmospheric pressure. At sea level on the earth's surface a column of mercury 760 mm long represents the mean atmospheric pressure: the *millibar* is now the unit in which atmospheric pressure is usually measured, 1013.2 mb being equivalent to 760 mm of mercury.

Another type of barometer is the aneroid barometer, which consists of a hollow metallic box or capsule nearly exhausted of air with its lid fluted so as to render it flexible; a lever is mounted with a needle to indicate on a graduated dial the variation in pressure on the lid. The aneroid barometer is used where convenience of handling is of greater importance than accuracy, as in the domestic wall or table barometer, and in the *barograph*.

barometric pressure. See *atmospheric pressure*.

barometric tendency. See *pressure tendency*.

barrage. A large structure erected across a river, usually to store water for irrigation. If hydro-electric power is also produced, the structure is generally termed a *dam*.

barranca, barranco (Spanish). A ravine or gorge sometimes formed, for instance on the lower slope of a volcano when heavy rain causes a torrent to sweep downwards and cut through the soft *volcanic ash*, e.g. on Tenerife (Canary Islands).

barrier beach, barrier island. A *bar* that is exposed even at high tide and is separated from the coast by a *lagoon*: common along the Atlantic coast of the USA from New Jersey to Florida and also along the coast of the Gulf of Mexico. Well-known seaside resorts, e.g. Palm Beach, Miami Beach (Florida), have developed on barrier beaches.

barrier reef. See *coral reef*.

barrow or **tumulus.** A mound dating from prehistoric times, built over a burial ground: commonly found in western Europe, including the British Isles.

barysphere or **centrosphere.** A term, now little used, which has been applied by some geologists to the *mantle* beneath the *lithosphere* or earth's crust, by others to the entire mass of the earth beneath the lithosphere, including both mantle and *core*.

basalt.* A dark-coloured, fine-grained *igneous rock*, formed by the solidification of *lava*. It belongs to the basic group of igneous rocks, containing a relatively small proportion of silica (on average 49 per cent). There are many types of basalt, widely distributed throughout the world and sometimes occurring in huge masses. Basalt may solidify in hexagonal columns, as in the Giant's Causeway, N Ireland.

base-level. The lowest level to which a stream can wear its bed. The length of time taken for the bed to reach base-level depends on the rate of erosion; generally speaking, this will be less for a large stream than for a small one and will be less over weak rock than over resistant rock. The permanent base-level is the level of the sea; a lake provides a temporary base-level, but the sediment deposited in it by the stream minimizes its effect.

basic lava. See *lava*.

basin. (1) A region in which the strata dip in all directions towards a central point. If coal deposits are present, it is called a *coal basin*: e.g. the Donets Basin or Donbas, USSR.

(2) The total area drained by a river and its tributaries, termed a *river basin*.

While the term is principally used in the above senses, it is also applied to an extensive hollow or trough in the earth's crust: if occupied by an ocean or a lake known as an *ocean basin*, a *lake basin* respectively. As specifically named, a *syncline* may be termed a basin: e.g. London Basin, Paris Basin. Again, the Great Basin of the SW United States is merely a large area partially enclosed by mountain ranges.

basin irrigation. See *irrigation*.

'basket of eggs' relief. A descriptive term for the type of *relief* created by a swarm or cluster of *drumlins*.

bart furan (Arabic). The season of 'sea open' in the Arabian Sea: the winter, or period of the NE *monsoon*, when the dominant feature of the pressure system over Asia is the Siberian anticyclone, winds being comparatively light over the Arabian Sea, and therefore favourable to native shipping.

bat hiddan (Arabic). The season of 'sea closed' in the Arabian Sea: the summer, or period of the SW *monsoon*, when off-shore winds from the Somaliland region cause the Arabian Sea to be so stormy that native shipping is laid up.

batholith or **bathylith.** A dome-shaped mass of igneous rock formed by the intrusion of *magma*, often consisting of *granite*. It is usually much larger than a *laccolith*, often extending over hundreds of square kilometres, and appears to have *replaced* rather than *displaced* the invaded rocks. Batholiths are revealed when the overlying rocks have been worn away. They form the sub-structure to mountain ranges, and appear to continue downwards to enormous depths.

bathyal zone. See *continental slope*.

bathyscaphe. A spherical steel chamber with observation portholes, used for exploring the deepest parts of the ocean (see *deep*); attached to it is a float shaped like a submarine.

bay. A wide indentation into the land formed by the sea or by a lake.

bay bar. A *bar* which extends across a bay; being attached to the land at both ends, it is thus distinct from a *spit*.

bayou. A marshy creek or offshoot to a river or lake; occurring in flat country, it remains swampy owing to floods, river seepage, and lack of drainage. The term is chiefly used in the southern United States, where it often signifies an *ox-bow lake*.

beach. The strip of land or terrace bordering the sea, sloping gently downwards from the land, usually recognized as that part which lies between high and low water marks, and formed by the action of the sea; it may consist of shingle, sand, or mud. A cliff standing on the landward side of the beach is gradually worn down by the sea, and the beach is thus widened, but when the waves can no longer reach the cliff, erosion by the sea practically ceases, and the beach no longer widens. See *raised beach*.

beach cusp. A small-scale pointed 'headland' on a beach, one of a series alternating with small 'bays', formed by wave action. The distance between cusps varies between about 5 m and 60 m.

bearing. The horizontal angle between the direction of an object and the *meridian* through the observer, measured in degrees (0°–360°) clockwise from true north; this is the *true bearing* of the object. The *magnetic bearing* is the corresponding angle measured clockwise from the magnetic north. The bearing of an object may be given in terms of the compass points, e.g. N 40° W, or 40° W of N, or approximately as N W, etc. See *azimuth*.

Beaufort scale. The series of numbers devised by Admiral Beaufort at the beginning of the nineteenth century to differentiate approximately between various wind strengths: e.g. 0 on the Beaufort scale represents a calm, the air being practically motionless, while at the upper end of the scale 12 represents a hurricane, the surface wind speed being greater than seventy-five miles (120 km) per hour. Between these two extremes, the numbers indicate the intervening wind speeds, which can usually be estimated approximately by such natural phenomena as smoke drift, leaves and twigs in constant motion, small waves on inland water, violent movement of trees, slight structural damage to buildings. The various wind velocities to which the numbers on the Beaufort Scale are equivalent have been internationally agreed upon.

beck. In N England, a small stream.

bedding plane. The surface which separates one layer of *sedimentary rock* from another.

bedrock. The solid rock beneath the soil, subsoil, and other loose rock material with which most of the land surface of the earth is covered. It is sometimes several hundred metres beneath the surface, but is usually found at a much smaller depth; in places, especially on steep slopes, it has no soil cover at all.

beheading. See *river capture*.

bench mark. In surveying, a reference mark of known elevation cut or set in stone, concrete, or other durable material and used in the determination of altitudes. In Britain it takes the form of a broad arrow with a horizontal bar across its apex, and on Ordnance Survey large-scale maps (e.g. 1:2500) is indicated by the broad arrow symbol, the letters B M, and the height in metres to two decimal places (formerly in feet). The mark is inverted when surveying below sea level, e.g. in mining. In the United States a bench mark takes the form of a metal disc indicating the elevation in feet.

benthos. The sedentary, bottom-dwelling marine organisms of plant and animal origin, as distinct from the *plankton* and the *nekton*; they include seaweeds, molluscs, and corals.

bergschrund (German). The gap or *crevasse* left around the upper rim of the glacier ice within a *cirque* as the ice moves downwards, thus separating the latter from the rock wall beyond; it usually provides a difficult obstacle to any attempt to climb from the snowfield to the mountain peaks beyond. The French term for bergschrund is *rimaye*.

berg wind. The warm, dry wind of *föhn* type experienced in South Africa, especially on the generally cool western coast, being most frequent in winter, when the plateau of the interior is covered by a strong anticyclone and pressure is low over the ocean. The winds thus blow outwards from the plateau, affecting all margins, and become heated by descent. The temperatures may rise above 100°F (38°C), and thus temporarily exceed those of midsummer. The berg wind may continue for two or three days, giving oppressive weather, and sometimes causing severe damage to crops; its direction and the season of its occurrence vary with situation.

bight. An indentation in the sea coast similar to a *bay* but either larger or with a gentler curvature: e.g. the Great Australian Bight, Bight of Benin.

bill. A narrow headland, or small *peninsula*.

billabong (Australian). In Australia, a term derived from the aboriginal, signifying a creek, water hole, or stagnant pool, generally in the bed of an intermittently flowing stream.

bioclimatology. The study of climate in relation to life and health, one of its objects being to determine the climatic conditions most favourable to human habitation, especially for invalids, and to define the areas where such climates exist.

biogeography. The study of the geographical distribution of plants and animals over the globe, being usually limited to the land surface; it is divided into *phytogeography* and *zoogeography*.

biosphere. A term sometimes applied to that portion of the *earth* occupied by the various forms of life, being additional, for purposes of classification, to the three main physical zones, the *lithosphere*, the *hydrosphere*, and the *atmosphere*.

bird's foot delta. See *delta*.

bise (French). A cold, dry wind from NW, N, or NE, experienced in southern France and Switzerland, often accompanied by heavy clouds.

bitter lake. A *salt lake* whose waters contain large quantities of chemical salts in solution and are therefore bitter in taste; e.g. the Great Bitter Lake in Egypt, linked to the Small Bitter Lake by the Suez Canal.

bituminous coal. The shiny black coal sometimes familiarly known as household coal, which according to classification of coals is of higher rank, i.e. has a higher fixed carbon content, than *lignite*, but lower than *anthracite*. It is the most abundant and most important type of coal, occurring in several forms which are named according to their main use, e.g. coking coal, gas coal, steam coal.

black cotton-earth. See *regur*.

black earth. See *chernozem*.

black ice. See *glazed frost*.

blind valley. In a *karst region*, a valley, either dry or still containing a stream, which ends suddenly in a cave or sinkhole, where the stream disappears underground.

blizzard. A storm of powdery snow, sometimes with small ice crystals, driven along by an abnormally high wind, reducing visibility practically to zero. Some of the snow falls from the clouds, but much of it is swept up from the ground. In Canada and the northern USA the blizzard, a special type of *cold wave*, often disturbs the calm of the winter anticyclone, coming with a northerly wind of gale strength in rear of an eastward-moving depression, and is most dangerous over the open prairies. In polar regions blizzards are frequent in some localities, at times excessively severe, and may continue for some days. Terre Adélie, in Antarctica, for instance, is specially subject to them, and has been called 'the home of the blizzard'. There a sudden rise of temperature occurs at the commencement of a blizzard in winter, as the surface *temperature inversion* is destroyed; in summer the temperature falls with a blizzard.

block lava. A sheet of *lava* which has solidified so that its surface is a mass of rough, jagged blocks; the Hawaiian term *aa* is sometimes used.

block mountain. A mountain mass formed by the uplift of land between *faults* or by the subsidence of land outside the faults. See *horst*.

blood-rain. Rain which is tinted a reddish colour, leaving a red stain on the ground. The colour is due to the imprisonment, in the drops, of dust particles which have been carried along in the upper air from a desert, often for long distances. It has been most often observed in Italy, the dust having originated from the Sahara, but has occurred as far afield as Great Britain.

blossom showers. The rains of March to May in the coffee-growing districts of the monsoon region of SE Asia; also called 'mango showers'.

blowhole. A hole near the sea-shore which has been formed in the roof of a cave, and through which air and possibly water are forced by the rising tide. The term *gloup* is sometimes used in Scotland.

blow-out. A hollow formed in light soil or in sand, e.g. in a *dune*, by *deflation*. Its formation may be initiated by destruction of the natural vegetation, or by over-grazing by animals, exposing loose, finely-divided material easily lifted by the wind.

blue mud. A marine deposit containing much decaying organic matter and also finely-divided iron sulphide; the latter gives it its characteristic dark blue or slaty colour. It covers much of the sea bed of the Pacific Ocean, the Arabian Sea, and the Bay of Bengal. See *green mud*, *red mud*.

bluff. A headland or cliff with a bold and almost perpendicular front, usually applied to the steep slopes bordering a river. These bluffs are often formed by the action of the river in cutting into the valley sides, e.g. on the concave side of a *meander*.

bocage (French). A type of farming country which is divided by hedges and trees into small fields, applied especially to NW France.

bog. An area of soft, wet, spongy ground, consisting chiefly of decayed or decaying moss and other vegetable matter. It often forms in shallow, stagnant lakes or ponds, and is largely produced by sphagnum moss; the latter spreads out from the shores, floating on the surface, and gives a deposit of vegetable matter on the bottom. In time the sphagnum moss will cover the entire surface of a lake or pond, a thick mass of decaying vegetation lying below; this is often called a *quaking bog*, for it quakes under foot. Eventually, peat is evolved. Bogs are also formed on cold, damp mountain surfaces. See *swamp*.

bogaz (Serbo-Croat). In a *karst region*, a long narrow chasm, enlarged by solution of the limestone, into which a surface stream may empty.

bohorok. The *föhn* type of wind experienced on the plains of Deli, Sumatra during the NE monsoon; being warmed and dried by descent on the lee side of the mountains, it may cause much damage to such crops as tobacco.

bolson. A basin of interior drainage in an arid or semi-arid region, whose floor is tending to be filled by a number of *alluvial fans* around its flanks. The term is chiefly used of Mexico and the SW United States.

Bonne's projection. A *map projection* which is a modification of the simple (one-standard) *conical projection*, and resembles the latter in appearance except that the meridians are curved. As in the simple conical projection, the central meridian is straight and is divided truly, the selected standard parallel is divided truly, and the other parallels at their true distances apart are drawn as concentric circles. The modification consists in the fact that *all* parallels are divided truly, i.e. the distances between the meridians along all parallels are made equal to those distances on the globe, and the meridians are formed by drawing curves through the corresponding points on each parallel – not, as in the simple conical projection, by joining the vertex to the points of division of the standard parallel. Thus the projection is *homolographic* or equal-area, and is on this account popular; it is not, however, suitable for the polar regions, and the more limited its extension in longitude the better.

bora. The cold and often very dry northerly or north-easterly wind experienced along the eastern coast of the Adriatic Sea and in northern Italy, mainly in winter; it occurs when atmospheric pressure is high over central Europe and the Balkans, and low over the Mediterranean. As it thus blows from the former area, it usually gives clear skies and cold, dry weather, but if it is associated with a depression over the

Bonne's projection.

Adriatic, it may be accompanied by heavy cloud and rain or snow. If the continental anticyclone is well established, the bora may continue for several days. It often blows with great strength, with violent gusts and squalls, sometimes exceeding 150 km per hour. See *mistral*.

bore. A high tidal wave experienced in a narrow river estuary, advancing upstream like a wall of water. It is produced by the sudden retardation of the normal tidal wave, when it reaches shallow water and meets the river current; this causes the water to pile up across the river, the crest falls over, and the water moves along like a large broken wave. A bore is experienced in the River Severn, England, where at the *spring tides* it is often as much as 1 metre high, and also in such rivers as the Seine, Hooghly, and Yangtse-kiang. It is sometimes known as an eagre or eger.

boreal. A term meaning literally 'belonging to the north': sometimes applied to the northern *coniferous forests* of N America and N Eurasia and to the corresponding climate (short warm summers, cold winters with snow).

boss. A term sometimes applied to a *batholith* of relatively small size, especially one which is approximately circular in outline. See *stock*.

bottom. In the USA an *alluvial plain*.

boulder clay or **till.** The mass of rocks and finely ground *rock flour* dragged along in the lower part of the ice of a glacier, and left behind when the ice melts. It is usually a tough, unstratified clay, loaded with stones, and it may be several metres thick, though only the upper few centimetres have been modified to form a soil. Some so-called boulder clay, on the other hand, contains little or no clay, but perhaps sand, and no boulders. Its composition, which is very variable, depends on the rocks from which it came. Boulder clay is well distributed over northern Europe, including the British Isles (except the extreme south), being the remains of the ground *moraines* of glaciers of the *Ice Age*.

bourne. An intermittent stream, applied especially to the chalk regions of southern England. The bed is usually dry except in winter, when the *water table* rises above its level. See *winterbourne*.

brae. In Scotland, a hillside or bank overlooking a valley.

braided stream. A network of small shallow interlaced streams derived from a single stream. It was formed after the original stream had deposited sediment, dividing and forming new channels, and then these channels had joined up, divided, and joined up many times.

brave west winds. The westerly *planetary winds* of the temperate region of the southern hemisphere, which, owing to the comparatively slight obstruction by land masses, blow with great force and regularity. Striking the western mountainous coast of southern Chile, Tasmania, and New Zealand they bring heavy rainfall, in places exceeding 2,500 mm annually. See *roaring forties*.

breaker. A wave breaking into foam as it advances towards the shore, where the water becomes so shallow that there is insufficient to complete the wave form; or a wave breaking against a rock or other solid object.

breakwater. A barrier built into the sea in order to break the force of the waves, and thus to serve as a protection against them.

breccia (Italian). Rock consisting of angular fragments cemented together in a matrix; it may consist of any type of material, and is formed in a large variety of ways. See also *conglomerate*.

breeze. A term usually applied to a current of air which is too light to be called a wind, or more specifically, to certain types of wind of regular occurrence, e.g. *land breeze, sea breeze*.

brickearth. A fine-grain deposit which overlies the gravel in parts of the London Basin, England, i.e. on some of the Thames terraces; the name was originally given because of its use in brick-making.

brickfielder. The hot wind experienced in south-eastern Australia caused by the movement of tropical air southwards, especially during the summer, and often bringing clouds of dust. Hot spells many days in duration, with temperatures daily exceeding 100°F (38°C), often occur while the brickfielder blows. It blows ahead of a *depression* or a *trough of low pressure*, and precedes the *southerly burster*.

bridge, natural. See *natural bridge*.

bridging point. The point where a river is or can be bridged: used particularly of the *lowest* bridging point, i.e. the lowest point in the course of a river where it is bridged and thus frequently the location of an important route centre.

brigalow scrub. A type of *scrub*, consisting largely of a species of acacia known as brigalow, which covers much of central Queensland, Australia.

British Summer Time or **BST.** *Standard time*, first introduced in 1916, in use in the British Isles for about seven months each year (Mar-Oct), being one hour in advance of *Greenwich Mean Time* or GMT; 7 o'clock BST thus corresponds to 6 o'clock GMT. For a time (1968–71) it was adopted experimentally as British Standard Time for the whole year. Many other mid-latitude countries, including the United States, adopt a similar summer time system, which is often termed *daylight saving time*.

broad. In East Anglia, England, an extensive stretch of fresh water forming part of the course of a sluggish river, i.e. where it broadens out, or adjoining the river near its estuary, and probably due to the digging and removal of peat. The Norfolk Broads, which in fact extend into Suffolk, are associated chiefly with the Bure, Yare, and Waveney rivers; the district, sometimes known as Broadland, is popular with sailing and angling enthusiasts.

brocken, spectre of the. The greatly magnified shadow of an observer thrown on to a bank of cloud or a mist in a mountainous region: so called after the Brocken, a peak in the Harz Mountains, Germany.

Bronze Age. The period when men used implements and weapons made of bronze, an alloy of copper and tin. It does not necessarily denote a fixed chronological period in history, but marks a stage of human culture through which many peoples of the world passed, in their progress from *Stone Age* to *Iron Age*.

brook. A small stream or rivulet.

brown coal. See *lignite*.

Brückner cycle. The cycle of various climatic and other natural phenomena, recurring very irregularly, which include periods of warm and dry years alternating with cold and damp years, the advance and retreat of Alpine glaciers, the level of the Caspian Sea and its inflowing rivers, and a number of meteorological data. This cycle had been known before Brückner, but he rediscovered it in 1890, and calculated its average length at approximately thirty-five years; individual cycles, however, range in length from twenty-five to fifty years.

buffer state. A state, usually independent, situated between two other states, and therefore supposed to discourage hostilities between them:

Belgium used to be considered a buffer state between Germany and France, Poland between Germany and Russia, and Afghanistan between Russia and India.

built-up area. The area of a town that is covered with buildings and thus can only be subject to further development after the demolition of those buildings.

bund. Chiefly in India, an artificial embankment, dyke, or dam. In certain Chinese ports which have or have had commercial links with England, e.g. Shanghai, the Bund is the name given to the waterfront.

buran. The cold, fierce, northerly or north-easterly wind experienced in Siberia and Central Asia, mainly during the winter in rear of a depression, breaking the comparative calm of anticyclonic conditions, carrying with it snow and ice particles; it thus corresponds to the Canadian *blizzard*. It reaches gale force, often blows at temperatures of $-30°C$ ($-20°F$) or below, and is thus dangerous to both human and animal life, especially on the open steppes, as the blizzard is on the prairies. A strong north-easterly wind in summer is also called a buran. The winter buran is also termed the *purga*.

burn. In Scotland, a brook or small stream.

bush. A term used mainly in Australia, New Zealand, South Africa, and the United States for a region covered with scrub or woodland not yet cleared for cultivation; or, more loosely, any wild and uncultivated region, even though not wooded.

butte. A flat-topped hill, formed when a stratum of hard rock overlies weaker layers and protects them from being worn down. The butte is similar to but smaller than a *mesa*, and is often produced from a mesa when the latter is reduced in size through dissection and erosion: it is characteristic of the arid plateau region of the western United States.

Buys Ballot's law. The law, enunciated by Buys Ballot in 1857, which states that if an observer in the northern hemisphere stands with his back to the wind, the atmospheric pressure will be lower to his left hand than to his right, the reverse being true for the southern hemisphere. Expressed in a different way, the law states that in the northern hemisphere the winds move anti-clockwise round centres of low pressure and clockwise round centres of high pressure, the reverse being true, again, for the southern hemisphere.

C

caatinga. The *thorn forest* of N E Brazil, in a region of deficient rainfall, containing cacti, acacias, and other drought-resistant plants.

cacimbo. The heavy mist and low cloud, from which drizzle sometimes falls, occurring in the mornings and evenings along the coast of Angola. They are characteristic of the dry season, when they cause the air to become extremely moist, and die out in the rainy season. They correspond to the *smokes* of the Guinea Coast.

cadastral map. A large-scale map which shows individual properties. The term is also rather loosely applied to other maps on a similar large scale; for example, the OS map of Great Britain on the scale of 1:2500 (approx. 25 in. to 1 mile) is often regarded as a cadastral map, despite the fact that it does not show all property boundaries.

Cainozoic or **Kainozoic** or **Cenozoic era.** The New Life era, the third and latest of the major divisions of the geological scale of time (after pre-Cambrian time), extending over about the last 70 million years: that part of the earth's history dating from the close of the *Mesozoic era* to the present time. It is divided into the Tertiary (earlier) and Quaternary periods. Some geologists, however, regard it as being synonymous with the Tertiary, the Quaternary being considered a separate or fourth great era. The Cainozoic era is the era when mammals were widely distributed over the earth, and the abundant vegetation was beginning to resemble that of today.

cairn, carn (Gaelic). A mound or heap of stones, in ancient times erected for memorial purposes, but more recently often erected as a landmark. In Scotland it sometimes forms part of the name of a particular mountain, e.g. Cairn Gorm, Carn Mor.

calcareous. Containing a substantial proportion of calcium carbonate: generally applied to rocks and soils.

calcification. In an arid or semi-arid region, the deposition of calcium carbonate near the surface of the soil, brought about by the rise of water containing the salt in solution, through capillary action; the water evaporates, leaving behind an accumulation of solid calcium carbonate.

caldera.* A large basin-shaped *crater* bounded by steep cliffs, usually formed by the subsidence of the top of a volcanic mountain, and sometimes occupied by a lake. If the volcano is not yet extinct, one or more active cones may exist within the caldera. In one of the largest known calderas (23 km by 16 km), that of Aso-san, in Kyushu, Japan, for example, there is an active volcano (Nakadake). The best-known caldera in North America is at Crater Lake, Oregon, in which stands a small island which is a volcanic cone formed after the original volcanic summit had sunk.

calendar. A system by which time is divided into fixed periods, known as years, months, days, etc. The year, the month, and the solar days are natural periods of time which have always been used in the preparation of a calendar; they correspond respectively with the period of the earth's revolution round the sun – 365 days, 5 hours, 48 minutes, 46 seconds, the period of revolution of the moon round the earth, and the period of rotation of the earth on its axis. One obstacle to the production of a calendar is the fact that the year is not an exact multiple of the time of the moon's revolution round the earth or of the solar day.

To give a solar year of 365¼ days, three consecutive years of 365 days and a fourth or leap year of 366 days are arranged. But such a year is 11 minutes 14 seconds longer than the true year. The Gregorian calendar (New Style) now in use corrects this error by arranging that the centurial years shall be taken as leap years only when they are exactly divisible by 400. Thus 1700, 1800, and 1900 were ordinary years, but 2000 will be a leap year. The error is reduced by this means to less than one day in 3000 years.

In addition to the Gregorian calendar, which is in common use throughout the modern world, a number of other calendars have been devised: e.g. Chinese calendar, initiated long before the Christian era, Jewish calendar, Muslim calendar, French Republican calendar, and others.

calendar month. The interval of time in one of the twelve months into which the year is divided by the *calendar*: or, say, the interval between the 12th of one month and the 11th of the next month. See also *lunar month*.

calina. The haze which occurs during July and August in Mediterranean lands, reduces visibility, and turns the blue sky into a dull grey colour; it is caused by dust particles which have been swept up by strong winds.

calm. The state of the atmosphere when there is virtually no horizontal movement: the wind speed is less than 1 knot and is recorded as Force 0 on the *Beaufort scale*.

calms of Cancer. The region of calms and light winds within the belt of high pressure near the *Tropic of Cancer*. See *horse latitudes*.

calms of Capricorn. The region of calms and light winds within the belt of high pressure near the *Tropic of Capricorn*. See *horse latitudes*.

calving. The detachment of an *iceberg* from the front of a glacier, when the latter reaches the sea, or the detachment of a portion of an iceberg when the latter is afloat.

campos. The tropical grasslands or *savanna* of Brazil, situated south of the equatorial forests of the Amazon basin. They vary between open treeless grasslands and areas in which there are considerable stretches of woodland.

canal. An artificial watercourse, usually cut in order to facilitate the cheap transport of bulky goods by barge, when the time taken in transit is not an important factor. A canal is often cut between two important rivers, in order to improve the waterway systems of the area, e.g. the Rhine–Marne Canal. Canals are also often constructed to facilitate irrigation in regions which are deficient in rainfall. See also *ship canal*.

Cancer, Tropic of. See *Tropic of Cancer*.

canyon or **cañon.*** A *gorge*, relatively narrow but of considerable size, bounded by steep slopes. It has often been formed by a river cutting through the soft rocks of an arid region; the scantness of the rainfall prevents denudation of the canyon walls, and so maintains their steepness. The walls of a large canyon, however, rarely approach the vertical, and their irregularity of slope is due to inequalities in the hardness of the rock. For instance, the Grand Canyon of the Colorado River in the USA, the largest and best-known canyon in the world, has a depth of over 1.6 km, in places, but although it is very narrow at the bottom in these places, it is often 13 to 16 km wide at the top. A small ravine through which a tributary flows into the main river is known as a *side-canyon*.

cape. A headland, a more or less pointed piece of land jutting out into the sea.

Cape maquis. The *scrub* type of vegetation which prevails in southern Cape Province, around Cape Town, South Africa, similar to the *maquis* of the Mediterranean region of southern Europe.

Capricorn, Tropic of. See *Tropic of Capricorn*.

capture, river. See *river capture*.

carbonation. See *weathering*.

carbon dioxide. A gas composed of one part of carbon combined with two parts of oxygen, and normally occupying .03 per cent of the atmosphere.

Carboniferous period. The Coal Age: that part of the *Palaeozoic Era* when coal was extensively formed. Thick layers of partially decayed swamp vegetation, covering coastal lowlands, had become buried under marine deposits when the coastal lands sank. More swamps were formed when the water grew shallower, and the process was repeated. As the deposits became compressed and hardened, the vegetable matter formed coal. The coal thus occurs in seams separated by *sedimentary rocks*, such as limestone and sandstone, from the marine deposits. The term Carboniferous is also applied to the system of rocks formed during the period, including carboniferous limestone. In North America a different terminology is used, the rocks being divided into Mississippian and Pennsylvanian, corresponding respectively to the lower and upper Carboniferous divisions used in Europe.

cardinal points. The four main directions or points of the compass: north, south, east, and west.

carse. In Scotland, the low alluvial land bordering a river near to its mouth, e.g. Carse of Gowrie.

cartography. The art of drawing maps and charts.

cascade. A small *waterfall*, or a series of falls resembling steps.

cash crops. Crops which are produced for sale, and not for consumption by the farmer and his family. *Plantation* crops are of this kind. See *subsistence crops*.

caste. An exclusive and hereditary social group to which a person involved in the system is allotted, and to which he or she belongs throughout life. The caste system is particularly observed by the Hindus; it confers many privileges on the members of the higher castes, but condemns those of the lower castes, formerly known as the 'untouchables', to the most menial labour, such as scavenging, for life. There are now signs, however, that the rigidity of the system is gradually being broken down.

cataract. A great *waterfall* or series of falls, or sometimes, as on the River Nile, *rapids*.

catch crop. A crop sown in order to utilize land that would otherwise lie fallow; in general it grows and matures quickly: it may be grown, for example, between one main crop and the next. See also *cover crop*.

catchment basin or **drainage area.** The region which drains all the rain water that falls on it, apart from that removed by evaporation, into a river or stream, which then carries the water to the sea or to a lake; it may thus coincide with the *river basin*. Its boundary is defined by the ridge beyond which water flows in the opposite direction – away from the basin. See *watershed*.

Causses.* The region of limestone plateaux in the southern part of the Massif Central, in France, exhibiting many of the typical surface features of a *karst region*: the term being used for specific plateaux, e.g. Causse de Larzac. The name is derived from *cau*, the local version of the French word *chaux* (lime). The term is also sometimes applied to similar limestone regions elsewhere.

cave. A subterranean hollow space in the earth's crust which may be entered from the surface. A sea-cave may be produced by the action of the waves, and also by boulders and pebbles being thrown against a cliff by the sea. It may be formed, too, by the contraction and expansion of the air in a rock fissure as the waves advance and retreat; the air is compressed by the rise of each wave, and allowed to expand as the wave falls, so that in time the roof and walls of the cave may be broken up and the cave enlarged, even though the waves themselves have not actually come into contact with the rock.

Inland caves are often formed in a limestone region, where water containing carbon dioxide dissolves out underground channels, and enlarges them in places to the dimensions of caves, usually with a stream flowing through them. See *speleology*.

cavern. A term generally regarded as synonymous with *cave*, though sometimes implying one of large dimensions.

cay.* See *key*.

celestial equator. The imaginary circle formed by the intersection of a plane through the centre of the earth perpendicular to its axis and the *celestial sphere*; it thus corresponds in the celestial sphere to the terrestrial *equator* on the earth.

celestial sphere. A sphere of infinite radius, having its centre at some point within the solar system, as, for instance, at the centre of the earth, on to which all members of the solar system may be projected.

Celsius scale. A name often applied to the *centigrade scale* of temperatures, which was originally devised by the Swedish astronomer, Anders Celsius (1701–44). At first Celsius called the boiling point of water 0° and the freezing point 100°, but these two values were later reversed.

Cenozoic era. See *Cainozoic era*.

Centigrade or **Celsius scale.** The temperature scale used over most of the world. It is the simplest scale devised, the two 'fixed points', the freezing point and the boiling point of water, being respectively 0° and 100°. To convert a temperature on this scale to one on the *Fahrenheit scale*, it should be multiplied by 1.8, and then 32 should be added: $F = (1.8 \times C) + 32$.

centrosphere. See *barysphere*.

chain. A mountain system consisting of a collection of more or less parallel ranges, and possibly including plateaux, provided that the general longitudinal arrangement is maintained. The term is also loosely applied to other features when several of these occur in line, e.g. a *chain* of islands.

chalk. A soft white or greyish type of *limestone* which sometimes consists largely of the calcareous remains of small marine organisms and fragments of shells; in its purest form it may contain as much as 99 per cent of calcium carbonate.

chalybeate. Containing iron, e.g. a *mineral spring*.

channel. (1) A relatively narrow stretch of sea between two land masses, and connecting two more extensive areas of sea.

(2) A river bed.

(3) The deep, navigable part of a bay, harbour, etc.

chapada (Portuguese). In Brazil, an extensive plateau or tableland, e.g. Chapada Diamantina, in Bahía state.

chaparral. The low, dense *scrub*, principally shrubs and bushes, which is characteristic of regions having a Mediterranean climate: usually applied to that of California, USA, which enjoys this climate. It corresponds to the *maquis* of the Mediterranean area in Europe.

chart. (1) A map of any type. See *weather chart*.

(2) A map to facilitate navigation at sea by indicating noteworthy features, such as the depth of the ocean.

(3) A graph.

chase. An open (not enclosed) tract of land kept originally for hunting; it occurs in the names of certain rural areas in England, e.g. Cannock Chase, in the Midlands.

chergui. In Morocco, the hot dry easterly wind which blows from the Sahara and parches the soil. Farmers often protect their crops by erecting *windbreaks*.

chernozem (Russian) or **black earth.** A fine, fertile soil, black or dark brown in colour, covering an extensive area of the southern USSR north of the Black Sea, and part of Hungary and Romania, containing a large proportion of *humus* (in the A horizon) and some lime (in the B horizon). The soil is so rich in plant foods that it will take crops for long periods without the addition of fertilizers, and has no superior for production of cereals, etc. A similar soil also covers a belt of land extending from Saskatchewan, Canada, through N Dakota to Texas, USA. It is associated with a natural cover of grass.

chili. The hot, dry, southerly *sirocco* wind of Tunisia, N Africa.

chimney. A narrow cleft in a rock, especially in the Lake District, England, which a climber can ascend.

china clay or **kaolin.** A whitish clay formed by the decomposition of the *feldspar* in *granite* and extensively used in the manufacture of china or porcelain.

chinook. The warm, dry, *föhn* type of wind experienced along the eastern side of the Rocky Mountains in Canada and the USA. It normally blows on the southern side of a depression which is moving eastwards across the continent, and is south-westerly, though its direction is considerably modified by local topography; it is thus commonest during winter and spring. Being dried and warmed adiabatically by descent from the Rockies, the chinook raises the atmospheric temperature, sometimes by about 20°C (30°–40°F) in fifteen minutes, providing a great contrast to the anticyclonic cold, melts and dries up the winter snow, and so makes grazing possible almost throughout the winter. It is thus of major economic importance, especially in the pastoral regions, from southern Colorado, USA, as far north as the lower Mackenzie River, in Canada. Strong and frequent chinooks mean that the winter is mild, and pastures are available practically without interruption; absence of chinooks means a severe winter, and probably heavy losses of livestock.

chott (French). See *shott*.

chronometer. An extremely accurate timekeeper, such as is used to determine *longitude* at sea; in the latter case, it is poised so as to remain horizontal, whatever the position of the ship.

cinder cone. See *ash cone*.

cinders, volcanic. See *lapilli*.

cirque (French) or **corrie.** A deep, rounded hollow with steep sides, formed through erosion by snow and ice, and thus characteristic of regions which have been glaciated. In regions where glaciers still exist, *névé* often lies in the cirques, is reinforced by snow from the heights above, and feeds the glacier. In regions where glaciation took place in the distant past, numerous lakes often fill the cirques, and enhance the beauty of the mountain scenery. In Wales the term *cwm* is often used, in Scotland 'corrie' or 'coire' (Gaelic). See also *nivation*.

cirque glacier. A small glacier within a cirque.

cirrocumulus. A type of high *cloud*, made of ice crystals, and consisting of small flakes or globular masses, in groups or lines, sometimes known as a '*mackerel sky*'.

cirrostratus. A uniform, thin, milky veil of high *cloud*, which does not blur the outline of the sun or moon, but produces *halos*.

cirrus. A type of high *cloud*, consisting of detached pieces, delicate and feathery in appearance. See also *false cirrus*.

civil twilight. See *twilight*.

clay. (1) An exceptionally fine-grained substance, very retentive of moisture, often becoming plastic when mixed with water. Of the various types of clay, which differ according to texture and also origin but are all grouped together as *sedimentary rocks*, many contain large amounts of silicates of alumina. See also *boulder clay*.

(2) In pedology, a soil in which the diameter of the particles is less than 0.002 mm, irrespective of their mineral character. (Some soil scientists take 0.005 mm as the limiting diameter of the particles.)

clearing. A piece of land cleared for cultivation, especially the primeval forest.

cleavage. The splitting of a rock, which has been submitted to great pressure, into thin sheets or slabs. The direction of cleavage is occasionally parallel to the stratification of the rocks, but usually is inclined or at right-angles to it; like jointing, it is due to planes of weakness in the rock. See *joint*. Roofing slate provides an example of a rock in which cleavage is well developed.

cliff. A high and extremely steep rock face, approaching the vertical, either inland or along a coastline.

climate. The average weather conditions of a place or region throughout the seasons. It is governed by latitude, position relative to continents and oceans, and local geographical conditions. Broadly speaking, the interiors and the eastern parts of the great continents have a continental climate, with small rainfall, low humidity, and a great range of temperatures, both diurnal and seasonal, while oceanic islands and the western parts of continents have a heavier rainfall, higher humidity, and more uniform temperatures; there are numerous exceptions, however, and local climates are still further modified by altitude, proximity of mountains, etc.

Near to the equator, climate is almost synonymous with *weather*, as there is so little variation in the latter. But between the tropics and the poles, especially in the region of the *westerlies*, the weather is often so variable that the climate can scarcely be described in concise terms.

climatic region. One of the main areas into which the earth is divided according to *climate*. All geographers do not employ the same nomenclature, but the four principal climatic regions which are usually recognized are the tropical, subtropical, intermediate or temperate, and polar. These may then be sub-divided into other regions. In the tropical region, for instance, are the equatorial (see *equatorial forest*), *monsoon*, Sudan type (see *savanna*), and dry or hot desert regions (see *desert climate*). In the subtropical region are the dry subtropical or *Mediterranean climate* and the wet subtropical or *cotton belt climate*. In the intermediate or temperate region are various sub-divisions of the *maritime climate* and the *continental climate*. Finally, there is the polar or Arctic climate (see *ice-cap climate* and *tundra*). Where the normal characteristics of any of these regions are masked by altitude, a *mountain climate* may be said to prevail.

climatology. The science which treats of the various climates of the earth, and their influence on the natural environment.

climatotherapy. The treatment of disease through suitable climatic environment, often, but not always, found in recognized health resorts. As climate is subject to seasonal variations, the required environment may have to be sought in different localities at different periods of the year.

climograph. A graphical representation of the differentiation between various types of climate. Mean monthly values of the *wet bulb temperature* as ordinates are plotted against the *relative humidity* values as abscissae, and a closed, twelve-sided polygon, the climograph, is obtained. This reveals the type of climate at a glance: a climograph showing wet bulb temperatures and relative humidities which are all high, for instance, depicts a constantly hot, damp climate. Other types of climograph have also been devised, and the term is sometimes applied to the simple climatic graph in which mean monthly temperatures and mean monthly rainfall values are plotted. See *hythergraph*.

clinometer. An instrument for determining the difference in elevation between two points and therefore used in finding the *dip* of a rock stratum, the slope of an embankment, etc.

clint. A ridge of bare rock between *grikes* or fissures in a limestone region. The classic example of clints and grikes is seen in the limestone surface above Malham Cove, in Yorkshire, England.

cloud. A mass of small water drops or ice crystals, formed by the *condensation* of the water vapour in the atmosphere, usually at a considerable height above the earth's surface: the water vapour being created by evaporation of surface water – oceans, lakes, rivers, etc. Although clouds assume an almost infinite variety of forms, two main types are recognized, according to their shape and mode of formation: cumuliform or 'heap' clouds – clouds of great vertical depth – and stratiform or 'layer' clouds. Meteorological classification of clouds, internationally agreed upon, is more specific, however, and describes ten principal forms, which for convenience are separated according to their approximate height above the earth's surface as low, medium, and high clouds. About 2,000 m is usually taken as the upper limit of low clouds, medium clouds occurring within the range of 2,000 to 6,000 m, and high clouds from 6,000 to 12,000 m; these heights are applicable to temperate latitudes, for in the tropics they tend to be greater. The ten forms above-mentioned are:

(1) *Low clouds: stratocumulus, nimbostratus, cumulus, cumulonimbus, stratus.*

(2) *Medium clouds: altocumulus, altostratus.*

(3) *High clouds: cirrus, cirrostratus, cirrocumulus.*

There are, in addition, certain sub-divisions of these.

cloudburst. An abnormally heavy downpour of rain, usually associated with a *thunderstorm*; in temperate regions it is necessarily short-lived, for the available supply of water vapour is soon exhausted by it. During this short time, however, it may cause considerable damage, tearing up the ground and transforming gullies into raging torrents. Cloudbursts, though possible anywhere that rain falls, are most frequent in mountainous districts. There they are sometimes caused by the sudden stopping of the upward movement of heated air as a storm crosses a mountain range; with the cutting off of this supply of rising air, the raindrops and hailstones which had been supported by it fall in a much shorter space of time than if the supply had been maintained.

cloudiness. The state of the sky with respect to clouds, or, in meteorological and climatological terms, the amount of sky covered by cloud, irrespective of the type; it is estimated visually, and is usually expressed in eighths of sky covered. By this scale, 0 represents a cloudless sky, and 8 a sky entirely covered by cloud. A map of mean annual cloudiness shows two belts of high cloud amount, corresponding to the equatorial and circumpolar low pressure belts; areas of very low cloud amount are shown, of course, in the hot deserts. See *isoneph*.

cloud seeding. The injection of a substance into the clouds from an aircraft or from the ground (e.g. by rocket), usually in order to induce the clouds to give *precipitation*. Seeding agents include solid carbon dioxide ('dry ice') and silver iodide, their particles acting as nuclei for the formation of raindrops; the degree of success, however, has been extremely variable.

cluse (French). A narrow gorge or *transverse valley* cut through a mountain ridge; the term is used chiefly of the Jura Mountains. See *val*.

coaling station. See *fuelling station*.

coal measures. The series of rocks which include both the coal seams and the intervening strata of clay, sandstone, etc., in a coalfield. Some geologists, however, assume the term to refer to the upper Carboniferous system of rocks (see *Carboniferous period*), roughly equivalent to the Pennsylvanian of North America, whether actual coal seams are present or not.

coast. That part of the land which borders the sea or other extensive tract of water, and so comes under the direct influence of the waves. See *concordant coast*, *discordant coast*.

coastal plain. A plain which borders the sea coast and extends from the sea to the nearest elevated land. It may be formed by the deposition of solid matter by rivers, by denudation by the sea, or by the emergence of part of the former *continental shelf* owing to a relative fall in sea level.

coastline or **shore-line.** The coastal outline of the land, which includes bays, but crosses narrow inlets and river mouths.

cockpit. In a tropical *karst region*, a *doline* or *sinkhole*, especially in the 'cockpit country' of Jamaica.

col. (1) A depression in a range of mountains or hills, usually providing a pass through the range. It may be formed by two streams on opposite sides of the ridge cutting back towards one another, thus lowering the *water-parting*, or by the continuing erosion of an *arête* between two cirques on opposite sides of the ridge.

(2) The region situated between two *depressions* which face one another, and also between two *anticyclones* which face one another, the depressions and anticyclones being placed alternately; the nearly uniform pressure in a col is therefore higher than in the two depressions which it separates, and lower than in the two anticyclones. Sometimes on a weather chart only the two anticyclones appear, the col being an area of relatively low pressure between them – like a pass between two mountains; sometimes, too, only the two depressions may be shown. On the edge of the col, the winds circulate in different directions round the anticyclones and depressions, and within the col are light and variable. The weather associated with a col in summer is sometimes fine, but there is a pronounced tendency to the development of thunderstorms; in winter, conditions are liable to be dull or foggy.

cold desert. A term applied to the *ice sheet* of Arctic and Antarctic regions, where vegetation is prohibited by low temperatures and some-

Cold
Air

Warm
Air

Rain

Upward movement of warm air at a cold front (broken arrow) and direction of movement of the front.

times extended to the *tundra*, where vegetation is severely restricted by the climate.

cold front. The boundary line at the earth's surface between a mass of advancing cold air and a mass of warm air, beneath which the cold air pushes like a wedge. The frontal surface rises at a steeper angle than in the case of the *warm front*, the average slope being about 1 in 40. The passage of a cold front through a place is normally marked by a rise of atmospheric pressure, a fall of temperature, a veer of wind, a heavy shower, and sometimes a *line squall*, perhaps with thunder.

cold pole. A popular name sometimes applied to Verkhoyansk, in E Siberia, where excessively low temperatures have been reached; the mean midwinter temperature is −50°C, and the lowest reading then taken on the earth's surface, −70°C, was recorded in 1892. This is due, in the first place, to the development during winter of an intense anticyclone over Siberia, and, in these quiet weather conditions, the accumulation of a vast pool of abnormally cold air. The village of Verkhoyansk, situated almost on the Arctic Circle, lies at the bottom of a steep-walled valley carved into the plateau. The already cold air on the plateau is still further chilled by contact with the snow, which loses heat by radiation very rapidly in the clear, dry atmosphere – a loss which continues throughout the long polar night; this chilled air then sinks into the valley, and gives the excessively low temperatures at Verkhoyansk. In recent years temperatures as low as −88°C have been recorded at Vostok, the Soviet base in Antarctica.

cold wave. A burst of cold air, usually of polar origin, often experienced after the passage of a depression, behind the *cold front*. Such cold waves are specially prevalent in North America and Siberia, for during winter a reservoir or pool of cold air has accumulated over the great continental land masses; in the southern hemisphere the cold waves are comparatively mild, for the smaller land masses there do not permit such a vast accumulation of cold, anticyclonic air. See *southerly burster*, *pampero*. Cold waves are always menacing to crops.

As employed by the United States Weather Bureau, the term cold wave signifies a specific fall of temperature over twenty-four hours to a minimum below a certain temperature, the amount of fall and the minimum limit varying according to the season and the locality.

collision hypothesis. See *planetesimal hypothesis*.

colony. A human settlement formed by a body of people in a territory far from their native land, usually in an undeveloped and sparsely inhabited country; as used in the political sense (not, for instance, as in speaking of the French colony in London), the term signifies the country so settled – and in this sense the colony is subject to the country from which the colonists hailed.

combe, coomb, coombe. In southern England, a hollow or short valley in the side of a hill, e.g. in the chalk downs. In the Lake District the term is sometimes applied to a *cirque*.

comb rock, coomb rock. In SE England, the mass of rock fragments which often partly fills the dry chalk valleys and *combes*, probably as the result of *nivation*.

comet. A heavenly body revolving round the sun in an eccentric orbit, consisting of a solid nucleus and a luminous, gaseous tail, and small in comparison with a planet. One of the best-known comets is Halley's Comet, named after Edmund Halley (1656–1742), the English astronomer, who first observed it in 1682; it became visible again in 1758, and then periodically, e.g. in 1985–6, appearing every 76 years.

common. A tract of land which belongs to the local community as a whole, and is open to common use.

compass, magnetic. An instrument consisting of a magnetized needle, which, by being balanced on a fine point, is free to rotate in a horizontal plane; the needle always swings to such a position that one end points towards the north magnetic pole – *not* the north geographical pole. See *magnetism, terrestrial*. In the mariner's compass, the magnetic needle is fixed to a circular card, likewise free to rotate in the horizontal plane, which is graduated into thirty-two divisions of $11\frac{1}{4}°$ each – the thirty-two points of the compass.

composite landscape. A landscape which exhibits topographic features that have developed in more than one *cycle of erosion*.

composite volcano or **stratovolcano.** The most typical kind of *volcano*, taking the form of a conical mountain, built up during many eruptions of alternate layers of lava with ash, cinders, etc.: e.g. Stromboli (Italy), Rainier (USA), Fuji-san (Japan).

concordant coast. A coastline that is roughly parallel to the mountain ranges immediately inland, and is generally regular. When submergence takes place, the sea occupies former valleys, and the mountain

A concordant coast with coastal ranges: the Adriatic coast of Yugoslavia.

ranges become lines of islands, e.g. along the coast of Yugoslavia, in the Adriatic Sea. Alternative terms are longitudinal coast and Pacific coast, the latter because such a high proportion of the coasts around the rim of the Pacific Ocean are of this type. See *discordant coast*.

condensation. The process by which a substance changes from the vapour to the liquid state. Clouds, for instance, are formed by the condensation of water vapour in the atmosphere; air containing water vapour rises from the earth's surface, expands, and is cooled till the water vapour condenses into drops of water. When larger drops have collected and begin to fall as rain, they may evaporate again before reaching the earth's surface. The opposite process to condensation, in fact, is *evaporation*. See *dew point*.

condensation trail, contrail or **vapour trail.** A long, cloud-like trail that forms behind an aircraft owing to the condensation of water vapour produced by the combustion of its fuel. In the tropics trails

40

Conical projection with two standard parallels.

only form at heights exceeding about 10,000 m, in the latitude of Britain at about 6,000 m (winter) to 8,500 m (summer), and in high latitudes in winter they may form at ground level. The trails sometimes spread until they assume the appearance of *cirrus* clouds.

condominium. A territory governed jointly by two or more countries: e.g. the former New Hebrides, governed by Great Britain and France, from 1980 the Republic of Vanuatu.

cone, ash or **cinder.** See *ash cone*.

configuration. The form of a part of the earth's surface with respect to both its horizontal outline and its elevation.

confluence. The point at which one stream flows into another, or where two streams converge and unite.

confluent. A stream flowing into another of roughly equal size.

conglomerate. A rock composed of rounded pebbles cemented together in a matrix of finer material, sometimes called 'pudding-stone'; it is thus consolidated *gravel* or *shingle*. See also *breccia*.

conical projection. The type of *map projection* produced when the globe is imagined as being surrounded by a paper cone, the apex above the pole; the map is projected on to the cone, and the latter then unrolled. Straight lines radiating from the apex of the cone represent meridians, concentric circles represent parallels of latitude. Only along the parallel where the cone touched the globe are the distances on the two equal, so that the projection is accurate only along this one parallel, and is known as the 'one-standard parallel' projection. It is therefore used only for sections of the globe, the distortion being inconsiderable for a small area.

Errors are reduced in several modified conical projections, e.g. the 'two-standard parallel' projection, in which distances are made accurate along two parallels. The latter are selected, one towards the top, the other towards the bottom of the map, and both are made the correct length and the true distance apart. This scale is correct along all meridians and along the selected standard parallels, and the projection is thus superior to the 'one-standard parallel' projection for all maps having a substantial extent of latitude.

coniferous forest.* A forest of mainly evergreen coniferous or cone-bearing trees carrying needle-shaped leaves. From such forests is obtained the valuable softwood timber of commerce. The most important and extensive coniferous forests of the world stretch in a huge belt across northern Canada and northern Eurasia, with 'tongues' of forests extending southwards on the higher land, e.g. along the Rocky Mountains, and 'islands' of forest land in other mountainous areas farther south, e.g. in the Alps. These coniferous forests form the home of many valuable fur-bearing animals.

conjunction. (1) The apparent proximity to each other of two heavenly bodies.

Diagram to illustrate consequent (C), obsequent (O), and subsequent (S) rivers.

(2) The position of two heavenly bodies when they are in the same or nearly the same direction as viewed from the earth.

connate water. Water which was imprisoned in sedimentary rocks during their formation and has been held there: sometimes known as *fossil water*.

consequent river. A river which flows down the initial slope of land, i.e. in the direction of the *dip*, and is thus a necessary consequence of that slope. See *obsequent river*, *subsequent river*.

conservation, soil. See *soil conservation*.

continent. (1) One of the larger, unbroken masses of land into which the earth's surface is divided – Europe, Asia, Africa, North and South America, Australia, and Antarctica.

(2) In a colloquial sense, the mainland, applied particularly to Europe by the people of the British Isles.

continental climate. The type of climate experienced in the interior of the great continents, especially in the intermediate or 'temperate' zone of the northern hemisphere. Its influence also extends to eastern coasts of the continents and neighbouring islands, which are exposed in winter to the prevailing winds from the interior. It is a climate characterized by extremes of temperature, with maxima and minima occurring soon after the summer and winter *solstices* respectively. In addition to the great range of temperatures experienced, both diurnally and seasonally, other features of the climate are a relatively small rainfall and low humidities. See *maritime climate*.

continental divide. See *watershed*.

continental drift. The supposed horizontal displacement of portions of the original continent which comprised the entire land mass of the world to form the present-day continents, enunciated in the *displacement theory* and notably described in Wegener's Hypothesis (1910). According to this theory, the original land mass of *Sial*, which Wegener named *Pangaea*, fractured, and parts of it drifted away to form separate continental islands. Part of the evidence was the fact that the shores of opposite continents, e.g. the western coast of Africa and the eastern coast of South America, fit together fairly well, like the pieces of a jig-saw puzzle, and exhibit geological similarities. In the 1960s important developments in the theory were brought about by the study of *plate tectonics*, supported by considerable evidence derived from *palaeomagnetism*. Pangaea is believed to have broken up into a number of large plates about 60 km thick, which carried the continents and drifted about on the denser molten rock of the earth's interior. From 1968 onwards investigations were carried out on the sediments of the ocean basins, mainly in the Atlantic and Pacific Oceans, from a specially designed deep-sea drilling vessel, the 'Glomar Challenger', launched by the USA, and have helped to confirm the theory of continental drift. See also *mid-oceanic ridge*.

The continental shelf round the British Isles indicated by the 100-fathom isobath.

continental glacier. A term used by some geographers and glaciologists for an *ice sheet*.

continental platform. The approximately level part of the earth's crust which is raised above the depressions in which the oceans lie, and includes both the lower land areas of the continents themselves and also the *continental shelf* which borders the continents.

continental shelf. The sea bed, bordering the continents, which is covered by shallow water, in general 100 fathoms or less in depth; it thus takes the form of a shelf or ledge sloping gently downwards from the coast, and is approximately outlined by the *isobath* of 100 fathoms. At the edge it varies in depth from about 65 to 200 fathoms, however, and it also varies considerably in width, reaching in some places 160 km (100 miles) or more. Where it is widest, the angle of slope is usually least,

Diagram to illustrate the construction of contours on a map.

and may be less than 1°; where the coast is mountainous, it is usually narrow, and there is a quick transition from high land to deep water. Beyond the continental shelf there is a drop in the sea bed to a depth of 2,000 fathoms or more, so that the shelf has a relatively steep edge (see *continental slope*). As the land slopes continuously down-wards on to the continental shelf, with no change of angle at the water-line, it is widely held that the edge of shelf represents the former boundary of the continent; the shelf may have been formed by a rise in level of the sea or a fall in level of the land, or by the *denudation* of the fringe of the land by the sea or by the *deposition* of solid materials beneath the water by rivers, etc.

continental slope or **bathyal zone.** The relatively steep slope which de-scends from the edge of the *continental shelf* to the deep ocean bed. Its actual gradient is in fact gentle, usually not more than 5°.

contour. A line drawn on a map to join all places at the same height above sea level; a number of contours therefore depict on a flat map the relief of the land over the area covered. The intervals between contours may represent height differences of say 50 ft as on a British OS map (1:50,000), though heights are now given in metres, or 20 m, for instance, on the Swiss Landeskarte series (1:50,000), or of as much as many hundreds of feet (or metres) on a small-scale map of a large

45

area in an atlas. Heights and intervals on maps published in most countries are given in metres. On physical maps, the areas between adjacent contours are often shown in different colours; usually lowlands are coloured green, higher lands brown, the shades deepening progressively with height, while still higher land is often coloured red and finally white. Similar lines showing the depths of the sea bed are called *isobaths*, areas between them being coloured in varying shades of blue.

conurbation. An area which is occupied by a mass of streets, factories, dwellings, etc., possibly enclosing small isolated rural localities, and formed by the growth of several neighbouring and formerly separate towns. The recognized conurbations of England and Wales are Greater London, Tyneside, W Yorkshire, SE Lancashire, Merseyside, W Midlands, and SE Wales. Some authorities, however, apply the term also to much smaller 'built-up' areas.

convection. The transmission of heat from one part of a liquid or gas to another by the movement of the particles themselves. When the lower portion of a mass of fluid is heated, it expands, its density is reduced, and it rises, carrying its heat with it – to be replaced by cool fluid which in its turn is heated. A familiar example of convection is the upward movement of air which has been heated by contact with the earth's surface; this air is said to rise in a convection current. See *advection*.

convectional rain. Rain which is caused by the process of *convection* in the atmosphere. When the surface layers of the atmosphere are heated, the moisture-laden air rises in a convection current, and in rising is cooled till the *dew point* is reached, and its water vapour condenses and forms cloud; the convection current is sometimes so strong that the cloud attains great vertical depth, and its water content becomes so considerable that heavy rain is deposited. Thus the thundery rain of a summer afternoon in temperate regions is typical convectional rain. See *rainfall*.

coomb, coombe. See *combe*.

coppice. A small wood, or plantation of trees, which is periodically cut to provide posts, fuel, etc.

copse. A small wood or thicket.

coral island. A *coral reef* situated far from any other kind of land. It may consist simply of a mound of sand resting on a flat coral reef, in which case it may be several miles (km) long and quite broad, but will have only slight elevation. When there has been an uplift of the land, however, the reef itself may be above sea level, and the island may reach a considerable altitude. By various agencies a coral island may receive seeds which become established and at length cover it with a rich vegetation.

coral polyp.* A small marine creature, constructed like a sea anemone, which has a hard skeleton formed by the solidification of the base and side-walls of the body, and can only live in shallow tropical seas. The skeleton is made of calcium carbonate extracted from the sea water in which the polyp lives, and the solidification of its base fixes it to the surface to which it is attached. When the coral polyp dies, the softer parts of the body decay and are washed away, but the skeleton is left behind. The increase in numbers of the coral polyps causes the masses of coral to grow to enormous size, forming *coral reefs* and *coral islands*.

coral reef.* A chain of rocks lying at or near the surface of the sea, and built up principally by immense numbers of *coral polyps*; both on and behind the reef, fragments of shells, coral, and coral sand are piled up by wind and wave, and new land is thus formed. Three more or less distinct kinds of coral reef are recognized: fringing reefs, barrier reefs, and *atolls*.

A *fringing reef*, formed by corals and other calcareous organisms growing on the bed of the shallow seas round a continent or island, lies near the shore; its surface comprises a rough, uneven platform at about the level of low water, and its outer edge slopes downwards into the sea. The corals grow outwards from the shore to a depth of about 30 fathoms, and upwards to low water level, so that the edge of the platform lies at approximately the 30-fathom line. As the outer corals grow most freely, they may reach the surface first, leaving a shallow channel or lagoon between the platform and the land.

A *barrier reef* lies at some distance from the shore, its outer side rises from deep water where no reef-building corals live, and the lagoon is wide and deep. There are two possible explanations of its formation: either its foundations were not laid by corals, or the depth of the sea has increased since the corals built them; both may be true. See *atoll*.

corded lava. See *ropy* or *corded lava*.

cordillera. A series of more or less parallel ranges of mountains together with the intervening plateaux and basins: applied especially to the Andes of South America, first named by the Spaniards Las Cordilleras de los Andes. In South America the term is applied to individual ranges, e.g. Cordillera de Mérida (Venezuela). It is applied, too, to the group of mountain systems in western North America, from and including the Rocky Mountains to the Pacific coast.

core. The central part of the earth, below the *mantle*, about 6,900 km (4,300 miles) in diameter, with a high density and probably consisting of nickel-iron. The behaviour of earthquake waves on reaching the zone suggest that it consists of an inner solid core surrounded by an outer liquid core.

coriolis force. See *geostrophic wind*.

corn belt. The belt of land in the United States, situated south and south-west of the Great Lakes, where maize – known to the Americans as corn – is principally grown. The states which lead in corn production in this area are Iowa, Illinois, and Nebraska.

corn belt climate. The type of climate experienced in the *corn belt* of the United States, and in other regions similarly situated on the continents of Europe and Asia which together produce most of the world's corn crop: e.g. the plains of the Danube basin, and northern China. The climate may be regarded as the long-summer type of the cool intermediate climate, or as the long-summer sub-division of the humid *continental climate*.

corona. (1) The fringe of radiant light surrounding the sun which is plainly visible round the dark rim of the moon during a total eclipse.

(2) A number of coloured rings round the sun or moon, comprising a bluish inner region and a reddish outer ring. Usually this, the aureole, is all that appears; sometimes, however, there is a complete corona, the aureole being surrounded by a series of coloured rings, from violet on the inside through blue, green, yellow, to red. Thus the corona is distinguished from the *halo* by the fact that its colour sequence is opposite; it is produced by the diffraction of light by water drops, while the halo is due to refraction.

corrasion. The mechanical *erosion* caused by loose solid material during its *transportation*: e.g. that effected by the solid material carried down by a river, in wearing away fragments from its bed and its banks. Corrasion of the bed, thereby causing a deepening of the channel, is called *vertical corrasion*, while corrasion of the banks is called *lateral corrasion*. Although a stream of clear water will not affect solid rock, it will cause considerable corrasion if the bed and banks consist of loose material. Most of the corrasion effected by a river, however, is due to the pebbles and sand that it drives along its bed. Another example of corrasion is the wearing away of the surface of desert rocks by wind-borne sand.

corrie. See *cirque*.

corrosion. The wearing away of rocks by chemical action, e.g. by solution, as distinct from *corrasion*, which is a mechanical process.

coseismic line. See *homoseismal line*.

cotton belt. The belt of land in the south-eastern United States which produces more of the world's cotton crop than any other area; the rich black soils of Texas, Mississippi, and Alabama have the highest output, but most of the state of Florida lies outside the cotton belt.

cotton belt climate. A term used by some geographers to signify the type of climate experienced in the American *cotton belt*, which forms part of the *subtropical region*. The climate, in fact, may be regarded as one of the two sub-divisions of the subtropical climate – the humid or wet subtropical climate. It differs from the dry subtropical or *Mediterranean climate* in being usually located on the eastern sides of the continents, in having a heavier rainfall, and in having its rainfall well distributed throughout the year or concentrated in the warm season. The climate is characteristic of southern China as well as the American cotton belt.

counter-trades. See *anti-trades*.

course. See *river*.

cove. A small creek, inlet, or bay; a steep-sided hollow or recess inland, e.g. in the side of a mountain.

cover crop. A quickly-growing crop sown chiefly to protect the land against *soil erosion*. A leguminous plant is often favoured because it also restores nitrogen to the soil, and for this reason may be termed a *green manure crop*.

crag. A rough, steep rock or point of rock. In high mountain regions crags are often formed by the action of frost in *weathering*.

crag-and-tail. A hill or crag having a steep, often precipitous face on one side, and sloping downwards comparatively gently on the other side. When the crag-and-tail has been formed glacially, there is a hollow on one side of the crag and a long 'tail' of broken rock material on the other side. This is due to the fact that the crag or mass of rock, lying in the bed of a glacier, has obstructed its flow; the ice has then worn away the rock on the upstream side, and deposited the waste on the downstream side.

crater. * The funnel-shaped hollow at the top of the cone of a *volcano*. The bottom of the funnel opens into the channel or pipe through which the erupted material finds its way to the surface. The term is also sometimes applied to the hollow caused by the fall of a *meteorite* on to the earth's surface.

crater-lake. A sheet of water collected in the *crater* of an extinct volcano. See *caldera*.

creek. (1) A narrow coastal inlet.

(2) A small stream, tributary, or branch of a river.

Creole. A person born in the West Indies, but not of the aboriginal race; also applied to such persons born in certain areas of the American mainland (particularly Central America) and some European colonies. The term is thus used sometimes of the descendants of European settlers, sometimes of Negroes; nowadays it is often associated, however, with people of mixed blood.

crepuscular rays. The beams of sunlight seen radiating from the position of the sun just after sunset, the dark bands representing shadows cast by clouds or hills below the horizon. The term is also applied to similar clearly defined beams diverging upwards from behind a cloud, or passing through gaps in a layer of low cloud.

crescent dune. See *barkhan*.

crevasse. * A deep, vertical crack in a glacier. It may be formed when the slope down which the glacier is moving steepens, for there the glacier begins to move more quickly. When the slope becomes gentler again, the crevasse tends to close up, but it rarely makes the surface of the ice smooth once more; the sun has melted some of the ice while the crevasse has been open, and so widened its upper part, and the two opposite faces do not fit when the crevasse closes. A crevasse is also formed when the glacier has to turn a sharp corner. Both these kinds of crevasses are transverse to the glacier, and, since it moves more rapidly in the middle than at the sides, they become curved outwards in the direction of movement. More or less longitudinal crevasses may be formed when the valley widens and the glacier spreads; oblique crevasses may also develop, owing, for example, to the difference between the velocity in the middle and at the sides of the glacier. The term is also applied to a wide crack in the raised bank or levee of a river or canal. See also *icefall*.

croft. A small farm-holding in the highlands or islands of Scotland, consisting of a piece of land used primarily for cultivation, usually adjoining the house. When combined with fishing and possibly other occupations, the craft is reckoned to supply all essential family needs in food, fuel, and clothing, though its average size, excluding the common hill pastures over which the few cattle and sheep can roam, is only about five acres (2 hectares).

cromlech. A prehistoric structure, consisting of a large flat stone resting on upright stones; in Great Britain the term is practically synonymous with *dolmen*, while in France it is applied to a circle of small *menhirs*.

crust, earth's. The outermost portion of the earth, lying above the *Moho*, and thus about 8–40 km (5–25 miles) in thickness, and composed largely of *igneous rocks*; it comprises two layers, the upper discontinuous *sial* and the lower continuous *sima*. See *lithosphere*.

crustal movements. The movements of the outer parts of the solid *lithosphere*, as manifested by *raised beaches, earthquakes*, etc.

cuesta (Spanish). A ridge, or belt of hilly land, formed on gently dipping rock strata, e.g. on a *coastal plain*, from the more durable layers, which resist *denudation* better than the weaker layers, and are thus left behind as uplands; it has a gentle *dip* slope on one side, and a relatively steep *scarp* on the other.

cumulonimbus.* A heavy, dark *cloud* of great vertical depth, towering upwards in huge, voluminous masses, the tops being about 4,500 m (15,000 ft) or more above the base, often spreading out aloft in the form of an anvil. Below the base, very low, ragged clouds frequently trail. It is the typical thunderstorm cloud, and usually gives showers of rain, snow, or hail.

cumulus. A *cloud* of considerable vertical development, though less so than in the *cumulonimbus*. The upper parts are dome-shaped, and have 'cauliflower' heads, while the base is practically horizontal. Two types are generally recognized: the fair-weather cumulus, small, white, detached puffs typical of fair weather, and heavy cumulus, which has much greater depth, and often develops later into cumulonimbus.

current. See *ocean current*.

cuspate foreland. A roughly triangular foreland or cape, with the apex extending out into the sea, usually formed by the joining up of two curved spits, which have themselves been constructed by two opposing sets of waves. Well-known examples include Cape Hatteras, North Carolina, and Cape Kennedy (formerly Cape Canaveral), Florida, USA, and Dungeness, Kent, England.

cut-off. See *ox-bow lake*.

cwm. In Wales, a term used principally for a *cirque*, but occasionally for other types of valley.

cycle of erosion. The series of changes through which *erosion* causes a newly uplifted land surface to pass, from youth through maturity to old age. In youth, streams occupy steep-sided V-shaped valleys. *Corrasion* is rapid, and such features as rapids, waterfalls, and lakes are often apparent. In maturity, or middle age, when erosion has proceeded farther, the valleys are broad and gentler in slope, and rivers have begun to meander. In old age, valleys are very broad, rivers are sluggish, and the region becomes a *peneplain*.

cyclone. A region of low atmospheric pressure, of which there are two types. The first, characteristic of temperate latitudes, is now usually referred to as a *depression*; the second, a much more violent phenomenon, though in general covering a smaller area, and typical of the tropics, is usually called a *tropical cyclone*. The two types are similar in the fact that their winds in the northern hemisphere circulate in an anti-clockwise direction, and in the southern hemisphere in a clockwise direction.

cyclonic rain. Rain associated with the passage of a cyclone or *depression*, and caused by a warm, moist air mass moving upwards over colder, heavier air. See *rainfall*.

cylindrical projection. The type of *map projection* produced if a paper cylinder is imagined as surrounding the globe, and, after all relevant points on the latter are projected on to the former, the paper is then opened out. On this kind of projection the poles cannot be truly depicted, as their points have been extended to occupy the whole width of the map, and, as a result, all territories lying near to the poles are much exaggerated in size. This is a serious disadvantage, and with the one exception of *Mercator's projection* cylindrical projections are not in common use.

D

dale. A wide, open valley, mainly in northern England and southern Scotland.

dam. A man-made structure built across a river in order to control the flow of water. In general the purpose of constructing a dam is to provide a supply of water, particularly for irrigation, and to manufacture electricity cheaply by utilizing the head of water thus artificially produced; flood control is also ensured. See *barrage*. The term is occasionally used of an obstruction formed by a glacier or by another natural agency across a river or stream so as to produce a lake.

datum level. The zero with reference to which the altitudes of land surfaces and the depths of the sea are determined. See *mean sea level*.

dawn. The faint light which illuminates the various regions of the earth before sunrise; the time when light appears in the sky; the interval during which the atmosphere is illuminated before sunrise. See *twilight*.

day. See *sidereal day* and *solar day*, *mean*.

daylight saving time. See *British Summer Time* or *BST*.

dead ground. A term applied, chiefly in surveying, to ground which is hidden from the observer by intervening land, e.g. by a ridge.

dead valley. The term used, particularly by French geographers, for a *dry valley*.

débâcle. A term, now little used, for the breaking up during spring or summer of the ice formed on rivers during the winter, chiefly applied to the great rivers of the USSR and North America. In general it takes place at successively later dates with increasing distance from the equator: in the southern USSR about mid-March, but in extreme northern Siberia not until June. The débâcle has a duration of two to six weeks, and during this time the rivers often overflow their banks and inundate the surrounding country.

debris or **detritus.** A collection of material formed by the disintegration or wearing away of rocks.

deciduous forest. A forest consisting of trees which lose their leaves at some season of the year. In the case of the *monsoon forests*, such as those of India and Burma, the trees shed their leaves during the hot season in order to protect themselves against excessive loss of moisture by evaporation. In the case of the deciduous forests of the cool intermediate lands, such as those of north-west Europe, the trees shed their leaves during the autumn (appropriately called the 'fall' in America because then the leaves are falling), in order to protect themselves against the cold and frost of winter. From the deciduous forests is obtained much of the valuable hardwood timber of commerce: from the monsoon forests such extremely hard wood as teak, from the cool intermediate forests such wood as oak, elm, and beech.

declination. The angular distance of a heavenly body from the *celestial equator*, measured on a meridian passing through the body.

declination, magnetic or **variation, magnetic.** The angle at any point on the earth's surface between the magnetic meridian (the direction in which a freely pivoted compass needle points) and the geographical meridian (the true geographical north). At most places on the earth's surface the compass points either west or east of true north, and the declination could be expressed, for instance, as 10° W. See *agonic line*. Magnetic declination is subject to a regular diurnal variation, to irregular, comparatively short-period changes, and to secular change. See *magnetism, terrestrial*.

declination of the sun. The angular distance of the sun either north or south of the equator. At the summer *solstice*, about 21 June, the *north* declination of the sun is thus $23\frac{1}{2}°$, and about 22 December the sun's *south* declination is $23\frac{1}{2}°$. A sailor, by observing the sun's zenith distance in degrees, and allowing for the declination (found from the Nautical Almanac), can thus find his latitude at noon on any day; if he is north of the Tropic of Cancer, for instance, and the sun is north of the equator (i.e. in summer), he will calculate his latitude by adding the sun's declination to its zenith distance.

deep. One of the deepest parts of the ocean, forming a depression in the sea floor of limited area, and having relatively steep sides. The deeps are not usually found in the middle of the oceans, but towards the margins, generally where volcanoes are still active and earthquakes common. Most of the deeps, in fact, occur as narrow, trough-like depressions around the shores of the Pacific; among them are the Tuscarora Deep off Japan and the Atacama Deep along the coast of South America. There are others along the edges of some of the plateaux which rise from the *deep-sea plain* – one extending from the Tonga Islands almost to New Zealand. A *sounding* of 10,497 m was recorded north-east of Mindanao in the Philippines, and in 1960 the US *bathyscaphe* 'Trieste' descended to 11,022 m in the Marianas Trench. In the Atlantic, where there are fewer deeps, a sounding of 9,220 m was recorded in the Milwaukee Deep, north of Puerto Rico, and the only other deep with soundings above 8,000 m is the South Sandwich Trench, in the South Atlantic, where a depth of 8,428 m was recorded.

deepening. In meteorology, the term for decreasing atmospheric pressure at the centre of a *depression*: the opposite of *filling*.

53

deep-sea or **abyssal plain.** The extensive and fairly level area, about 4,000 to 6,000 m below the surface, which forms the majority of the ocean floor. In places it descends to the *deeps*. See also *guyot, seamount*.

defile. A term rather loosely used, but usually applied to a gorge, ravine, or narrow pass.

deflation. The lifting and conveyance of particles of sand and dust by the wind.

deforestation. The process of clearing forests.

degradation. A process which tends to wear down the land surface; it is usually applied to a river, and involves the deepening of its valley by the river. When the load of loose, solid material entering a stretch of river, for instance, is less than the amount it can carry there, the river wears away from its bed a greater amount than it deposits. The term is also applied to a glacier. See *aggradation*.

degree. (1) The unit of temperature, varying according to the scale employed, e.g. *centigrade* (*Celsius*), *Fahrenheit*.

(2) The unit of measurement of *latitude* or *longitude*, usually employed to indicate position on the earth's surface. As a degree is geometrically equal to 1/360 of a circle, the distance between the equator and the pole, which is one quarter of the earth's circumference, is taken to be equal to 90° of latitude; a degree of latitude is thus equal to 1/360 of the earth's circumference. Similarly, a degree of longitude is also equal to 1/360 of the earth's circumference *at the equator*, but decreases in length in passing from the equator to either of the poles, becoming zero at the poles. Each degree of latitude or longitude is divided into 60 minutes (′), and each minute into 60 seconds (″).

dell. A small wooded valley; dale. Generally a literary term.

delta. The fan-shaped alluvial tract formed at the mouth of a river, when it deposits more solid material there than can be removed by tidal or other currents: the name being originally applied by the Greeks to the alluvial tract thus produced by the Nile, owing to its resemblance in shape to the fourth letter of their alphabet. As material is deposited, it becomes easier for the river to divide and flow to each side, each new branch forms new banks, then divides and sub-divides, and the deposit grows outwards in the shape of a fan or triangle, which finally becomes covered with a network of channels; the apex of the triangle is called the head of the delta. A fan-shaped delta, such as that of the Nile, is known as an *arcuate delta*. A lobate delta, such as that of the Mississippi, is known as a *bird's foot delta*. A small delta is sometimes built where a river enters a lake, or at the confluence of two rivers, especially where a swift stream heavily laden with sediment joins a slow river. Many of the great deltas of the world are extensively cultivated, and some support dense agricultural populations. When the delta streams make sudden great changes of course as they are liable to do, disastrous

Sketch map of the delta of the Nile.

floods may affect these populations. In the Hwang-ho flood of 1887, at least a million people were drowned and many villages destroyed. In addition to the Nile, the Mississippi, and the Hwang-ho, other well-known deltas include those of the Ganges-Brahmaputra, the Rhine, and the Rhône.

demoiselle (French). See *earth pillar*.

dendritic drainage. The type of drainage produced when a *consequent river* receives a number of tributary streams, which in turn are fed by smaller tributaries, the whole forming a dendritic or tree-like pattern. (See Fig. p. 56.)

dendrochronology. The study of past climatic changes as revealed by the annual growth rings of trees, being specially concerned with variations in temperature and rainfall: applied particularly in the field of *geochronology*.

density of population. The average number of inhabitants living within a specified unit of area – usually the square kilometre or the square mile – in a certain region.

denudation. The wearing away of the land by various natural agencies: the sun, the wind, the rain, frost, running water, moving ice, and the sea. The heat of the sun causes the rocks to expand, crack, and break up; the wind carries loose particles, and with sand helps to wear away rocks; the rain loosens and carries away soil; frost freezes water in the cracks of rocks, causes the cracks to widen, and the rock to break; rivers and streams wear away the land, especially in their upper courses, where their slopes are steep; moving ice in the form of

Pattern of streams illustrating dendritic drainage.

glaciers also wears away the land; the sea along the coasts wears away the rocks. In addition, water, especially if it contains carbon dioxide, has a strong solvent action on parts of the earth's crust. Rock salt is readily and completely soluble, limestone more slowly and less completely soluble; most rocks, however, are only partially dissolved. The process of denudation may thus be classified as *weathering, transportation*, with its accompanying *corrasion*, and solution. Denudation is one of the two major processes responsible for earth sculpture, or the change in form of the earth's surface, the other being *deposition*.

dependency. A territory which is governed by a state from which it is remote.

deposition. The laying down of solid material which has been carried from a distant part of the earth's crust by some natural agency. Rivers, for instance, deposit mud and pebbles; the winds carry much sand and dust, which are deposited when they die down, and fall either on the land or into the sea; glaciers carry along boulders and stones, which they deposit where they end owing to the melting of the ice; the sea deposits sand and pebbles, Deposition is one of the two major processes of earth sculpture, the other being *denudation*.

depression. A region where the atmospheric pressure is low relative to

A typical depression showing isobars and surface winds; also occlusion
(O), warm front (W), and cold front (C) (N hemisphere).

that of its surroundings, sometimes known as a low or a cyclone. On
the *weather chart* it is represented by a number of closed *isobars*, more
or less oval or circular in shape, the isobar of lowest pressure being the
nearest the centre of the depression. Both the size and the velocity of a
depression are very variable; it may be 150–3,000 km (100–2,000 miles)
across, it may be practically stationary or moving at about 900–1,100
km (600–700 miles) per day. A 'deep' depression is one in which the
pressure is very much lower at the centre than at the edges, a 'shallow'
depression one in which these pressures are not very different from
each other. The winds of a depression, which in the northern hemisphere circulate round the centre in an anti-clockwise direction, in the
southern hemisphere in a clockwise direction, are generally much
stronger than those of an *anticyclone*, the *pressure gradient* being
steeper.
According to modern meteorological theory, the depressions which
are so prominent a feature of the weather of temperate regions originate where warm tropical air meets cold polar air, the former ascending
over the latter with the formation of frontal surfaces. See *front, cold
front, warm front.* Unsettled weather is characteristic of depressions,

and the rainfall which accompanies them is due to the ascent of the warm air over the cold air, and the formation of extensive cloud systems. See *cyclonic rain*. With depressions are often associated *secondary depressions*. (See Fig. p. 57.)

desert. An almost barren tract of land in which the precipitation is so scanty or so spasmodic that it will not adequately support vegetation. A desert in which absolutely nothing grows, however, is uncommon; it may be extremely poor grassland or extremely poor scrub. A rock desert is one in which the rock has been exposed owing to the strong erosive action of the wind, with only slight deposition. In a stony desert, the rock surface has been broken up by temperature changes, and the ground covered by a layer of fragments, from which the smaller particles have been carried away by the wind. A sandy desert usually has an undulating surface of *dunes* with intervening hollows.

The deserts of the world are often sub-divided into tropical or hot deserts and mid-latitude deserts; of the former, probably the best known are the Sahara and the Arabian Desert, of the latter the deserts of Gobi and Turkestan. An area of high latitude or high altitude whose lack of vegetation is due to low temperatures is sometimes called a *cold desert*. See *desert climate*.

desert climate. The type of climate of which the salient feature is aridity, or lack of regular precipitation; it may thus occur within a wide range of latitudes, the two principal climatic divisions being the tropical or hot desert and the mid-latitude desert. The *isohyet* of 250 mm (10 in) may be taken as a rough guide to the limit of the desert climate, though in the far north of Canada and Siberia a rainfall of 250 mm is actually sufficient to promote forest growth. Character of rainfall, in fact, is as important as amount: in some desert areas there may be a rainfall of over 500 mm during the year, but it falls in violent thundery showers, and is mostly lost by *run-off* and evaporation. Associated with the aridity of the desert climate are such characteristics as amount of sunshine, range of temperatures, and relief of land – all of which combine to distinguish it from other climates, in whatever latitude it is situated. Its most significant feature is its unproductiveness, its inability to support settled, independent communities.

One of the main causes of the aridity of the desert climate is distance from marine influence, so that it occurs principally in continental interiors. Another is the system of *planetary winds*, with which areas of a permanent or seasonal high pressure in the *horse latitudes* are associated; high atmospheric pressure is unfavouable to precipitation, and the greatest areas of desert climate in the world are thus situated in these areas of high pressure – the Sahara, Arabia, central Australia, the Kalahari and the Atacama Deserts, etc.

desert pavement. A relatively smooth, mosaic-like area in a desert region.

consisting of pebbles closely packed together after the removal of finer material. See *reg*, *serir*.

detritus. Fragments of material removed by disintegration and other processes from the surfaces of rocks.

dew. The moisture deposited on the earth's surface, or on objects near to the earth's surface such as blades of grass, when nocturnal radiation from the earth has cooled the lower layers of the atmosphere below the *dew point*, and the water vapour present has condensed into drops. The greater the amount of water vapour in the air, and the lower the temperature of the ground, the more abundant the dew. For dew to form, the air must be calm or nearly so, in order that it may remain long enough in contact with the ground to be cooled to the *dew point* – unless that temperature has already been practically reached. A warm day favours evaporation, increasing the amount of water vapour in the air, and lack of clouds favours radiation at night; thus calm weather and a clear sky provide the best conditions for production of dew. See *hoar frost*.

dew point. The temperature at which the atmosphere, being cooled, becomes saturated with water vapour, and by *condensation* the latter is deposited as drops of *dew*.

dew pond. An artificially constructed pond, lined with cement or clay, situated at high level on chalk downs, e.g. in southern England, which retains its water for unusually long periods, even during drought, and is therefore useful for watering cattle. The name suggests that the water supply is maintained by dew, but in fact little is derived from this source.

diastrophism. The disturbance and dislocation of the earth's crust, including its bending, folding, and breaking, which has resulted in the major inequalities of its surface. See *epeirogenesis*, *orogenesis*.

diathermancy. The thermal permeability, or the ability to transmit radiant heat, of a body such as the atmosphere.

diatom ooze. One of the *oozes* which cover a large proportion of the ocean bed. It is of vegetable origin, consisting of the siliceous parts of microscopic diatom plants or algae which mainly inhabit the cold waters of the earth; they have shells of silica, from which the ooze is formed. There is a broad belt of diatom ooze extending round the earth in the southern ocean.

dikakah (Arabic). Terrain which is characteristic of the low-lying plains of N E Saudi Arabia, consisting chiefly of sand with scattered bushes and hummocks of grass, creating an uneven surface at ground level.

dike. See *dyke*.

dingle. A small, narrow, well-wooded valley; generally used in a literary context.

dip. (1) The maximum slope of an inclined stratum of rock measured

Rock strata illustrating dip and strike.

A discordant coast with coastal ranges: the S W coast of Ireland.

from the horizontal, and stated in terms of the angle in degrees and the direction as a point of the compass, e.g. 5° NW.

(2) The angle between the direction of the earth's magnetic field and the horizontal at any point on the earth's surface.

discordant coast. A coastline that extends across the trend of the mountains and valleys immediately inland, and, unlike the *concordant coast*, is generally irregular, with many inlets: e.g. the coast of S W Ireland. Alternative terms are transverse coast and Atlantic coast, the latter because such a high proportion of the coasts around the Atlantic Ocean are of this type. (See Fig. above.)

dismembered rivers. Rivers which were originally the tributaries of another, but now enter the sea independently, owing to the submergence (by the sea) of the lower part of the river system.

displacement theory. See *continental drift*.

dissected plateau. A *plateau* into which a number of valleys have been carved by erosion; its origin as a plateau is patent, however, when the tops of the mountains and ridges are seen to be level against the skyline, showing that they once formed part of a continuous surface.

distributary. A branch or outlet which leaves a main river and does not rejoin it, carrying its water to the sea or a lake. It is usually applied to the numerous channels into which a river divides on its *delta*, or on an *alluvial fan*.

diurnal range. The amount of variation between the maximum and minimum of any element, such as air temperature, during 24 hours.

divide. See *watershed*.

doab. Chiefly on the Indo-Gangetic Plain of India and Pakistan, the alluvial tract of land between two adjacent rivers, e.g. the Rechna Doab, between the Chenab and Ravi rivers. In Urdu and Persian the term means literally 'two waters'.

doctor, the. A name given locally to a number of different winds in various parts of the world, on account of their moderating effect on the otherwise unpleasant and unhealthy weather conditions; the *harmattan* of West Africa and the regular summer sea-breeze of the coast of Western Australia are often so-called.

doldrums. The equatorial belt of low atmospheric pressure where the N E and S E *trade winds* converge on and meet each other, producing calms and light surface winds and a strong upward movement of air. Thus, in spite of the calms and light winds, the doldrums are characterized by turbulent and stormy weather, with heavy rains, thunderstorms, and squalls: on account of their lack of wind, they used to be avoided as far as possible by sailing-ships, for the latter were often becalmed for several days. The doldrums are variable both in position and extent, usually moving northwards and southwards with the sun; their movement, however, is much less than that of the sun, being about 5° on each side of the mean position, with a lag of one or two months behind the sun. Along coasts in the doldrums, the alternating *land breeze* and *sea breeze* are important. See *intertropical convergence zone*.

doline or **dolina.** A closed hollow in a *karst region*, formed by the solution of the limestone near the surface, and subsequent subsidence; it is often rounded or elliptical in shape, and sometime has a *sinkhole* into which surface water flows.

dolmen. A prehistoric structure consisting of a large, unhewn stone resting on several upright stones; in Great Britain the term is practically synonymous with *cromlech*.

dolomite. A semi-transparent crystalline mineral consisting of the double

61

carbonates of calcium and magnesium; also a rock, often known as magnesian limestone, in which the mineral is the chief constituent.

dome. A curved stratum of rock in which the *dip* is in all directions away from a central point rather than an axis, as in an *anticline*. See also *salt dome*.

donga. In South Africa, a steep-sided gully or dry watercourse, similar to the *wadi* or *nullah*.

down. A tract of open, mainly treeless, hilly land, especially applied to the chalk hills of southern England, sparsely covered with soil and mainly used for pasturing sheep.

downland. A term sometimes applied to the mid-latitude or temperate *grasslands* of Australia and New Zealand.

drain. An artificial channel for carrying away (draining) surplus water from land, common in low-lying parts of England, and sometimes used in names of certain channels: e.g. in the Fens, Hobhole Drain, Lincs.; in Somerset, King's Sedgemoor Drain.

drainage area. See *catchment basin*.

dreikanter. See *ventifact*.

drift. (1) A slow movement of surface water at sea, on a lake, etc., caused by the wind; the similar movement of sand, etc.

(2) Any deposit on the earth's surface which has been transported, e.g. by the wind, but generally applied to one transported by a glacier (glacial drift) or by the water issuing from a glacier.

(3) In South Africa, an important ford on a river.

drift-ice. Detached portions of ice-floes or icebergs carried by currents into the open sea, beyond the limit of the pack-ice.

drift mining. The extraction of a mineral, such as coal, through an opening at ground level which leads down an incline to the seam (or ore vein); this incline may be quite steep (e.g. 1 in 4), and the mineral may be removed by belt conveyor or by wagons hauled by a locomotive. See *adit*.

drizzle. Rainfall in which the water drops are extremely small, like a fine spray, of diameter about 0.2 to 0.5 mm.

drought. An extended period of dry weather; extreme dryness due to lack of rain. A drought is liable to cause most distress in a region on the boundary between one which has an abundant or at least reliable rainfall and one in which the rainfall is adequate in most years but from time to time fails – as in some of the densely populated parts of India and China. In the less populous parts of the interior of Australia, North and South America, the losses due to drought are mainly confined to livestock. Certain definitions of types of drought have been adopted. See *absolute drought*, *partial drought*, *dry spell*.

drowned valley or **submerged valley.** A valley which has been submerged by the advance of the sea or a lake, owing to the sinking of the land or the rise of the sea or lake. See *ria*.

drumlin. An elongated hill or ridge of *boulder clay*, usually oval and shaped like half an egg; it occurs in a previously glaciated region, the long axis lying parallel to the direction of flow of the ice, with the thick, steep end facing the direction whence the ice came. The exact manner of formation of drumlins is somewhat uncertain, but they are probably fragments of ground *moraine* which were compressed by ice movements into their characteristic shape. Whenever they are found, they occur in large numbers. Some of the best-known groups of drumlins are those situated in Northern Ireland, e.g. Co. Down, northern England, e.g. Eden valley, and northern USA, near Madison, Wisconsin, and south of Lake Ontario in central New York State. See also *rock drumlin*.

dry farming. A method of farming without irrigation in an area of limited rainfall, the land being treated so as to conserve the moisture it contains; the term is usually confined to the raising of crops. Specially adapted plants that will best utilize the available moisture are cultivated. Other features of dry farming are the removal of weeds that would take up some of the moisture, and the preparation of a mulch to resist capillarity and protect the moist earth from the heat of the sun. A common practice is the formation of a dry, powdery surface soil by frequent use of the plough, the harrow, and other implements, and to this procedure is sometimes added the artificial production of a hard, impervious sub-surface layer of soil. Even stones may be used as a mulch, as in the drier parts of the Mediterranean region. In Siberia, where melting snow provides valuable moisture for the spring-sown crops, the soil is ploughed in the autumn; this conserves the snow in the furrows, and prevents it from being swept from the ground by the strong winds of winter, and thus being lost to the soil. In the drier regions of India, USSR, USA, Canada, and Australia, dry farming methods have long been employed.

dry gap. See *wind gap*.

dry spell. In the British Isles, a period of at least fifteen consecutive days, none of which has received as much as 1.0 mm of rain, The definition has not been internationally accepted, however, and a dry spell is often defined, not by any specific set of climatological data, but by its effects on plant life. See *wet spell*.

dry valley. A valley in chalk or limestone country, from which the stream has disappeared, or may appear only very temporarily, e.g. after heavy rain (see *bourne, winterbourne*). There are various theories as to their formation, including the lowering of the *water table* and the diversion of the original stream by *river capture*.

dune.* A mound or ridge of sand formed, either in a desert or along the sea coast, through transportation by the wind. The sand particles are carried along by the wind and piled into a heap, which gradually increases in size till it becomes a mound or ridge; the dune is often commenced where an obstacle of some kind exists, and the sand is heaped against this until it is covered and the sand falls over on the leeward side.

In a desert there are two main types of dune, the crescent-shaped dune or *barkhan*, and the long, narrow, ridge-like dune, or *seif dune*, extending in the direction of the prevailing wind. By the action of the wind, the shape and size of a dune are always changing. When the winds are variable, it has no fixed shape, and its movements are irregular. When the winds are fairly constant in direction, however, the sand on the windward slopes is blown over the top and falls over on the leeward side, and the dune thus travels slowly forwards. On the margin of a sandy desert, this movement of the dunes has caused cities to be buried and has devastated once fertile land. Often, however, it is only the smaller dunes which move: when the occasional rain of the desert does fall, much of the water is conserved in the deeper parts of the large dune, evaporation being restricted to the surface layers; this moistness of the lower layers thus helps to fix the position of the dune.

Along the sea coast the dunes somewhat resemble in profile those of the desert, but in a non-arid climate they do not usually travel far inland, largely because they become overgrown with vegetation, e.g. marram grass. In the *landes* of SW France movement of the dunes was deliberately checked by sowing plants and later coniferous trees.

dust. Solid matter consisting of minute particles, smaller than sand particles, and occurring everywhere in the atmosphere; it is often carried immense distances by the wind, and is constantly being deposited on the earth's surface. The sources of dust are various: in and near to industrial areas, the smoke from factory and domestic chimneys charges the atmosphere with particles of carbon and other substances; in the deserts, dust is raised from the ground by the wind (see *duststorm*), while volcanic dust enters the air during an eruption. Particles of *hygroscopic dust* act as nuclei for the condensation of water vapour in the atmosphere.

dust bowl. A type of man-made desert, a region subject to severe *drought* from which topsoil has been removed by wind erosion, usually because of over-grazing or the ploughing and cultivation of such climatically unsuitable land: originally and still mainly applied to the dust bowl of the western United States, e.g. in Colorado, Kansas. See *soil erosion*.

dust counter. An instrument for counting the number of dust particles present in a given volume of air.

dust devil. A local whirl of dust, usually not more than a few metres in diameter, in which the particles are swept round and round the centre, and are lifted to considerable heights – sometimes to 600–900 m (2,000–3,000 ft) above the earth's surface. It is caused by excessive local heating by the sun in an arid region, a strong convection current being formed. Dust devils usually move over the desert at 8–24 km (5–15 miles) per hour, though speeds of over 50 km (30 miles) per hour are sometimes reached, and as many as five or six of them may often be counted by the observer. Being so limited in size, they are harmless even to aviation – unlike the *duststorm*.

duststorm. A storm in which a thick mass of dust obscures the atmosphere, and reduces visibility very considerably – sometimes practically to zero. It causes acute discomfort on the surface, and is a danger to aviation. It is caused by a turbulent wind blowing over an arid, dusty surface, and its approach is usually heralded by a wall of dust which extends upwards to a considerable height – sometimes to over 3,000 m. In advance of the storm, the wind is light and variable, but increases in strength as the storm approaches. Duststorms are frequent in such arid desert regions as the plains of Iraq, North Africa, and N W India, and are especially liable to occur in thundery weather; the atmosphere is so dry that the rain associated with the thunderstorm often evaporates before reaching the ground, but if it does not, the dust is washed down with it, and the duststorm is thus much shortened in duration and restricted in scope. It should be distinguished from a *sandstorm*. See also *haboob*.

dust-well. A hollow, containing dust, in the surface of a glacier; it is formed when a patch of dust, blown on to the ice, absorbs heat from the sun more rapidly than does the ice itself, and causes the latter to melt, a depression being thus created.

dyke or **dike.** (1) A vertical or highly inclined sheet of igneous rock, formed when molten rock material or *magma* from the interior of the earth has forced its way towards the surface through a cleft, or by melting a passage for itself, and has there cooled and solidified. The dyke may change its direction, or branch away into smaller dykes, or give rise to *sills*; its thickness may vary from a few centimetres to hundreds of metres.

(2) A ditch.

(3) A bank of earth, stones, etc., constructed to prevent low-lying land from being inundated by the sea, a river, etc.

E

eagre. A tidal wave or *bore*, usually applied to that of the R Trent, England.

earth. The fifth in size of the nine major planets, and the third in distance from the sun. The solid outer crust of the earth, known as the *lithosphere*, is partially covered by an extensive area of water, known as the *hydrosphere*, and around the earth is a gaseous envelope known as the *atmosphere*. Although the earth is often regarded as being a sphere, it is actually an oblate spheroid, being slightly flattened at the poles; the polar diameter is about 43 km shorter than the equatorial diameter, the former being approx. 12,714 km in length.

earth pillar, demoiselle (French), or **hoodoo.** A tall column of earth, often 6–9 m (20–30 ft) high, capped by a large boulder. The boulder has originally lain on the soil; when most of the soft surface material surrounding it has been gradually worn away by rain, it has protected the earth beneath it, and has remained perched on a long pillar of this

Diagram of an earth pillar, typical of those seen in the Tirol.

earth. Earth pillars occur frequently in mountain valleys, and well-known examples are those of the Tirol and the Bad Lands, USA.

earthquake. A movement or tremor of the earth's crust which originates naturally and below the surface. It sometimes causes a permanent change of level at the surface, but often the damage done by the shaking provides the only lasting visible effect. It may be produced by a volcanic explosion; earthquakes, in fact, are common in most volcanic areas, and often precede or accompany eruptions. It is more likely, however, to be of *tectonic* origin, and probably due to the existence of a *fault*.

At least three distinct sets of waves are set up by an earthquake, and at a considerable distance from the place of origin these are felt separately; close to the place of origin, however, they all reach an observer at approximately the same time. As these waves pass a place, the ground may be felt to rock, and buildings sway backwards and forwards. Maximum damage is not done always at the *epicentre*, where the movement is up and down, but at places where the wave reaches the surface obliquely yet which are still close enough to the origin for it to have lost little of its force. A large earthquake is usually followed by a series of other shocks. An earthquake which originates below or near to the sea causes great disturbance of the water, and sometimes large waves emanate from it and travel a considerable distance; on occasion these waves have caused a greater loss of life, by flooding coastal regions, than the earthquake itself. See *tsunami*.

In the main earthquake regions, many of which have active volcanoes in their midst, an earthquake of some kind takes place practically every day; on Hawaii, for instance, hundreds of minor shocks are recorded during the year. There are extensive areas on the earth's surface, however, where earthquakes are very rare. The three great regions where earthquakes have taken place more or less frequently are (1) the west coast area of North and South America, (2) a belt across southern Europe and southern Asia, and (3) a belt in the Pacific Ocean which includes Japan, the Philippines, and most of the East Indies. Of the thousands of earthquakes which are recorded annually, only a hundred or so cause damage. Nowadays the magnitude of an earthquake is normally measured on the *Richter scale*.

earthquake period. The period during which a region is subject to earthquake shocks without any extended respite.

ebb-tide. The receding or falling tide, i.e. after high tide and before low tide. See *tides*.

echo-sounding. See *sounding*.

eclipse, lunar. The obscuration of the light of the moon when the earth, passing between sun and moon, casts her shadow on the latter. It can thus occur only at the time of full moon, when the moon is in opposition. It does not occur at every full moon, however, for the moon's orbit is not in the plane of the *ecliptic*, but is inclined at about 5° to it.

ECLIPSE, SOLAR

Simplified diagram to illustrate solar eclipse and lunar eclipse.

If the moon is completely obscured there is said to be a *total eclipse*, if partially, a *partial eclipse*. Lunar eclipses are far less frequent than solar eclipses, but in a given area many more of them are visible than of solar eclipses. This is because at every place where the moon is above the horizon at the time of the eclipse, the eclipse is visible, whereas a solar eclipse is visible only over a limited area. In a lunar eclipse the *penumbra* is scarcely visible. A total lunar eclipse may last as much as two hours. See *eclipse, solar*.

eclipse, solar. The obscuration of the light of the sun when the moon, passing between earth and sun, casts her shadow on the former. It can thus occur only at the new moon, when the moon is in conjunction, but it does not occur at every new moon because of the inclination of the moon's orbit to the plane of the *ecliptic*. If the sun is completely obscured, there is said to be a *total eclipse*, if partially, a *partial eclipse*; when the moon's shadow does not even reach the earth, an *annular eclipse* is given – a ring of light is visible round the circular disc of the moon. Solar eclipses are much more frequent than lunar eclipses, but they can be seen only over a very limited area: the cone of the moon's shadow becomes so narrowed across the space between moon and earth that a total eclipse is observed along a narrow belt. The average diameter of the shadow of a total eclipse, in fact, is 145 km (90 miles). Unlike the lunar eclipse, however, its *penumbra* is visible, and a partial eclipse is seen over a much wider area. On account of the restricted area from which any total solar eclipse is visible, at any single place the phenomenon is rare, and expeditions are organized to the locality from which it can be observed; its duration is only a few minutes.

ecliptic. The apparent track of the sun throughout the year, as a result of the motion of the earth round it, being a great circle on the *celestial sphere*. The *plane of the ecliptic* is the plane passing through this path, and is coincident with the plane of the earth's *orbit*; it thus meets the celestial sphere in the ecliptic.

ecology. The science which treats of organisms in relation to their environment; it is frequently sub-divided into human ecology, animal ecology, plant ecology, and bio-ecology, the last-named dealing with the interrelationship between animal life and plant life. Ecology lies on the frontiers of so many other subjects, including various branches of geography, that its limits have not yet been precisely defined.

ecosystem. A term, used mainly in *ecology*, coined in 1935 by A. G. Tansley from 'ecological system': a community of plants and animals, together with their immediate environment, including the inanimate part of that environment.

edaphic. Relating to the soil.

elbow of capture. See *river capture*.

elevation. (1) The raising of a portion of the earth's crust in relation to its surroundings. See *subsidence*.

(2) The altitude or angular height of an object such as a heavenly body above the horizon.

eluviation. The removal of material in solution or in suspension from the upper or A horizon of the soil to the B horizon through the downward percolation of water. See *illuviation*.

enclave. An outlying territory belonging to one country which lies wholly within the territory of another country: it is an enclave with respect to the country in which it is located. See *exclave*. The term is sometimes used to denote an area which is *almost* enclosed in this way: e.g. one which is bordered by the sea on one side.

end or **terminal moraine.** See *moraine*.

englacial. A term meaning 'within the ice', applied e.g. to a *moraine* or a stream in a glacier. See *subglacial*.

entrenched or **intrenched meander.** See *incised meander*.

entrepôt. A place or district which acts as an intermediary centre for trade between foreign countries: that is, for the receipt of goods from one part of the world and their distribution to another part; or a place where goods are temporarily stored. Two well-known examples of seaports outstanding in entrepôt trade are Singapore and Hong Kong.

Eozoic. Usually synonymous with *pre-Cambrian*.

epeirogenesis. Continent-building: large-scale changes in the level of the earth's crust, in which the surfaces of continents have been simply elevated or depressed, with little or no folding. The formation of a *plateau* provides an example. See *orogenesis*.

epicentre or **epicentrum.** The point on the earth's surface which is vertically above the point of origin or *seismic focus* of an earthquake. Here the earthquake vibrations first reach the surface, and then seem to spread outwards. If the time of arrival of the earthquake is observed for several different places, the position of the epicentre may usually be determined. See *homoseismal line*.

epicontinental sea. A shallow sea which rests on the *continental shelf*, e.g. the North Sea.

epiphyte. A plant which grows on another plant but is not parasitic, obtaining its essential foods from the atmosphere. Epiphytes are typical of the *equatorial forest*, and certain orchids provide the best-known examples.

epoch. A sub-division of a *period* in the geological scale of time.

equal-area projection. See *homolographic projection*.

equator. The imaginary circle, lying midway between the poles, formed at the surface of the earth by a plane drawn through the centre perpendicular to its *axis*; as its centre is also the centre of the earth, it is a *great circle*. It is also the longest circumference of the earth.

equator, celestial. See *celestial equator*.

equatorial climate. The type of climate experienced on lowlands within about 5° to 10° latitude of the equator. Throughout the year temperatures and humidity are uniformly high, and seasonal changes are slight: mean monthly temperatures are about 75°–80°F (25°–27°C). Rainfall is heavy and well distributed, with no marked dry season; much of the precipitation consists of *convectional rain*, falls during the afternoons, and is often accompanied by violent thunderstorms. The characteristic natural vegetation is *equatorial forest*, and the main areas where the climate prevails are the Amazon basin (S America), the Zaire basin and the Guinea coast (Africa), and the Malay peninsula, Indonesia and the Philippines (Asia).

equatorial forest or **tropical rain forest.*** The hot, wet, evergreen forest of the equatorial region, where rainfall is very heavy and where there is no dry season; it extends in parts into the typical monsoon areas. Owing to the extreme heat and moisture, the growth is dense and luxuriant. Many of the trees grow to tremendous heights, and in the struggle to reach the sunlight *lianas* climb up other trees; *epiphytes* are also found abundantly in the equatorial forest. Individual species of trees are very scattered, but among them are such valuable tropical hardwoods as mahogany and ebony; the wild rubber tree is also a native of the equatorial forest. Typical equatorial forest regions include the basins of the Amazon and Zaire, and much of the East Indies.

equinox. The term for the two points of intersection of the apparent annual path of the sun with the plane through the equator; the time of the year when the sun appears vertically overhead at noon at the equator. It is thus the time when the illuminated half of the earth just includes the two poles, and when all places on the earth have equal day and night – twelve hours each. The sun rises exactly in the east and sets exactly in the west everywhere. There are two equinoxes each year, one, falling about March 21, being called the *spring* or *vernal equinox*, and the other, falling about September 22, the *autumnal equinox* (northern hemisphere).

equipluve. A line joining all places which have equal *pluviometric coefficients*. A map showing such lines thus illustrates the raininess of a particular month or other period over a given area.

era. One of the principal divisions in the geological scale of time (after *pre-Cambrian* time) being itself sub-divided into *periods*. Many geologists recognize three eras – the *Palaeozoic*, *Mesozoic*, and *Cainozoic eras*, which thus extend over about the past 600 million years.

erg (Arabic). In the Sahara, that part of the desert whose surface is covered with sand *dunes*. See *reg*, *hammada*.

erosion.* The wearing away of the land surface by various natural agencies, the most important being those consisting of water – the sea, rivers, and rain. Ice, in the form of glaciers, frost, and melting snow, also assists in the process of erosion, as does the wind. Some geographers regard erosion as synonymous with *denudation*.

erratic block or **erratic.** A boulder which has been transported from its source by a glacier, sometimes over a considerable distance, and has been left stranded when the ice melted; it is thus, often, of a different type from neighbouring rocks. In some areas, such as parts of South Dakota, Minnesota, and other northern states of the USA, erratic blocks have been so numerous as to impede agriculture.

eruption, volcanic. The forcing of materials in solid, liquid, or gaseous form from the interior of the earth on to its surface by a *volcano*. See also *fissure eruption*.

escarpment or **scarp.** An inland cliff or steep slope: the steep face of a *cuesta*, or possibly formed as a direct result of a *fault*; sometimes regarded as equivalent to cuesta.

esker. A long, narrow ridge of sand and gravel which was once the bed of a stream flowing beneath or in the ice of a glacier, and was left behind when the ice melted. See *ås*.

estuary. The mouth of a river where tidal effects are evident, and where fresh water and sea water mix. If the land consists of soft rocks, the funnel-like shape of the estuary may be due to the scouring action of the river and the tide, but in most cases it is due to subsidence of coastal lowland. The river valley has been flooded by the sea, and the tides have maintained rather than actually created the shape of the estuary. Many estuaries, such as those of the Thames, the Elbe, the Plate, are the sites of important seaports.

étang (French). A shallow pool or lake lying among sand dunes and gradually becoming filled with silt: applies especially to those along the coasts of Aquitaine (Landes) and Languedoc, in France.

etesian winds or **meltemi.** The strong, constant, northerly winds of summer experienced in the eastern Mediterranean, blowing round the great trough of low atmospheric pressure which extends westwards from NW India. From about mid-May to mid-October they regularly blow at 15–50 km (10–30 miles) per hour, sometimes rising to over 60 km (40 miles) per hour. During the day they increase in strength, as the insolation over the hot land to the south and east temporarily raises the *pressure gradient*, then at night they often decline and die away. On land they sometimes carry considerable dust. Despite the prevailing heat, however, their dryness causes them to be quite refreshing. Their strength and dryness are such that orchards often have to be protected from them by a *windbreak* such as a row of cypresses set on the northern side. (See also *trough of low pressure*.)

ethnography. The subject which deals with the regional distribution of the races of mankind, and their history.

ethnology. The science which treats of mankind as distributed over the earth in racial units.

eustatic movement. A large-scale rise or fall of sea level. Such a movement may be caused, for instance, by the decay or development of *ice sheets*.

evaporation. The process by which a substance changes from the liquid to the vapour state. Evaporation of surface water by the heat of the sun, from the oceans, lakes, rivers, etc., is the cause of the water vapour in the atmosphere. As the atmosphere is seldom completely saturated, evaporation goes on almost all the time, the rate of evaporation being dependent on the air temperature, the amount of water vapour already in the atmosphere, the nature of the water surface, and the wind. Evaporation is thus greatest in the hot deserts of the world. The opposite process is *condensation*.

evaporite. A *sedimentary rock* which has been deposited by the evaporation of water from a concentrated saline solution, examples being rock salt (sodium chloride) and gypsum (calcium sulphate).

evapotranspiration. A term signifying the total loss of moisture from the soil in the form of water vapour, including that lost by evaporation from bodies of open water, e.g. lakes, reservoirs, and from the surface of soils and rocks, and also that lost by *transpiration* from growing plants. An estimate of the evapotranspiration from a certain area will assist in deciding on the necessity or otherwise for irrigation water.

exclave. An outlying territory belonging to one country which lies wholly within the territory of another country: it is an exclave with respect to the country to which it belongs politically. See *enclave*.

exfoliation. A *weathering* process which consists in the peeling off of thin layers of rock from the surface. In hot deserts it is caused by the heating of the rocks by day and their cooling by night, leading to alternate expansion and contraction. The corners of rock masses especially are broken off, and the surfaces assume a rounded form. The process is often assisted by others, such as the chemical weathering of the outer layers. The term 'onion weathering' is sometimes used for exfoliation.

exosphere. The outermost fringe of the *atmosphere*, its base 500–1,000 km (300–600 miles) above the earth's surface, and so beyond the *thermosphere*, where the gases are so rarefied that individual molecules may escape into space.

exotic river. A river that owes its flow to water received in another region, usually applied to one flowing across a desert, e.g. the Nile,

Tigris, Euphrates, each of which is swollen by precipitation deposited in the upper basin.

exports. Goods which are dispatched from a country in trade, normally because they are surplus to its requirements; from the national standpoint, they may be regarded as goods exchanged for *imports*. They have usually been produced in the exporting country, but sometimes they may have been purchased abroad and re-exported. See *entrepôt*. See also *invisible exports*.

extensive cultivation. A system of farming by which the cultivator expends a limited amount of labour and capital on a relatively large area. See *intensive cultivation*.

extrusive rocks. Rocks formed by solidification of *magma* above the earth's surface, e.g. volcanic *lava*; they are thus *igneous rocks*. See *intrusive rocks*.

'eye' of the storm. See *tropical cyclone*.

F

Fahrenheit scale. The temperature scale devised by the German physicist Gabriel Fahrenheit (1686–1736) and much used in English-speaking countries. The 'fixed points', the freezing point and boiling point of water, are 32° and 212° respectively. Thus, to convert a temperature on the Fahrenheit scale to one on the *centigrade scale*, 32 must first be subtracted from the former, then the result divided by 1.8: $C = (F - 32) \div 1.8$.

fall. The term used in the United States for autumn, signifying the season of 'the fall of the leaf'.

fall line. The line joining the waterfalls on a number of approximately parallel rivers: especially applied to the line running along the sudden increase of slope – where the waterfalls thus occur – from the Appalachian Mountains to the Atlantic coastal plain in the eastern USA. The fall line marks the point where each river leaves the uplands for the lowlands, and thus the limit of its navigability. For this reason, and because water power is available there, many important industrial centres have become established along the line, e.g. Philadelphia, Baltimore, Richmond.

false cirrus. A type of cloud often associated with the upper part of a *cumulonimbus* cloud, from which it may become detached, and in appearance denser than normal *cirrus*.

fan, alluvial. See *alluvial fan*.

fata morgana. A type of *mirage* in which an object appears to be elongated vertically, owing to the fact that it is observed through several horizontal layers of air of different refractive indices.

fathom. The unit of length, equal to 6 ft, used mainly in determining the depth of the sea.

fault. A fracture in the earth's crust along which movement has taken place, and where the rock strata on the two sides therefore do not match. Although the movement is usually more or less vertical, a fault may take place in any direction, including the horizontal. The change of level on one side compared with the other, known as the *throw*, varies from less than a centimetre to hundreds of metres; the amount of lateral displacement is known as the *heave*. The side of a fault where the strata have moved relatively downwards is known as the *downthrow* side, the other being the *upthrow* side. A *normal fault* is

Diagram to illustrate the arrangement of the rock strata in a fault.

one in which the *fault plane* is vertical, or is so inclined that the downthrow is on the dip side of the fault plane. See also *tear fault*, *thrust fault*.

fault plane. The surface along which a *fault* has taken place.

fault scarp. A *scarp* situated where a *fault* has taken place, being due to the relative downward movement of the strata on the lower side of the fault.

fauna. The animal life of a region or of a geological period, corresponding to the term *flora* for plant life.

feldspar or **felspar.** A widely distributed group of minerals consisting of silicates of aluminium combined with potassium, sodium, calcium, and barium, and probably comprising almost half of the earth's crust. Although insoluble, feldspar undergoes chemical decomposition, *china clay* being a product.

fell. Chiefly in northern England, a bare, uncultivated hill or mountain. See *fjall*.

fellah (pl. **fellahin**) (Arabic). In Arabic-speaking countries, especially Egypt, a peasant; in Arabic the term means literally 'a ploughman'.

fen. A tract of low-lying, marshy land, in which *peat* is being formed beneath the surface and the soil is generally alkaline: applied especially to the region round the Wash in eastern England.

Ferrel's law. The law which states that a body moving in any direction over the earth's surface will tend to be deflected, owing to the earth's rotation, to the right in the northern hemisphere and to the left in the southern hemisphere; it is applied especially to the movement of large masses of air – the winds. Thus a wind which would blow from N to S if the earth were stationary becomes in the northern hemisphere N E, e.g. the N E trade wind.

fertilizer. A substance of natural or artificial origin which is added to the soil to increase its productivity, by supplying those chemical elements that are necessary to plant life.

fetch. At sea, the length of open water across which the wind is blowing,

Fiords along the coast of southern Norway.

i.e. the distance from the weather shore, which largely determines the height of the waves.

filling. In meteorology, the term for increasing atmospheric pressure at the centre of a *depression*: the opposite of *deepening*.

finger lake. A long, narrow lake lying in a hollow scooped out by an ice sheet or glacier and often dammed at the lower end by a *moraine*. Examples are the Finger Lakes, in New York state, USA, and lakes of the Lake District (England), the Scottish Highlands, and similar glaciated regions.

fiord or **fjord** (Norwegian).* A long, narrow inlet into the sea coast, with more or less steep sides. Owing to the occurrence of fiords along the edges of mountainous regions which were once heavily glaciated, e.g. along the coasts of Norway and Greenland, it is generally held that they were formed when glaciers, making their way to the sea, scooped out deep, trough-like valleys which may have been first cut by streams, so that the lower ends were filled by the sea. Usually a fiord is extremely deep, but becomes shallower towards the mouth, possibly because the glacier lost some of its power of erosion as it melted, or because a terminal *moraine* blocked the end. (See Fig. above.)

firn (German) or **névé** (French). The granular substance, intermediate between snow and ice, which is formed as the snow that has accumulated at the head of a glaciated valley is being transformed into *glacier* ice. As the glacier moves down the valley, the firn gradually becomes welded into a completely crystalline mass of ice. Many geographers and glaciologists prefer the term *firn* to *névé* because other terms can be more easily constructed from it, e.g. *firnification* (creation of firn).

firth. In Scotland, a long, narrow inlet into the sea coast, usually the lower part of an *estuary*, but sometimes a *fiord*; occasionally a *strait*, e.g. Pentland Firth.

fisheries zone. The belt of sea adjoining the coast which for the purposes of fishing is regarded as being under the territorial jurisdiction of the nation occupying the coast. Normally it is much wider than the belt of *territorial waters*, many nations having adopted the 200-mile limit during the 1970s.

fissure eruption.* A volcanic *eruption* in which *lava* is ejected through a long cleft or fissure, generally without explosive activity, and often producing a *lava plateau*.

five-year plan. In the USSR, one of a series of state plans each designed to be completed in five years and to develop the country's economy – primarily to stimulate industrialization and to collectivize agriculture – according to the overall plan of the Communist Party. The first such plan took effect and was declared fulfilled in 1932 under Stalin. Other countries, chiefly those subscribing to a like political régime, later inaugurated similar five-year plans.

fjall (Icelandic), **fjäll** (Swedish), **fjell, fjeld** (Norwegian). Corresponding Scandinavian terms for a mountain or hill, often but by no means always implying a plateau-like summit: while Dovrefjell, in Norway, is an extensive plateau, for example, Hverfjall, in Iceland, is a large volcanic crater. The corresponding English term is *fell*.

fjärd (Swedish). A long, narrow inlet into a low-lying coast, e.g. the E coast of Sweden, and so distinguished from a *fiord*.

flash-flood. A sudden, transient rush of water (a *flash*), amounting to a short-lived flood, usually but not invariably in a desert area, e.g. in a *wadi*, possibly caused by a violent rainstorm.

floe. See *ice-floe*.

flood-plain. A plain, bordering a river, which has been formed from deposits of sediments carried down by the river. When a river rises and overflows its banks, the water spreads over the flood-plain; a layer of sediment is deposited at each flood, so that the flood-plain gradually rises. It is usually highest near the river, at the natural *levee*. During the formation of a flood-plain, it is often characterized by *marshes*, meandering streams (see *meander*), and *ox-bow lakes*. If the drainage system is later diverted for some reason, the flood-plain may be left as a smooth and extremely fertile tract of land.

flood-tide. The advancing or rising tide, i.e. after low tide and before high tide. See *tides*.

flora. The plant life of a region or of a geological period, corresponding to the term *fauna* for animal life.

fluvial or **fluviatile.** Belonging to or relating to a river, e.g. fluvial deposits.

fluvioglacial or **glaciofluvial.** Caused by the action of streams issuing from the melting ice at the end of a glacier or at the edge of an ice sheet; applied especially to the deposits of an *outwash plain*. Many glaciologists prefer the term *glaciofluvial* because the action of the glacier precedes that of the streams.

fog. A dense mass of small water drops with smoke or dust particles, in the lower layers of the atmosphere. According to international meteorological practice, the phenomenon is termed a fog only when the obscurity is such that objects at a distance of 1 kilometre from the observer have become invisible. See *mist*, *haze*.

The condensation of water vapour in the lower layers of air, which is normally the cause of fog, is due to the cooling of the air below its *dew point*. This cooling may be due to *radiation* from the earth's surface, and the conditions most likely to produce a fog are thus a very light wind and a clear sky at night. The fog is then most dense shortly after sunrise, and often disperses before the afternoon; in winter, however, it may persist for several days. A fog may also be formed by the drift of air over a cold surface (see *advection fog*), or by the mixture of one *air mass* with a cooler air mass. Land fogs occur chiefly in autumn and winter, sea fogs chiefly in spring and summer. The sea fog is usually a type of *advection fog* and it is most prevalent in the vicinity of cold ocean currents: e.g. the frequent fogs of the Grand Banks off Newfoundland. The depth of a fog is very variable, but is usually below 300 m (1,000 ft); at sea it is sometimes so shallow that the masthead of a ship will project above it. A smoke fog, in which the poor visibility is due mainly to smoke particles, occurs in industrial areas where there is a continual emission from factory and domestic chimneys; but the worst type of fog in these areas is produced by a mixture of smoke and water drops (see *smog*). A dust fog is typical of a desert region.

fog bow. A white bow seen opposite to the sun in a fog; it resembles and is produced in the same way as an ordinary *rainbow*, but owing to the smallness of the water drops, the colours overlap and the bow is white – though the inner edge has a bluish tinge and the outer edge a reddish tinge. Sometimes a second bow is seen inside the first, the colours being reversed.

foggara (Arabic). In the Sahara, particularly Algeria, an underground irrigation channel. See *ganat*.

föhn wind. The warm, dry wind which blows down the leeward slope of a mountain, best known in the valleys of the northern Alps, where the

Diagram illustrating the formation of the föhn wind.

name originated. It occurs when a depression moving to the north of the Alps draws in air from the south. This air ascends the southern slopes, clouds are formed, and there is heavy rain; when it reaches the northern slope, it has lost most of its moisture but is still warm, and it is dynamically heated further as it descends, and so blows down the valleys as a very warm, dry wind – the föhn. It may raise the temperature by 8° to 11°C; snow is melted, trees, houses, etc., become excessively dry, avalanches may occur. The maximum frequency of the föhn in northern Switzerland is in spring, when it is useful in melting the winter snow from the pastures. In autumn, the season of second greatest frequency, it is useful in ripening the crops, especially the grapes. The föhn blows in the direction of the mountain valleys, but is usually a southerly wind and is strongest in valleys lying in a north–south direction. A similar type of wind occurs in all mountainous regions which are affected by depressions. See *chinook*, *nor'-wester*, *samoon*.

fold. A bend in rock strata caused by movements of the earth's crust. When the compression is relatively small, the strata are formed into a series of arches and troughs (see *anticline* and *syncline*); when the compression is greater, the folds bulge outwards at the top, and lower down dip inwards from both sides. *Denudation* takes place simultaneously with the folding, so that the outer parts of a fold may be worn away as it is produced. A *symmetrical fold* is one in which the axial plane is vertical, an *asymmetrical fold* one in which the axial plane is inclined. See also *monocline*, *nappe*, *overfold*, *recumbent fold*.

folded or **fold mountains.** Mountains which have been thrown up into a massive *fold* or ridge by earth movements. Often the mountains form an *anticline*, and the adjacent valleys are *synclines*, though where such mountains have been exposed to erosion for a long period there is a tendency towards the reverse, the anticlines to become valleys and the synclines to become hills, for the resistance of the latter to the denuding effect of water is greater than that of the former. Most of the important mountain ranges consist of folded mountains, including the Himalayas, the various Alpine chains, the Pyrenees, and the Apennines.

foraminifera. See *globigerina ooze*.

force. In northern England, a *waterfall*: e.g. High Force, on the River Tees. The term is derived from Old Norse, and the equivalent Swedish term is *fors*: e.g. Tannfors, on the upper Indal River.

ford. The shallow part of a river or other body of water which may be crossed by wading.

foreland. A headland or promontory, generally of low altitude, e.g. North Foreland and South Foreland, on the coast of Kent, England; see also *cuspate foreland*.

forest. An extensive area of land covered mainly with trees. See *coniferous forest*, *deciduous forest*, *equatorial forest*, *monsoon forest*, *thorn forest*. In economically developed areas some forests have lost much of their original character owing to clearances, though names have been retained: e.g. in England, Sherwood Forest, in Nottinghamshire. The so-called 'deer forests' of Scotland are areas of heath and moor.

fosse. A ditch or moat.

fossil. The remains or the form of a plant or animal which has been buried and preserved for a long period in the rocks of the earth's crust. The only organisms which have been thus preserved are those which were buried in *sedimentary rocks* soon after death, or were encased in a material which protected them from decay and the attacks of living organisms. See *palaeontology*.

fossil water. See *connate water*.

Foucault's pendulum. The apparatus by which Foucault demonstrated the rotation of the earth on its *axis*. A heavy ball was suspended by a fine wire from the dome of the Panthéon, in Paris, so that it could swing freely in any direction, and the pendulum was set in motion; gradually the direction of the swing appeared to change, and, as no external force had been applied to the pendulum, the rotation of the floor, and of the earth itself, was thus shown.

fractostratus. A type of cloud – literally broken *stratus*.

frazil ice. Surface ice which forms in spicules on rapidly flowing rivers, the movement of the water preventing the ice crystals from forming a solid sheet. The phenomenon has been best observed in the Canadian rivers, and the term is Canadian in origin.

free port. A port, or a zone within a port, at which goods, either imports or exports, may be loaded and unloaded without payment of customs duty. It is usually an *entrepôt*. Hong Kong is an example of a free port.

free trade. International trade which is not hampered by restrictions, such as customs duties, imposed by one or other participating country.

freshet. (1) A clear stream.

(2) A river flood caused by heavy rains or by rapidly melting snow.

friagem. The *cold wave* experienced on the tropical *campos* of Brazil during winter, caused by the development of an anticyclone. In the region of the middle Amazon, for instance, there is sometimes a cool spell during May or June lasting several days. The temperature may fall below 10°C, causing acute discomfort, and rendering the natives extremely vulnerable to colds.

frigid zone. A term formerly applied to the regions within the *Arctic Circle* and the *Antarctic Circle*. The sun's rays are always very oblique, so that the weather in general is never warm: in summer it is cool or cold, in winter it is extremely cold.

fringing reef. See *coral reef*.

front. The lines of separation at the earth's surface between cold and warm air masses. In general it is produced by the horizontal movement of two such air masses, which have originated from widely separated regions, e.g. tropical and polar air. This brings them into contact with each other, and from the line of the front on the ground a frontal surface, or surface of discontinuity, slopes upwards over the cold air; the warm air, being lighter than the cold air, is continually ascending this frontal surface. Usually a front lies along a *trough of low pressure*. See *depression*, *cold front*, *warm front*, *occlusion*.

frontier. That part of a country which borders on another country, i.e. adjoins the boundary-line between the two countries.

frontogenesis. In the atmosphere, the processes that bring about the formation or intensification of a *front*.

frost. (1) The particles of frozen moisture formed on the earth's surface when the air temperature has fallen as far as or below 0°C. See *glazed frost*, *hoar frost*, *rime*.

(2) An air temperature, at or below 0°C, which causes water to freeze; the intensity of the frost, i.e. the number of degrees of frost, is indicated by the number of degrees C that the air temperature falls below the freezing point of water (0°C). In temperate regions, e.g. the British Isles, a frost may be very local and transitory, owing probably to cooling by radiation, or it may continue for several days over an extensive area.

frost hollow or **pocket.** A hollow into which cold air, in conditions favourable to radiation, sinks from the adjacent slopes under the action of gravity and there accumulates, rendering the site liable to a greater frequency and severity of *frosts* than the surrounding area: thus a site to be avoided by fruit farmers and gardeners.

fruit belt. A strip of land about 50 km (30 miles) wide extending along the eastern shore of Lake Michigan, USA, where the lake so tempers the climate that grapes and similar fruits can be successfully grown, whereas their cultivation would be impossible in other districts in the same latitude. See *grape belt*.

fuelling station. A port, or a repository within a port, which supplies fuel in the form of oil (formerly coal) to ocean-going vessels which are unable to carry enough in their bunkers for their complete voyage.

fumarole. A hole in the earth's crust from which steam and gases, such as carbon dioxide, are emitted under pressure. It is frequently found in a volcanic region; the steam is produced by the *magma* beneath the surface, when the volcano itself has probably ceased to erupt. The most striking development of fumaroles in the world was in the Valley of Ten Thousand Smokes, near the volcano Katmai, in Alaska; here an area of several square miles was formerly riddled with fumaroles ejecting steam. See also *solfatara*.

funnel cloud. The cloud formed at the core of a *waterspout* or *tornado*, sometimes extending downwards as far as the earth's surface. Over land, the lower end is often darkened by dust and other debris swept up from the ground by the wind.

G

gabbro. A group of coarse-grained *igneous rocks* consisting essentially of a *feldspar* and one or more ferro-magnesian minerals.

gale. According to common usage, simply a very high wind, but according to usual meteorological practice a wind of Force 8 or more on the *Beaufort scale*: i.e. a wind of about 68 km per hour or more on the surface.

Gall's projection. A *cylindrical projection* in which the cylinder, instead of touching the globe only at the equator, is sunk into its surface, and coincides with the surface at 45°N and 45°S latitude. Between these latitudes the parallels are too close together, whereas on their poleward side the parallels are too far apart, but in the higher latitudes there is less exaggeration of areas and shapes than in *Mercator's projection*. It is a form of *stereographic projection*.

ganat or **qanat** (Persian). In Iran, an underground channel which carries irrigation water from the mountains where the rainfall is relatively plentiful, to the drier areas below. Its course may be clearly recognized from the air, for at intervals it has circular openings resembling miniature craters. It corresponds to the *foggara* of North Africa.

gangue. The material, of relatively small value, surrounding or accompanying a metallic *ore* in a lode or vein; it is usually non-metallic, such as quartz.

gap town. A town situated in or near a gap in a ridge and thus often an important route centre; examples in S E England include Guildford and Lewes, in U S A Harrisburg, Pennsylvania.

garden city. A term first used in the United States by A. T. Stewart (1869), applied to a town carefully planned so as to include facilities for industry whilst maintaining its favourable residential character, with a relatively low housing density and full cultural and recreational amenities. In England Ebenezer Howard's scheme for such towns led to the establishment of Letchworth (1903) and Welwyn Garden City (1920), which considerably influenced the official New Towns policy adopted after the Second World War. See *new town*.

garigue or **garrigue** (French). The scattered, low *scrub*, interspersed with extensive patches of bare soil, which prevails in limestone areas of the Mediterranean region, the land being too poor or too dry for the growth of normal scrub. The garigue, in fact, is even poorer than the *maquis*, and from the standpoint of agriculture is almost valueless, being suitable only for feeding goats. Many of the plants which constitute the garigue, such as broom and gorse, have bright but short-lived flowers; others, like lavender and thyme, are aromatic.

garua. The thick mist or drizzle experienced in western Peru during the winter, often covering the coastal region like a thick blanket of cloud; it provides almost all of the scanty rainfall of this region.

gauge, railway. The distance between the inner edges of the rails on a railway track. Gauges vary in different countries and are roughly classified as broad, standard, and narrow gauges. The broad gauges usually include those of 5 ft or more in width; the standard gauge, as used in Great Britain, is 4 ft 8½ in wide; the narrow gauges include the metre gauge, the 3 ft 6 in, and smaller gauges.

gauge, rain. See *rain gauge*.

gazetteer. A geographical dictionary; a list of places or topographical features, arranged alphabetically for ease of reference, together with information concerning the places or features.

geanticline. See *geoanticline*.

geest (German). The heath-covered sandy region of the glaciated northern lowlands of Germany, lying between the Elbe and the Ems; the soil is infertile and the population sparse.

geoanticline or **geanticline.** An *anticline* on a large scale, i.e. extending over several miles (km); its formation is very gradual, and erosion of the crest proceeds simultaneously.

geochemistry. The study of the 'chemistry of the earth' including not only the *lithosphere*, *hydrosphere*, and *atmosphere*, but also the *biosphere*; it thus links chemistry with geology, meteorology, and biology.

geochronology. The subject that deals with the study of the earth's history in terms of the geological scale of time, involving the dating in years of the various geological periods. Among the methods used in dating such periods are those of *dendrochronology*, *tephrochronology*, *varve* analysis, and *radiocarbon dating*.

geodesy. The science of the measurement of the shape and size of the earth, including its weight, density, etc., and also of the surveying of such large portions of the earth's surface that the curvature of the earth has to be considered.

geographical inertia. The tendency of a place or region to retain an economic activity after the original causes of that activity have been eliminated or modified: e.g. the manufacture of furniture at Grand Rapids, Michigan, USA.

geographical mile. A measure of length equal to one-sixtieth of a degree or one minute (1′) of latitude; it thus varies with latitude, but it approximately equals 6,080 ft, and this is the generally accepted value. See *mile, statute*; *nautical mile*.

geography. The subject which describes the earth's surface – its physical features, climates, vegetation, soils, products, peoples, etc., and their distribution. For its data it has drawn extensively on specialized sciences, such as geology, meteorology, astronomy, anthropology, and biology. To some American geographers the subject is the 'study of human *ecology*'. A number of sub-divisions of the subject are recognized, including the following: *mathematical geography*, which deals with the shape, size and movements of the earth; *physical geography*, which usually includes a study of *climate, natural vegetation* and *oceanography*, and is sometimes assumed, rather loosely, to be synonymous with *physiography*; *human geography*, which is sometimes regarded as synonymous with *anthropogeography*; *political geography*, which is concerned primarily with the world's political divisions; *economic* or *commercial geography*; and *historical geography*, the nature of which has been interpreted in a wide variety of ways.

geoid. A term sometimes used to signify the shape of the *earth*; the latter is often taken to be an oblate spheroid, but, in view of certain variations, the term geoid, which simply means 'earth-shaped body', has been introduced.

geology. The science of the composition, structure, and history of the earth. It thus includes the study of the materials of which the earth is made, the forces which act upon these materials and the resulting structures, the distribution of the rocks of the earth's crust, and the history not only of the earth itself but also of the plants and animals which inhabited it throughout the different ages. The subject is often sub-divided into *physical* or *dynamical geology* and *historical geology*; the former includes *mineralogy*, *petrology*, structural geology, and *geomorphology* or *physiography*, while the latter includes *stratigraphical geology* or stratigraphy, *palaeontology*, and *palaeogeography*.

geomorphology. The study of the landforms or physical features of the earth, and of the relationship between these landforms and the geological structures beneath. The term is sometimes regarded as being synonymous with the older term, *physiography*.

geophysics. The study of the physical processes relating to the structure of the earth, including not only the *lithosphere* but also the *hydrosphere* and the *atmosphere*. Strictly speaking, it signifies the 'physics of the earth'; it is thus a branch of experimental physics, and links the science of physics with that of geology. Such subjects as *meteorology*, *hydrology*, and *seismology* are closely allied to and in some respects are branches of geophysics.

geopolitics. An alternative name for political *geography*, derived from the German 'Geopolitik'. The latter, through the powerful teachings of Karl Haushofer (1869–1946), convinced the Germans that they were required to dominate, and led to the demand for *Lebensraum* as part of the creed of National Socialism.

85

geostrophic wind. A hypothetical wind formed as a result of two forces, the deflecting force due to the earth's rotation, the so-called geostrophic or *coriolis force*, which acts in accordance with *Ferrel's law*, and the force due to the *pressure gradient*. The geostrophic wind thus takes a direction parallel to the isobars, in accordance with *Buys Ballot's law*, and its velocity can be easily calculated from a *weather chart* by means of a wind scale: the closer the isobars, the greater the velocity of the geostrophic wind. Near the earth's surface friction reduces the geostrophic force, and the surface wind blows across the isobars; the geostrophic wind is of limited value in calculating the speed and direction of this wind. The wind speed and direction at a height of 600 m (2,000 ft) may be determined with a high degree of accuracy, however, by means of the geostrophic wind scale. Such calculations are extremely useful for areas where few actual wind observations are available.

geosyncline. A large depression or trough in the earth's crust, or a *syncline* on a large scale, i.e. extending for distances up to hundreds of km (miles). A fundamental difference in structure, however, is due to the fact that the geosynclinal trough gradually fills with sediment as its floor subsides, resulting in the formation of an enormous thickness of sedimentary rocks.

geothermal. Relating to the heat of the earth's interior, as demonstrated by the high temperature of its *magma*: in the Wairakei district of New Zealand, for instance, *geothermal energy* is utilized, electricity being produced by steam raised from the local *hot springs*.

geothermal gradient. The rate at which the temperature of the rocks of the earth's crust rises with depth below the surface, due to geothermal influence: the rate varies considerably with location, and a mean estimate is 1°C per 34 metres (1°F per 62 ft).

geyser.* A *hot spring* which at regular or irregular intervals throws a jet of hot water and steam into the air; sometimes the jet rises to a height of 30 to 60 m (100–200 ft). It occurs in a volcanic region, From the mouth of the geyser, a tube penetrates deeply into the earth, and fills with water, which percolates through from the surface. The water near the base of this tube is considerably heated by hot lava, but the tube is so long and narrow that convection cannot take place freely; the temperature of the water down below thus continues to rise, while that at the top of the tube is relatively cool. At the same time, the boiling point of the water at the base of the tube is raised by pressure, and the temperature has to reach well above 100°C before steam is formed. When this does take place, the water above is forced upwards and flows away. The sudden reduction of the pressure at the bottom of the tube lowers the boiling point of the water, and the latter is now rapidly converted into steam, which forms in such volume that the entire column above it is ejected well into the air. The action of a geyser is thus intermittent. The best-known geysers are those of New Zealand, Iceland, and Yellowstone National Park, USA. The famous Old Faithful geyser of Yellowstone National Park used to erupt with great precision every 66½ minutes, but now is acting with less regularity and at longer intervals.

geyserite. A siliceous deposit produced around the mouth of a *hot spring* or *geyser*. See *sinter*.

gibli. The hot, dry, southerly *sirocco* wind of Libya, North Africa.

gill. In the Lake District and Yorkshire, England, a mountain stream.

glacial drift. See *drift* (2).

glacial lake. A small lake enclosed between the ice along the margin of a *glacier* and the valley wall.

glaciation. The covering of an area, or the action on that area, by an ice sheet or by glaciers.

glacier.* A mass of ice which moves slowly down a valley from above the *snowline* towards the sea under the force of gravity. It is formed owing to the pressure of the immense depth of snow, which depresses the freezing point; the snow in the lower layers thus melts, and then solidifies again into granular ice, or *névé*, being later transformed by the continued pressure into clear ice.

From the snowfield, where it almost always originates, the glacier may extend far below the snowline. At its source, there is an abundant supply of ice and melting is slow, and the glacier is thus broad and deep; lower down the temperatures are higher and the supply of ice is smaller. The glacier thus decreases in size till the amount of ice melting equals the supply from above, and there the glacier ends. Usually, then, the glacier is tongue-shaped, being broadest near its source and narrowest where it finishes. Its general shape also conforms to that of the valley in which it lies. It curves with the valley, and to some extent its surface follows that of the valley floor. The centre of the glacier is usually higher than its sides, and the cross-section of its surface is thus slightly convex. The surface is often uneven, and sometimes cut by deep cracks or *crevasses*: one cause of the unevenness of the surface is the melting of the top layer of the ice during the summer, when the water wears channels in the ice. Again, the lower layers of ice may be protected from melting by stones or other solid matter, and mounds of ice covered with debris are thus formed on the surface. See *glacier table*.

The rate of movement or flow of a glacier is greatest in the middle, for it is retarded by friction at the bottom and sides, and the end of the glacier is convex. Along its course the glacier collects rock material, which it deposits when the ice melts; these accumulations of fragments are called *moraines*. See also *piedmont glacier*, *polar glacier*, *temperate glacier*.

glacier breeze. A cold breeze of *katabatic* type blowing down the course of a glacier, caused by the cooling of air in contact with the ice.

glacier burst or **jökulhlaup** (Icelandic). A flood of water with blocks of ice, rocks and mud, caused by the melting of ice in a glacier or ice-cap by hot *magma* during a volcanic *eruption*. Iceland has long suffered from glacier bursts, notably in 1349, when a glacier burst from Vatnajökull swept forty farms and their occupants into the sea.

glacier mill. See *moulin*.

'glacier mouse', polster. The term *'glacier mouse'* (jökla mys) is applied to a type of small moss-covered stone found on certain glaciers in Iceland; *polster* is applied to similar moss-covered patches of pebbles and silt a few cm in diameter found on glaciers elsewhere, particularly, for example, on Matanuska Glacier, Alaska, near its end.

glacier snout.* The tapering, convex end of a valley *glacier*, often with an arch from which flows a stream formed by the melting ice, and sometimes partially covered by a terminal *moraine*.

glacier table.* A block of rock standing on a pedestal of ice on the surface of a glacier; the rock protects the ice beneath it from melting so quickly as the surrounding ice, and thus becomes perched on a pedestal.

glaciofluvial. See *fluvioglacial*.

glaciology. The study of ice and the action of ice in all its forms, and therefore including *snow*.

glacis. A gently inclined slope or bank.

glade. An open space or passage in a wood or forest, either natural or produced by the felling of trees.

glazed frost. A coating of smooth ice, sometimes of considerable thickness, which forms on objects on to which rain is falling in an atmosphere having a temperature below freezing point. It is formed, too, when a warm, damp wind follows an extremely cold spell, the moisture condensing and then freezing on surfaces which are still below freezing point. Though not frequent in Great Britain, when it does occur it may be sufficiently heavy to bring down telegraph and telephone wires. The term *black ice* is generally used for glazed frost on a road surface. Some American geographers term a deposit of glazed frost an *ice storm*.

glei soil. A type of soil which is formed under the influence of poor drainage; the *water table* stands at or near the surface, and a so-called glei horizon is developed, greyish in colour and characterized by reddish-brown deposits of ferric hydroxide.

glen. In Scotland, a long, narrow valley, with steep sides, usually having a river, a stream, or lake at the bottom. It is narrower and steeper-sided than a *strath*, though the two terms are sometimes used indiscriminately.

globigerina ooze. A calcareous deposit which covers a large proportion of the ocean bed, consisting chiefly of the remains of foraminifera, the globigerina being the most abundant and widely-distributed genus.

The shells are minute, commonly about the size of a pin-head. Mixed with them are small amounts of the shells, etc., of other living organisms, and small traces of material derived from the land. Globigerina ooze is the most widespread type of ooze in the Atlantic and Indian Oceans, and covers much of the southern Pacific Ocean. It is most developed at depths of about 2,700 to 4,500 m (1,500–2,500 fathoms).

gloup. See *blowhole*.

gneiss. One of an extensive series of rocks with a banded structure, of *metamorphic* type, varying widely in chemical composition, and usually characterized by the most conspicuous dark mineral present, e.g. hornblende gneiss. The banding, due to the separation of light and dark minerals in crude layers, is the most characteristic feature of a typical gneiss.

gnomonic projection. A type of *zenithal projection*, in which the projection is made on to the tangent plane from the centre of the globe. Areas and shapes are so distorted that it would be altogether valueless except for the useful quality that every *great circle* on the sphere is represented by a straight line on the map; this enables great circle routes to be easily plotted.

Gondwanaland. The southerly of the two ancient continents into which the earth's land mass was once divided, comprising most of Africa, Madagascar, India, Australia, Antarctica, and parts of South America; the other ancient continent was *Laurasia*. Later, according to the theory of *continental drift*, Gondwanaland broke up and formed the continents of the present day.

Goode's interrupted homolosine projection. A type of equal-area or *homolographic projection*, in which the oceans are interrupted but the continents are clear and well-shaped. The parallels of latitude are straight lines. Such equal-area projection of the whole earth's surface is valuable for showing the world distribution of climatic regions, economic data, etc.

gorge.* A valley which is more than usually deep and narrow, with steep walls; there is no sharp distinction between a gorge and a *canyon*, though the latter is generally of much greater size. The sides of a small gorge are sometimes practically vertical.

graben (German). See *rift valley*.

gradient. Of a slope, e.g. along a road, railway, or hillside, the ratio of the difference in height between two points and the horizontal distance between them, usually expressed in the form '1 in X'. For inclines no steeper than about 1 in 3 the slope distance between the two points may be assumed equal to its horizontal equivalent. Gradients may be calculated from a large-scale map, making use of *contours* or *spot heights* and the *map scale*.

gradient, pressure. See *pressure gradient*.

granite. A coarse-grained *plutonic rock* which always contains *quartz* and *feldspar*, as well as other minerals. Its structure is so coarse that the different mineral grains can be plainly seen and distinguished from one another. It is one of the hardest and most durable rocks, the commonest plutonic rock, and one of the most abundant rocks in the earth; it often occurs in large masses or *batholiths*. It is widely used in building and ornamental work. Districts in Britain well-known for their granite include Land's End (Cornwall) and Dartmoor (Devonshire), in the United States the Sierra Nevada (California).

grape belt. A strip of land about 96 km (60 miles) long and several miles wide extending along the southern shore of Lake Erie, USA, having a long, mild autumn with unusually late frosts, and a less severe winter than areas in the same latitude but farther inland, owing to the tempering influence of the lake. See *fruit belt*.

grasslands. Those regions of the world where the natural vegetation consists of grass; the rainfall is too light to permit forest growth, but is less scanty and irregular than that of the deserts, and the grasslands are thus normally situated between the forest belts and the arid regions. Two main sub-divisions are recognized, the *tropical grasslands* or *savanna* and the *mid-latitude, temperate,* or *intermediate grasslands*, of which the *steppes*, *prairies*, and *pampas* are examples. Sown grassland, as distinct from the natural grasslands described above, now covers considerable areas in countries where *pastoral farming* is an important occupation, e.g. in New Zealand.

graupel (German). See *soft hail*.

gravel. A deposit of rounded stones, usually mixed with finer material such as sand or clay, and formed by the action of moving water – by a river or a lake, or by the sea. More specifically, it consists of rock fragments 2–10 mm in diameter; if the fragments exceed 10 mm in diameter, they are often classified as pebbles and boulders. When a gravel is consolidated, it becomes a *conglomerate*.

gravity anomaly. The difference between the observed and the calculated force of gravity at a place, due, for example, to the variations in density of the underlying rocks. If the observed force of gravity is greater than the calculated value, the gravity anomaly is positive; if it is less, the gravity anomaly is negative.

great circle. A circle on the earth's surface whose plane passes through its centre, and therefore bisects it into two hemispheres. Two opposing meridians together form a great circle; the equator is also a great circle. The shortest distance between any two points on the earth's surface is the arc of the great circle which passes through them. See *great circle route, small circle*.

great circle route. A route between any two points on the earth's surface which follows the *great circle* between them; it is thus the shortest distance between the two points, and is often followed by ships at sea, provided that it does not take them into dangerous waters, and also by aircraft on long-distance flights. A great circle route between two places of approximately the same latitude proceeds north of the parallel of latitude in the northern hemisphere, and south of the parallel of latitude in the southern hemisphere.

green belt or **greenbelt**. Chiefly in Great Britain, a belt of land round a city or town where the erection of houses and other buildings is severely restricted and the open character of the country is preserved, in the form of woods, commons, fields, farms, etc.

green flash. The green light from the sun observed in a clear atmosphere at sunrise and sunset, lasting for two or three seconds. The blue and green light in the sun's rays is refracted more than the yellow and red light, and when the sun is so low that no red light from it can reach the observer, only a green light is seen; the blue light is generally absorbed or diffracted by the atmosphere.

'greenhouse effect'. A feature of *insolation* due to the earth's atmosphere: the latter permits the passage of short-wave solar energy to the earth's surface, which is thereby heated, but greatly absorbs the long-wave radiation from the earth, particularly when there is a substantial cloud cover. Temperatures at the earth's surface are thus maintained at a higher level than they would otherwise have, the atmosphere acting like the glass of a greenhouse.

green manure crop. See *cover crop*.

green mud. A marine deposit which contains much fine clay and also some grains of a mineral, glauconite, a silicate of iron and potassium, from which it derives its green colour. The shells of foraminifera, whose remains are found in the green mud, are often filled with glauconite. Green mud is found particularly on the continental slope off subtropical coasts where few large rivers enter the sea: e.g. off the coasts of south-eastern USA, California, and Portugal.

Greenwich Mean Time or **GMT.** *Standard time* for the British Isles, though replaced by *British Summer Time* Mar–Oct each year; it is *local time* at Greenwich, London, on the zero *meridian*.

gregale. A strong wind from the NE direction in the south central Mediterranean area, blowing mainly in the cool season. It occurs most frequently when pressure is high to the north over central Europe and the Balkans and relatively low to the south over Libya; this type brings little or no rain and the temperature does not fall much below the normal. Similar names (e.g. grégal in S France) have been applied to strong winds from a similar direction in other Mediterranean areas.

grike or **gryke.** A fissure between *clints* in the surface of the rock in a limestone region, formed when the limestone dissolves in rain water containing carbon dioxide from the atmosphere; it is often formed when an open joint is widened by solution. The term is especially used of such fissures in the N Pennines of England.

grit. A rock, mainly of quartz, resembling a *sandstone*.

grotto. A large cave produced in a limestone region by the solvent action of underground streams and percolating water; the term is sometimes loosely applied, too, to other types of cave.

ground frost. In the British Isles, a temperature on the grass of 0°C (32°F) or below: a term sometimes used in weather forecasts to indicate that at ground level a frost may occur while the air temperature remains above freezing point.

ground moraine. See *moraine*.

ground water. Water which exists in the pores and crevices of the earth's *mantle rock*, having entered them chiefly as rain water percolating through from the surface, and so feeds *wells* and *springs* – as opposed to the rain water which occurs within a few hundred metres of the earth's surface, for at great depths the pressure must be so great that all pores and crevices are closed. It has important chemical effects upon the rocks which it penetrates, for it may dissolve some of the rock material, it may deposit some of the mineral matter with which it has been overcharged elsewhere, or it may modify minerals by chemical combination. See *water table*.

grove. A small, shady wood; a cluster of trees set about a small open space.

growing season. That part of the year in a specific region when the growth of the indigenous vegetation is made possible by the favourable combination of temperature and rainfall. In general, its duration decreases with distance from the equator: in the *equatorial forest*, for instance, the growing season is continuous throughout the year, while in the *tundra* it lasts for only two or three months. Many cultivated plants demand growing seasons of special character; cotton, for example, requires about 200 frostless days, maize (corn) about 150 frostless days.

groyne or **groin.** A low wall built out into the seas, roughly perpendicular to the coast-line, to resist the travel of sand and shingle along a beach, or to minimize erosion by the sea.

gryke. See *grike*.

gulch. A narrow, deep ravine with steep sides formed by a torrent, chiefly applied to such a ravine in the western United States.

gulf. A large, deep bay; an extensive inlet penetrating far into the land. It may have been formed either by fracture of part of the earth's crust, or by the sea overflowing depressed land.

gully.* A long, narrow channel worn out by the action of water, particularly on a hillside; it is smaller than a *ravine*, and much smaller than a *valley*. The term is often used, too, of a channel produced in *soil erosion*; such a gully normally carries water only during or immediately after rain or the melting of snow.

gully erosion. See *soil erosion*.

guyot. A flat-topped mountain on the ocean floor, of which hundreds of examples are known in the Pacific. They are believed to be truncated volcanoes, which were eroded by wave action near the surface, to sink later to their present levels. See *seamount*.

gyre. A system of *ocean currents* which circulates around the subtropical *anticyclones* in the Atlantic and Pacific Oceans, clockwise in the northern hemisphere and anti-clockwise in the southern hemisphere. The Gulf Stream, for instance, forms part of the gyre in the North Atlantic, the Kuro Shio part of that in the North Pacific Ocean.

H

haar. A sea fog which is driven over the eastern coastal districts of Great Britain by an easterly wind, most frequently during the summer.

habitat. The natural environment of a plant or animal; it is often expressed as one of the main natural regions which are recognized in geography, or one of their sub-divisions, e.g. the equatorial forest, the tundra.

haboob. A type of *duststorm* experienced in north and north-east Sudan, being most frequent near to Khartoum. It is commonest in the afternoon and evening, and is rare in the morning; it occurs chiefly between May and September, but is possible at any time of the year. The haboob is usually accompanied by a sudden increase in wind strength and a change of direction, a marked fall in temperature, and an extremely poor visibility caused by the raising of the dust; it is often followed by heavy rain and sometimes thunderstorms.

hachures. Short lines of shading drawn on a map to represent differences in the slope of the ground. If the slope is steep, the lines or hachures are thick and close together; if the slope is gentle, they are thinner and farther apart. The darkest portions of a hachured map, then, represent crags and very steep slopes, while the lighter shades depict the gentler slopes; the white parts show plateaux, level mountain tops, hillside shelves, or level valley bottoms. Such a map, hung at a distance from the eye, thus gives a fairly good impression of the configuration of the land. The hachures are drawn from the highest point of a mountain to the foot, and should be perpendicular to the *contour* lines. Unlike the contour lines, they give no indication of the actual height of land above sea level.

hade. The angle between a *fault plane* and the vertical.

Hadley cell. A supposed element in the general circulation of the atmosphere, first described by the English meteorologist George Hadley in 1735 in part explanation of the *trade winds*, operating approximately between latitudes 30° N and 30° S. The cell comprises the following movements: a rise of air at the equator, a poleward flow at high altitude, a descent of air at about 30° N (or 30° S), then a flow back to the equator at the surface.

haff (German). A *lagoon*, formed at the mouth of a river owing to the presence of a sandy bar or *spit*, and usually so shallow as to be

Haffs along the southern shores of the Baltic Sea.

accessible only to small vessels: applied especially to the Baltic coast of the former East Prussia (now East Germany and Poland), where the spit is known as a *nehrung*.

hail. The hard pellets of ice with a diameter of 5 mm or more which fall from *cumulonimbus* clouds, and are often associated with thunderstorms. They are of various shapes and may reach considerable size; individual hailstones have been known to weigh over 1 kg. They are caused by the rapid ascent of moist air; the water drops freeze, and the size of the pellets increases as more water vapour freezes on to their surface. When the pellets are heavy enough to overcome the resistance of the ascending air currents, they fall; in their downward journey, they may still grow by assuming fresh layers of ice from the supercooled water drops in the moist air. A severe hailstorm is capable of causing immense damage to growing crops. See *soft hail*.

halo. A ring of light which surrounds the moon or sun when the latter is seen through the ice crystals of a thin veil of high cloud. When the solar halo is formed, it is rarely seen with the naked eye owing to the brightness of the sun, but is visible through darkened glass. The commonest type is that in which the angular distance between moon and halo is 22°. It is formed by refraction of light through the ice crystals of the cloud. The halo is usually white, but if the ring is very sharply defined it is coloured, having a reddish tinge on the inner edge. The colour sequence is thus opposite to that of the *corona*.

halophyte. A plant which grows naturally in a *salt-marsh* or other saline environment; it is often adapted, like the *xerophytes*, to conserve water.

hamlet. A small village or group of houses in a rural area.

hammada or **hamada** (Arabic). The type of desert, particularly in the Sahara, in which the surface consists principally of bare rock, having been swept clear of sand and dust by the wind. See *erg, reg*.

hanging glacier.* A *glacier* which is perched on a high shelf above a valley and appears to hang over the latter. It is always a potential danger to climbers, for a mass of ice, or ice *avalanche*, may break away and hurtle down into the valley below.

hanging valley. A tributary valley which enters a main valley from a considerable height above the latter, so that a stream flowing down it enters the main valley by a waterfall or rapids. Hanging valleys are particularly common in glaciated regions. One explanation is that the main valley was much more deeply eroded by its large glacier than the tributary valley was by its smaller glacier, and the opening of the tributary valley was thus left at some height above it. Hanging valleys are not always due to glaciers, however; they are formed when-ever the main valley has been eroded more quickly than the tributary valleys.

harbour. A stretch of water on the coast which affords shelter to sea-going vessels; it may have been formed naturally, or artificially, or by artificial improvement of a natural feature. See *port*.

hardpan. A hardened or cemented layer of soil, impervious to drainage, lying at or below the surface. It may consist of a layer of clay, or it may be due to cementation by iron oxide, or calcium carbonate, or some other substance.

harmattan. A strong north-easterly wind experienced in West Africa. Blowing direct from the Sahara, it is hot, very dry, and dusty – so hot and dry that it sometimes splits the trunks of trees. When it penetrates to the Guinea coast, it provides a welcome relief from the moist heat, and is beneficial to health; it is a relatively cool wind to that area, in fact, for by reason of its extreme dryness it promotes evaporation and therefore cooling. See *doctor, the*. On the other hand, it carries with it abundant dust from the desert, and a thick haze is sometimes formed and impedes river navigation; it may cause severe damage to crops; far inland, it is so dry and dusty as to be often injurious to health. Its average southern limit in mid-winter, when the equatorial belt of low pressure is along or just south of the Guinea coast, is about 5° N; in mid-summer it is about 18° N. It has a much greater duration in the north of the area than in the south.

haze. A mass of minute solid particles of dust, smoke, etc., which obscures the atmosphere near to the earth's surface so as to reduce the visibility below 2 kilometres, but not below 1 kilometre. See *mist, fog*.

headland. A steep crag or cliff jutting out into the sea.

head of navigation. The farthest point up a river to be reached by vessels for the purposes of trade.

headward erosion. The action of a river in cutting back and thus lengthening its valley upstream, perhaps leading eventually to *river capture*.

heat equator. See *thermal equator*.

heath or **heathland.** An extensive tract of open, uncultivated ground, more or less flat and covered with small shrubs such as heather or ling.

heat wave. A term commonly used to signify an unbroken spell of abnormally hot weather. In the British Isles, for instance, a period of several successive days when the temperature exceeded 27°C (81°F) would constitute a heat wave.

heave. See *fault*.

helium. One of the rare gases contained in the atmosphere, all of which together constitute only about .01 per cent of dry air; the proportion of helium is about one part in 200,000.

helm wind. A strong, cold wind which blows down from the summits of the hills in northern England, especially down the western slopes of the Cross Fell Range in Cumbria. When it blows, a heavy, helm-shaped cloud, the 'helm', forms over the Cross Fell Range, and a few kilometres away and parallel to the 'helm' appears a thin roll of cloud known as the 'helm bar'; the helm wind blows as far as the 'helm bar'. The helm wind usually occurs when the general direction of the wind is easterly or north-easterly, and is most common in late winter and spring. See *banner-cloud*.

hemisphere. One half of the earth's surface, formed when a plane through its centre bisects the earth. The earth is usually divided into northern hemisphere and southern hemisphere, the former being that half of the earth's surface which is north of the equator, the latter that half which is south of the equator. See *land hemisphere, water hemisphere*.

hide. In England, historically, the extent of land needed for the support of a peasant family. The area varied considerably according to the quality of the land, and ranged, for instance, from about 50 acres to 100 acres.

high. A region of high atmospheric pressure. On a *weather chart* the centre of an *anticyclone* is usually indicated by the word 'high'. See *anticyclone*.

hill. A small portion of the earth's surface elevated above its surroundings, of lower altitude than a *mountain*. In general, an eminence is not considered a mountain unless its elevation from foot to summit is well over 300 m, but the distinction is arbitrary. The Normandy Hills (Collines de Normandie) in France, for instance, rise to 417 m, while the Black Mountains (Montagnes Noires) of Brittany rise to only 326 m. The Anaimalai Hills of S India rise to 2,695 m.

hill fog. A meteorological term for a low cloud which covers elevated ground, e.g. hill slopes, and to observers within it resembles a *fog*.

hillock. A mound or small *hill*.

hill shading. In *cartography*, a method of depicting relief which has been widely used on topographical maps in conjunction with *contours*, giving a three-dimensional effect similar to that of a relief model. Oblique rather than vertical shading is commonly employed. The generally accepted convention is that light should appear to strike the various relief features from the NW, so that the slopes facing E and S are shaded.

hill station. A mountain resort in or near the tropics, originally established, e.g. in India, to accommodate European families who wished to escape the fierce summer heat of the plains. Simla (India) and Garut (Indonesia) were examples.

hinterland. The land which lies behind a seaport or seaboard and supplies the bulk of the imports of that seaport or seaboard. The seaport to which an inland region is the hinterland is sometimes determined by the outline of the land. West Yorkshire, England, for example, is part of the hinterland of Liverpool for trade with America, but for trade across the North Sea is part of the hinterland of Hull, Goole, and Grimsby. Sometimes the hinterlands of different seaports overlap, even in relation to the same sea; this may be due to variations in the facilities for shipping at the seaports and in facilities for communication with the hinterland; Hull, for instance, is capable of taking large sea-going ships, while Goole, only accessible to smaller vessels, has the advantage of nearness to their hinterland. The extent and importance of a hinterland may be much increased by improvements in its seaport or in inland transport facilities. The German word *hinterland*, meaning 'back country', originally referred to the territory, beyond the occupied coastal districts, over which a colonial power claimed jurisdiction, especially applied in the late 19th century to parts of Africa; the word was adopted by geographers and changed to the above.

hoar frost.* The deposit of ice crystals formed on objects near the ground when water vapour in the atmosphere solidifies without first passing through the liquid state: it is formed instead of *dew* when the *dew point* is below the freezing point. It often consists partly of frozen dew and partly of ice formed directly from water vapour.

hogback or **hog's back.** A long, narrow ridge in which both *dip* slope and

Section through a hogback showing inclination of strata.

Cape Cod, Massachusetts, showing the hook at its tip.

scarp slope are steep, owing to the steep inclination, or dip, of the beds, and thus differing from a *cuesta*.

homolographic or **equal-area projection.** A type of *map projection* in which the area bounded by any two adjoining parallels and two adjoining meridians is equal to any other area similarly enclosed; in other words,

Diagram illustrating the formation of a horst.

the ratio between any area on the map and the corresponding area on the globe is constant.

homoseismal line or **coseismic line.** A line drawn through places which are affected by an earthquake at the same time. Such lines are usually elliptical, the mid-point of the ellipse being the *epicentre*.

hoodoo. See *earth pillar, demoiselle*.

hook. A *spit* which is curved at one end; the curvature may be caused by the action of the waves in rolling material to the sheltered side of the spit. (See Fig. p. 99.)

horizon, rational, true or **astronomical.** A *great circle* on the *celestial sphere*, parallel to the sensible or visible horizon of an observer. See *horizon, sensible* or *visible*.

horizon, sensible or **visible.** The more or less circular line bounding an observer's view of the earth (or sea), where earth (or sea) and sky appear to meet. On land this line is broken by surface obstructions; at sea the line is a perfect circle, the observer being at the centre. The distance of the horizon is determined by the height of the observer. Allowing for refraction, and ignoring obstructions, the actual distance of the sensible horizon from an observer placed at an elevation of 30 m is about 22 km; this distance varies as the square root of the height of the observer.

horizon, soil. A layer of soil which lies more or less parallel to the surface and has fairly distinctive soil properties. See *profile, soil*.

horn (German).* A pyramidal peak, formed when adjacent *cirques* have been cut back into a mountain, the faces being bounded by sharp, steep *arêtes*. The classic example is the Matterhorn, in Switzerland.

horse latitudes. The sub-tropical belts of high atmospheric pressure over the oceans, situated in both hemispheres between the *trade winds* and the *westerlies*. They move north and south with the sun. They are regions of calms and light variable winds, of comparatively dry air, and quiet, stable weather conditions. The name may have originated from the practice, in the days of sailing ships, of throwing overboard horses which were being transported to America or the West Indies when the ship's passage was unduly prolonged.

horst (German). An elevated block of rock between parallel *faults* which has reached its position either through uplift between the faults, or through the sinking of the beds outside the faults.

horticulture. The cultivation of flowers, fruit, or vegetables, usually on small plots of land, and thus a form of *intensive cultivation*.

hot spring or **thermal spring.*** A stream of hot water issuing from the ground, often after being heated by *magma*, and therefore commonly occurring in a volcanic region when eruptions have ceased. Hot springs are not confined to volcanic regions, however, as water sinking far enough into the earth may become heated and rise to form springs. Mineral substances which have been held in solution are often deposited around the hot springs. See *fumarole, geyser, travertine*.

huerta (Spanish). Land in Spain which, owing to prolonged high temperatures and irrigation, produces two or more crops per year; it is situated mainly in the south-east, in the provinces of Valencia, Murcia, and Granada, and yields abundant oranges, pomegranates, figs, and almonds, occasionally even sugar-cane and cotton. The efficient cultivation of the huerta contrasts with the poverty and neglect of much of the interior plateau of Spain. See *vega*.

hum. In a *karst region*, a small mass of limestone standing above the surrounding country because of greater resistance to erosion. The term is also applied to a remnant of limestone which is resting on non-calcareous rocks and is being gradually worn away by solution.

humidity. The state of the atmosphere with respect to the water vapour it contains. See *absolute humidity, relative humidity*.

humus. The decomposed and partly decomposed organic matter, of animal and vegetable origin, in the soil. In uncultivated land the humus is derived from the natural decay of previous generations of plants; in ploughed and cultivated land the humus is supplied as some kind of manure. The humus of ordinary soil is black, and is thus responsible for making the soil darker than the subsoil. (See *soil colloids*.) It plays an important but very complicated part in maintaining the fertility of the soil. The amount of humus in different soils varies considerably; some, like the peat soils, consist largely of slightly decomposed organic matter which has not yet become humus.

hundred. In parts of England, historically, a sub-division of a county or shire, into which most counties were divided, corresponding in other parts to a *ward* or *wapentake*, and known as early as the tenth century.

hurricane. (1) A wind of Force 12 on the *Beaufort scale* of wind strengths: i.e. a wind having a mean velocity of over 120 km (75 miles) per hour.
(2) The *tropical cyclone* or revolving storm of the West Indies and Gulf of Mexico. It usually originates east of the islands, occasionally as far east as the Cape Verde Islands, and takes a westward course, sometimes causing extensive destruction on one island after another; it then generally recurves to the north-east. Besides the West Indies, the Gulf coasts

of the United States and the eastern side of Central America as far south as the Mosquito Coast of Nicaragua are affected by hurricanes; Costa Rica, Panama, and the northern coast of South America, however, lie outside the hurricane region. The name is also given to the tropical cyclone experienced off the coast of Queensland, Australia.

hydro-electric power. Energy obtained from natural or artificial waterfalls and utilized for the generation of electricity in dynamos worked by turbines.

hydrography. The subject that treats of the waters of the earth's surface, particularly with reference to their physical features, position, volume, etc., and the preparation of charts of seas, lakes, rivers, contours of the sea bed, shallows, deeps, currents, etc.

hydrologic cycle. See *water cycle*.

hydrology. The science that treats of water, especially in relation to its occurrence in streams, lakes, wells, etc., and as snow, and including its discovery, uses, control, and conservation.

hydrophyte. See *hygrophyte*.

hydrosphere. All the water of the earth, as distinct from the *atmosphere* and the *lithosphere*. It includes both the comparatively shallow layer of water (in liquid and solid form) which covers nearly three-quarters of the earth's surface, forming the oceans, seas, lakes, ice sheets, etc., and also the water that is present in the atmosphere.

hyetograph. A self-recording instrument, very similar to a *rain gauge*, which registers the rainfall. The collected rainfall is usually made to raise a float, to which is attached a pen writing on a chart that is wrapped round a clock-driven drum.

hygrogram. The continuous record of the *relative humidity* of the atmosphere, as measured by the *hygrograph*, usually to cover a period of a week.

hygrograph. A self-recording *hygrometer*, in which the *relative humidity* of the air is continuously traced on a chart fixed to a rotating drum, actuated by clockwork. The ordinary hair hygrograph, which is in common use at meteorological stations, depends on the expansion and contraction in length of human hair with variations in relative humidity, these changes being then transferred to the rotating chart, or *hygrogram*, by a pen. It is not an accurate instrument, but is useful for recording any considerable or sudden changes in the amount of moisture in the atmosphere, and the time at which they occur.

hygrometer. An instrument designed to measure the *relative humidity* of the atmosphere. It usually consists of two thermometers, a *dry bulb thermometer*, measuring the actual temperature of the atmosphere, and a *wet bulb thermometer*; the bulb of the latter is kept permanently moistened by a piece of muslin wrapped round it and an attached length of wick dipping into a reservoir of water. Evaporation from the wet bulb causes the temperature of the wet bulb thermometer to be

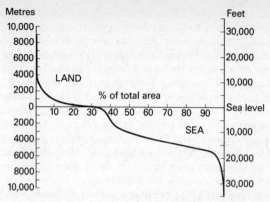

Hypsographic curve representing the earth's surface.

lower than that of the dry bulb thermometer, and the difference between the two temperatures – sometimes known as the wet bulb 'depression' – affords a measure of the relative humidity of the air. More complicated forms of hygrometer have been devised, but are not in general meteorological use. See *hygrograph*, *psychrometer*, *wet bulb temperature*.

hygrophyte or **hydrophyte.** A plant which thrives only when a considerable amount of moisture is available, and therefore lives either in water or in a very humid region such as the *equatorial forest*. The stem is usually long and comparatively fragile, and contains little woody fibre; the leaves are large and thin, and the roots shallow. The banana plant provides an example.

hygroscope. An instrument for showing the changes in the humidity or dampness of the air, usually by means of the changes in appearance or dimensions of a substance. In a crude wall instrument like the 'weather-house', containing the figures of a man and a woman, the state of the air is indicated by the twisting and untwisting of a piece of catgut in response to changes of humidity.

hypabyssal rocks. Those *igneous rocks* which have risen towards the earth's surface, but have failed to reach it, solidifying in fissures as *dykes*, *sills*, etc. They are thus intermediate between the *plutonic* or *abyssal rocks* and the *lavas* or volcanic rocks.

hypsographic or **hypsometric curve.** A diagrammatic curve in which heights are plotted against areas, often being used to represent the average form of the earth's surface: the various heights of the land and the depths of the ocean are represented by vertical distances above and below a horizontal line which signifies mean sea level, and the areas which the heights and depths cover on the earth's surface are represented by lengths along this horizontal line. Heights and depths

103

are much exaggerated. The salient facts illustrated by this curve are: first, the predominance of two levels representing the general bed of the oceans and the general, comparatively level surface of the continents, and second, the relative steepness of the *continental slope* joining these two predominant levels. Such curves can also be drawn for any defined area on the earth, e.g. a continent or country.

hypsometer. An instrument which measures altitude. Usually it is an instrument in which the boiling point of water is accurately measured; as this temperature varies with the atmospheric pressure, the latter can be calculated from it, and from this the altitude can be obtained. In order to obtain the height to within 3 m, the temperature of the boiling point of water must be measured to within one hundredth of a degree on the absolute scale. See *temperature*.

hythergraph. A graphical representation of the differentiation between various types of climate. Mean monthly temperatures are plotted as ordinates against the mean monthly rainfalls or humidities as abscissae, and a closed, twelve-sided polygon, the hythergraph, is obtained. This reveals the type of climate at a glance. See *climograph*.

ice. The solid form of water, with a density of 0.9 (approx.) gm per cc, so that it floats on water (see *iceberg*). It has been estimated that all but about 1 per cent of the ice on the earth's surface is represented by the *ice sheets* of Antarctica and Greenland. Ice also occurs in the form of minute crystals as *snow*, *hail*, and *frost*.

Ice Age. A geological period in which ice sheets and glaciers covered large areas of the continents, reaching the sea in places and lowering the temperature of the oceans. The latest Ice Age began early in the Quaternary Period (see *Cainozoic era*), when the ice covered much of Europe and North America; the present *ice sheets* of Greenland and Antarctica are relics of this Ice Age.

iceberg. A mass of land ice which has been broken off or 'calved' from the end of a glacier or from an ice shelf, and is afloat in the sea. When a glacier enters the sea, the ice is buoyed up by the water, and a portion of the glacier is easily broken off and floats away. Such a glacier berg is irregular in shape; a berg from an ice shelf is rectangular in shape, flat-topped or 'tabular', often very large, and is characteristic of the Antarctic.

The main sources of icebergs are the great ice sheets which cover Greenland and Antarctica. The Greenland icebergs, which break off from glaciers, are carried south by the Labrador Current towards the Grand Banks, off Newfoundland. They often project 60 m or more above the surface, and are sometimes several hundred metres long. The icebergs from the Antarctic ice shelf are sometimes over 60 km (40 miles) long and project more than 100 m above the surface. The number of icebergs varies considerably from year to year; when they are particularly numerous, they may be encountered far beyond their usual limits.

Only about one-ninth of the mass of an iceberg is visible above the water, so that the depth of a berg below the surface is far greater than its height above the surface. An iceberg gradually decreases in size owing to melting, erosion, and *calving*. The melting is caused both by the sun and by the entry of the iceberg into warmer waters. Erosion is caused by the swell, the waves, and rain. Calving often disturbs the balance of the iceberg and causes it to roll over. An iceberg often carries with it boulders and other rock material which came from the glacier: when melting takes place in the water, this debris sinks to the sea bed.

ice blink or **iceblink.** A white glare on the under-surface of a distant cloud, caused by the reflection of light from a mass of ice at ground level which may itself be too far away to be visible.

ice cap. A term regarded by some geographers as synonymous with *ice sheet* but by others considered to apply only to the smaller masses of permanent ice and snow, such as those on Spitsbergen and other Arctic islands.

ice-cap climate. The type of climate to be found over the polar ice caps or *ice sheets* of Greenland and Antarctica, which may be regarded as cold deserts of snow and ice; it is the least known of climatic types, and data are sparse. The mean monthly temperature throughout the year is below 0°C. The mean annual temperature of the interior of the Greenland ice sheet is estimated at −32°C, and that of the Antarctic interior is probably lower. The small precipitation consists almost entirely of dry, granular snow. In Antarctica, especially towards the margins of the ice sheet, severe blizzards occur, with wind speeds well over 80 km (50 miles) per hour.

icefall.* The steepened part of a *glacier*, where the sudden change of slope has caused *crevasses* running in different directions to intersect and break the ice surface into a mass of *séracs*. An outstanding example is the Great Khumbu Icefall, below Everest; there are others on Alpine glaciers, e.g. the Séracs du Géant, on the Glacier du Géant, which leads down to the Mer de Glace.

icefield. A uniform, unbroken *ice-floe* of great extent, i.e. several km (miles) across. The term is also sometimes applied to large areas of land ice, e.g. the Columbia Icefield, in the Rocky Mountains of Canada.

ice-floe. A mass of floating ice, detached from the main polar ice, and of large or small extent. A *light floe* is one in which the ice is only 1 metre thick or less, a *heavy floe* one in which the ice is thicker.

ice-foot. A mass of ice projecting into the sea on an Arctic or Antarctic shore. It sometimes becomes very thick, with its upper edge some metres above sea level. The first stage in its formation takes place during the autumn, when snow accumulates along the shore; water thrown up by the waves freezes on to this snow, and forms a mass of ice. This is later augmented by lumps of sea-ice, likewise forced on land by tides and waves. Fragments of rock often collect on the ice-foot, and protect the ice from melting so that parts of it remain till the following autumn.

ice sheet. A vast mass of ice and snow which covers large land areas in the polar regions; its surface is almost flat. The ice sheets of Greenland and Antarctica are the only large ones now in existence. The former covers the whole of Greenland except for a narrow fringe; only along

Sketch-map of Antarctica showing the major ice shelves.

this fringe does any uncovered rock appear. The Antarctic ice sheet, unlike that of Greenland, extends beyond the land surface which it covers, and projects out to sea in some parts (see *ice shelf*). The thickness of the Greenland ice sheet and of the Antarctic ice sheet has been estimated to be 3,000–4,000 m in places. Sometimes the Greenland ice sheet is described as an 'Arctic Sahara', or a 'cold desert'; it is more of a desert than the Sahara, however, for it is even more deficient in plant and animal life. The term *ice cap* is sometimes regarded as being synonymous with ice sheet. See *ice-cap climate*.

ice shelf. An extensive sheet of floating ice, on the margin of and attached to a coastline, e.g. the Ross Ice Shelf in Antarctica, which covers about 414,000 sq km (160,000 sq miles) of sea.

ice storm. Term used in the USA for *glazed frost*.

igneous rocks. Rocks which have solidified from a molten *magma*, and

107

form one of the three main types of rocks which comprise the earth's crust. They may have solidified after reaching the surface (*lavas* or volcanic rocks), or in channels connecting the molten reservoirs with the exterior (*hypabyssal rocks*) or well below the surface under pressure (*plutonic* or *abyssal rocks*). In many of them the various minerals have crystallized separately, and the rock is a mass of interlocking crystals. They do not usually occur in distinct beds or strata, and they are not fossiliferous. There are many kinds of igneous rocks, owing to the varying conditions under which the original magma solidified. See *metamorphic rocks*, *sedimentary rocks*.

illuviation. The deposition, usually in the B horizon, of material removed by *eluviation* from the upper or A horizon of the soil. A *hardpan* is sometimes formed in this way.

impermeable rocks. Rocks which, being non-porous or practically so, do not allow water, e.g. rain water, to soak into them. Granite provides an example; this rock may be pervious, however, owing to joints and fissures. Some geographers assume the term to be synonymous with *impervious rocks*.

impervious rocks. Rocks which do not allow water, e.g. rain water, to pass through them freely; they may be porous, like clay, or practically non-porous, like unfissured granite. Some geographers use the term *impermeable rocks*.

imports. Goods which are brought into a country in trade, being obtained from another country which has a surplus; the usual reason is that the first country finds them impossible, or difficult, or uneconomic, to produce at home. Sometimes climate prevents or restricts the domestic production of goods; tropical fruits, for instance, cannot be grown in the intermediate zone. Sometimes land and labour can be more profitably devoted to the production of other goods, and the commodities are imported; wheat and meat, for instance, are leading imports into Great Britain. In general, imports may be regarded as goods obtained in exchange for *exports*.

inch, innis (Gaelic). In Scotland, a small island; the term has been used in place-names: e.g. the island of Inch Kenneth (off the coast of Mull), Innis Mhòr (in Dornoch Firth).

incised meander.* An old *meander* which has become deepened by *rejuvenation*. Two types of incised meander are usually recognized: the *entrenched* or *intrenched* meander and the *ingrown meander*. In the entrenched or intrenched meander vertical erosion has predominated, so that the valley sides are steep and in cross-profile the valley is symmetrical. In the ingrown meander lateral erosion as well as vertical erosion has taken place, so that one valley side is steep and the other much gentler and in cross-profile the valley is asymmetrical.

Indian summer. A spell of calm, mild weather sometimes experienced in autumn in Great Britain and the United States, somewhat reminiscent of the balmier days of summer. Such warm spells do not necessarily occur every year. The term is supposed to have originated in North America towards the end of the eighteenth century; it is attributed to the fact that the area where the weather conditions were first observed was still inhabited by American Indians.

ingrown meander. See *incised meander*.

inlet. A small opening into the coastline or into the shore of a lake.

inlier. A mass of old rocks surrounded by geologically younger rocks. See *outlier*.

inselberg (German). An 'island mountain'; an isolated hill in an arid or semi-arid region. It usually has a rounded summit and steep sides of bare rock, and may be regarded as a type of *monadnock*; it may rise to well over 300 m (1,000 ft) above the surrounding plain.

insolation. The radiant energy received from the sun by the earth and other planets. It varies considerably over different parts of the earth's surface. The amount of insolation reaching any place during any one day depends on the *solar constant*, the area of the surface and its inclination to the sun's rays, the transparency of the atmosphere, and the position of the earth in its orbit. This amount varies throughout the day with the changes in the angle of incidence of the sun's rays; and the length of time that the sun remains above the horizon is a determining factor. At the *equinoxes*, that time is twelve hours per day everywhere on the earth's surface, but towards the summer *solstices* the longer days of the higher latitudes more than compensate for the great obliqueness of the sun's rays. Thus the total insolation per day is not at its maximum at the latitude where the sun is highest at noon, but at a rather higher latitude where the daily duration of sunlight is greater. For the year as a whole, however, insolation is greatest at the equator; it decreases at first slowly then more rapidly, then slowly again towards the poles. Insolation shows the least variation throughout the year at the equator, and varies very considerably at the poles.

instability. The condition of an *air mass* in which the *lapse rate* is greater than the dry adiabatic lapse rate of 1°C per 100 metres: air which is rising, e.g. because of surface heating, has a tendency to continue its ascent, for its temperature remains higher than that of its environment. Instability in humid air may thus lead to the formation of cloud of great depth and the development of thunderstorms.

insular climate. The type of climate experienced on islands and in coastal regions where the sea rather than one of the great land masses is the dominating influence. In contrast to the *continental climate*, the insular climate is thus characterized by a relatively small range of temperatures, both diurnally and from summer to winter. See *maritime climate*.

intensive cultivation. A system of farming by which the cultivator expends much labour and possibly capital on a relatively small area. Land may be kept continually under cultivation, without being allowed to lie fallow at any time. Intensive cultivation is practised in countries such as Denmark and England, where land is relatively valuable, and high crop yields are sought and obtained. See *extensive cultivation*.

interfluve. Strip or ridge between two adjacent river valleys.

interglacial period. A period of relatively warm climate between two periods of glaciation and cold climate during the *Ice Age*.

interior drainage. See *internal drainage*.

interlocking spurs. In a V-shaped *valley* down which a river with a winding course is flowing: the portion of the valley walls which project from both sides to the concave bends of the river and so obscure the view upstream.

intermittent spring. A *spring* from which the flow of water is intermittent, generally owing to changes in the height of the *water table* caused by a fluctuating rainfall.

intermontane or **intermont.** A term used to describe the location of a feature 'between mountains', e.g. intermontane plateau, intermontane basin. An example of the latter is the Great Basin of W. United States, between the Sierra Nevada and the Wasatch Mts.

internal or **interior drainage.** Drainage in which the waters have no outlet, and so do not reach the sea. An example is the Great Basin of Nevada and western Utah, USA, where the streams flow into basins and create *salt lakes*, from which the water continually evaporates or sinks into the ground.

International Date Line. The line approximating to the meridian 180° W (or E) where the date changes by one day as it is crossed: the date is one day earlier to the E of the line than it is to the W. A traveller crossing the date line westwards thus 'loses' a day; he has to advance the calendar, for example, from Saturday to Sunday. Similarly, a traveller crossing the date line eastwards 'gains' a day; he has to put back the calendar, for example, from Saturday to Friday. This is because on a journey eastwards from the Greenwich meridian, local time advances till 180° E is reached, when it is 12 hours ahead of GMT; similarly moving westwards, local time is retarded till 180° W is reached, when it is 12 hours behind GMT. Thus there is approximately 24 hours' difference in time between two points placed just each side of 180° W (or E) longitude – the International Date Line. Some deviations of the line from the 180° meridian have been agreed upon in order to avoid confusion of dates in island groups and land areas that are cut by the meridian.

Intertropical Convergence Zone or **Intertropical Front.** A zone of low atmospheric pressure near and more or less parallel to the equator, where the NE and SE *trade winds* meet, being thus associated with the *doldrums*. As the term 'front' is therefore not strictly correct, the term Intertropical Convergence Zone (ITCZ) is preferable.

Temperature-height curve to illustrate a temperature inversion: at ground level the air temperature is equal to that at about 630 m.

intrazonal soil. A soil which has been influenced in its development less by climate and vegetation than by other factors, such as defective drainage, excessive evaporation, or an unusual parent material.

intrenched meander. See *incised meander*.

intrusive rocks. Rocks which solidified from *magma* before reaching the earth's surface; they are thus *igneous rocks*. See *extrusive rocks*.

inversion, temperature. An increase of temperature with height above the earth's surface, being the reverse of the normal situation, in which the temperature falls with height; it may occur from the earth's surface or at altitudes far above the surface. A surface inversion is commonly experienced in hollows and valleys, especially in winter on calm, clear nights, when radiation has caused considerable cooling and the cold air has sunk down into them; a pool of cold air thus lies there, while on the mountain slopes above the air is warmer. When the sky has been clear and the wind light for some time, it is also usual in fairly level areas in temperate latitudes for a temperature inversion to develop above the surface at night. In winter, during anticyclonic weather, the inversion may reach a considerable height, and may persist for several days.

inverted relief. A type of relief in which land that was once at a relatively high level, e.g. an *anticline*, has been eroded so severely that it is now at a lower level than land previously below it, e.g. a neighbouring *syncline*.

invisible exports. Items representing services rendered to a foreign country which take the place of normal exports but do not involve the actual transfer of goods. Examples are the trade conducted for foreign countries by national shipping, expenditure in the country by foreign tourists, the interest on national capital invested in foreign countries.

ionosphere. A part of the *atmosphere* which extends upwards from about 60 km above the earth's surface: so named because it contains ions and free electrons, produced by solar radiation, which cause it to reflect radio waves.

Iron Age. The period subsequent to the *Bronze Age* when iron replaced bronze in common use for implements and weapons, marking a stage in human culture among different peoples rather than a definite chronological period. It became well established in some areas while the Bronze Age continued elsewhere.

irrigation. The artificial distribution of water on the land in order to facilitate the cultivation of crops where otherwise, owing to a deficiency of rainfall, agriculture would be impossible. There are two main types of irrigation, *basin irrigation* and *perennial irrigation*. With basin irrigation, long associated with the R. Nile, the flood waters of the river are led on the basin-shaped plots of land, each of which is surrounded by embankments. Sufficient moisture remains in the soil for the crop that is later planted to reach maturity. With perennial irrigation water may be led on to the fields at any time. In some areas the ancient method of baling water by hand is still practised, and a number of simple mechanical devices such as the *shaduf*, the *sakia*, and the Archimedean screw are employed. The modern method, however, is for a dam or barrage to be built across a river, creating an artificial lake; canals from this reservoir, then branch canals and distributaries, lead the water under control over the cultivated ground. This method is widely utilized in the United States, India, Egypt, and elsewhere. Irrigation water can be much more profitably used than an equal amount of rain water, for it can be stored until needed, instead of much of it being allowed to sink into the ground to a great depth and be lost to agriculture. There is a smaller loss, too, from evaporation. In Iran evaporation is almost entirely prevented by distributing the water through underground channels known as *ganats*. Although costly, irrigation has many advantages. It ensures a regular supply of water when most needed, and thus increases the productivity of the land; it helps to fertilize the land by distributing sediments; it often permits more valuable crops to be grown than would be possible by utilizing only rainfall; it often permits cultivation for a longer period, and enables several crops to be grown. On much of the irrigated land of the world, the density of population is therefore high.

isallobar. A line drawn on a *weather chart* through places at which the same change of pressure or *pressure tendency* has taken place during some period of time; it is obtained by plotting the change in atmospheric pressure which has taken place between two sets of observations. Isallobars are drawn to indicate regions of rising and of falling atmospheric pressure.

isanomalous line. A line on a map joining places having equal departures from the normal in some meteorological element. A map of isanomalous lines joining places of equal *temperature anomaly*, for example, shows at a glance the regions which are abnormally warm for their latitude, having a positive temperature anomaly, and those which are abnormally cold for their latitude, having a negative temperature anomaly. As the effects of latitude and altitude are eliminated, such a map gives a simple picture showing the influence of the land and sea, ocean currents, and prevailing winds.

island. A piece of land surrounded by water, in an ocean, sea, lake, or river. It may be formed in one of several different ways, e.g. by *diastrophism*, or movement of the earth's crust: the sea bed may have risen or the sea subsided till parts of the bed have emerged, or part of a coastal plain may have been submerged by the rise of the sea or the sinking of the land. Alternatively, a volcano may have built up its core till the top projects above the sea; a coastal region may have been eroded by the sea or by glaciers; sediment may have been deposited along the sea shore or in a river to form a low, sandy island; the island may have been built up by coral polyps. Again, two or more of these different processes may have combined to form an island.

Islands in the sea are often classified as *continental* or *oceanic*. A continental island is one which was formed by separation from the mainland, an oceanic island one which was formed in the ocean, independent of the mainland. An island which was volcanic in origin is called a volcanic island, and one which was built up by coral polyps a *coral island*.

island arc. A long, curving chain of islands, associated with which there is often a long, narrow trench in the ocean floor on the seaward side; the weakness in the earth's crust along it is manifested by great earthquake and volcanic activity. Examples are the Kuril Islands and the Aleutian Islands in the Pacific Ocean.

islet or **isle.** A small island.

isobar. A line on a map or chart joining places having equal atmospheric pressure. To render the pressure readings comparable with one another, they are usually corrected by reducing to mean sea level. In climatological studies, isobars may be drawn to show the average pressure distribution in an area or throughout the world during a certain period. For meteorological purposes, in connection with weather forecasting, isobars may be drawn on *weather charts* to show the pressure distribution at a certain time on a certain day. In the latter case they are almost invariably drawn at intervals of 2 or 4 millibars; the isobars drawn are those of even number, 1000, 1002, 1004 millibars, etc, their positions being found from the actual readings by interpolation.

isobath. A line on a map joining points on the sea bed which have equal depth. Such lines thus show the relief of the sea bed, just as *contours* show the relief of the land by joining places of equal altitude.

isoclinal folding. The folding of rock strata in which the *folds* are so

113

tightly packed together that the limbs of each fold dip in the same direction and at approximately the same angle.

isogonic line. A line on a map joining places having an equal magnetic declination. See *declination, magnetic*.

isohaline. A line on a map joining points in the oceans which have equal *salinity*.

isohel. A line on a map joining places having equal duration of *sunshine*.

isohyet. A line on a map joining places having equal depth of *rainfall* over a certain period.

isoneph. A line on a map joining places having equal average *cloudiness* over a certain period.

isopleth. A line on a map drawn through places having the same value of a certain element. Such lines show the geographical distribution of the elements. Familiar examples of isopleths are *isobars, isohyets, isotherms*.

isoseismal line. A line on a map joining places which have suffered an equal intensity of shock from an earthquake. Such lines usually form closed curves round the *seismic focus*. They are often very irregular, for earthquake damage depends to some extent on the type of foundations on which buildings rest, as well as on their distance from the origin. If a number of isoseismal lines are drawn, however, it is usually possible to determine the approximate position of the *epicentre*.

isostasy. The state of equilibrium that is said to exist between the highlands and the lowlands of the earth, due to the fact that the former are made of lighter rock materials than the latter. According to the theory of isostasy, known as the isostatic theory, the *continental platforms* are made of lighter material and are, as it were, floating at a higher level than the material of the ocean floor. See also *sial, sima*.

isostatic theory. See *isostasy*.

isotherm. A line on a map joining places having the same temperature at a particular instant, or having the same average temperature over a certain period; the temperature is normally reduced to mean sea level in order to eliminate differences due to altitude. The isotherms most commonly used in geography are those joining places having the same mean monthly temperature, especially for January and July, which show the average temperature conditions in midwinter and midsummer. The isotherms of mean daily maximum and mean daily minimum temperatures are also extremely useful.

isthmus. A narrow strip of land joining two large land areas, e.g. two continental land masses, or joining a peninsula to the mainland; examples are the Isthmus of Panama and the Isthmus of Suez.

J

jebel or **jabal** (Arabic). A mountain or range of mountains.

jet stream. A strong wind blowing from west to east at high altitude, usually near the level of the *tropopause*. Two main types of jet stream are recognized: the polar-front jet stream of middle latitudes and the sub-tropical jet stream.

joint. A crack in a mass of rock which has been formed along a plane of weakness or *joint plane*; unlike a *fault*, little or no movement has taken place between the blocks. Where the rock is exposed to the weather, joints have much influence on the shape of cliffs and crags. In sedimentary rocks, usually one set of joints is parallel to the *dip* of the rock strata and another set is parallel to the *strike*. The joints of igneous rocks are variable in form. *Basalt*, for instance, often breaks into hexagonal columns, as on the Giant's Causeway, Ireland, where there are often also transverse joints across the columns.

jökulhlaup (Icelandic). See *glacier burst*.

jökull (Icelandic). In Iceland, a mountain or plateau permanently covered with snow and ice; an *ice cap* of relatively small dimensions.

jungle. A popular term, which originated in India, for wild, uncultivated land with a dense undergrowth; it is sometimes applied, with little justification, to the typical *monsoon forests*.

juvenile gas. A gas which emanates from the earth's interior, probably from a volcanic source, and reaches the surface for the first time. See *juvenile water*.

juvenile water. Water which has risen to the earth's surface from a considerable depth and appears there for the first time, e.g. via a *hot spring*, and has not therefore come from the *hydrosphere* or the *atmosphere*.

K

Kainozoic era. See *Cainozoic era*.

kame. A mound of gravel and sand which was formed by the deposition of the sediment from a stream as it ran from beneath a glacier. Kames are thus often found on the *outwash plain* of a glacier. The term has lost favour owing to the variety of meanings attached to it, and the general term *esker* is often used for all such *fluvioglacial* deposits.

kampong (Malay). In Malaya and Singapore, a settlement or small village, usually containing vegetable gardens, coconut palms, fruit trees and fish ponds as well as dwellings.

kaolin. See *china clay*.

karaburan. The hot north-easterly wind experienced in the Tarim basin of Xinjiang, when the interior of the Asiatic land mass is strongly heated; it sets in during the early spring in Central Asia, and continues by day till the end of summer. It is strong, often blowing with gale force, and sweeps up clouds of dust from the desert, darkening the air and causing acute discomfort. The coarse sand is not carried beyond the deserts, but the lighter dust particles are conveyed long distances, cause a characteristic haze, and on settling on the ground form *loess*. The sand blown along by the karaburan is one of the principal causes of the changes in the courses of rivers through the desert.

karez (Baluchi). In Baluchistan (chiefly Pakistan), underground irrigation channels similar to the *ganat* of Iran and the *foggara* of North Africa.

karren (German). See *lapiés*.

karrenfeld (German). In *limestone* country, an area in which the rocks exhibit ridges and deep flutings, being known as *karren* or *lapiés*.

karst region of **karstland.** A limestone region in which most or all of the drainage is by underground channels, the surface being dry and barren: named after the karst limestone district of the Dinaric Alps, near the Adriatic coast of Yugoslavia. The calcium carbonate in the limestone is carried away in solution by rain water containing carbon dioxide from the atmosphere, and only the insoluble material is left to form a covering to the rocks. In parts the surface may consist of bare rock, or may be covered with a thin soil, except in the valleys, where a greater depth of soil may accumulate. Few streams are visible on the surface, for the rain water tends to disappear, possibly by a *swallow-hole*, into underground channels. It is the solution of the limestone by this water, before and after it sinks, which gives rise to the uneven topography of the region – the typical karst topography; it also leads to the formation of underground caves. Even when water does appear at the surface as a *spring*, the stream often flows for a short distance and then disappears underground. Other karst regions besides that in Yugoslavia include the *Causses* (France) and parts of the Pennines (England).

katabatic wind. A local wind caused (often at night) by the flow of air, cooled by radiation, down mountains slopes and valleys; it is also caused by the flow of cold air down the slopes of ice caps, such as those of Antarctica and Greenland. With the rapid loss of heat by radiation, the mountain or ice cap becomes cold, and the air above is chilled and moves downwards under the action of gravity. The direction of flow is controlled almost entirely by orographic features. See *mountain wind*, *anabatic wind*.

kettle hole or **kettle.** A hollow or depression in an *outwash plain*, probably formed because an ice block has been covered by gravel borne by streams emerging from the glacier, and has subsequently melted, allowing the debris to settle.

key or **cay.** A sandbank, reef, or low island, more particularly so named in the neighbourhood of the West Indies, e.g. Florida Keys (USA), Grand Cays (Bahamas).

khamsin (Arabic). The hot, dry, southerly wind experienced in Egypt, corresponding to the *sirocco* of North Africa. According to the Arabs, it blows during a period of fifty days, from April to June, the name khamsin being the Arabic word for fifty. It blows ahead of the depressions which move eastwards along the Mediterranean or across North Africa, and often carries with it a considerable quantity of dust from the interior. In the Middle East the name is also rather loosely applied to any hot, dry wind blowing off the desert.

khor (Arabic). In Sudan, a normally dry watercourse which only occasionally contains water: synonymous with *nullah*, *wadi*.

klong (Thai). In Thailand, one of the many canals which made Bangkok, the capital, the 'Venice of the East'. With the construction of roads, the klong has lost much of its former commercial importance.

kloof (Afrikaans). In South Africa, a ravine or narrow valley.

knick point. A break, or change in slope, in the profile of a river (see *profile, river*), which may be due to uplift of the land, causing *rejuvenation*.

knob-and-kettle. A descriptive term, used principally by US geographers, for a terminal *moraine* which exhibits knolls (knobs) alternating with hollows (kettles), resulting in an extremely irregular ('knob-and-kettle') topography.

knoll. A small, rounded hill or mound.

knot. A unit of speed equal to one *nautical mile* per hour. In the days of sailing ships, the knot was a length of knotted string, attached to the log-line; the number of knots, arranged at regular intervals along the line, which ran off the reel in a certain time indicated the ship's speed in nautical miles per hour.

koembang (Indonesian). A *föhn* type of wind experienced in Java, which sometimes damages sensitive crops such as tobacco.

kopje or **koppie** (Afrikaans). In South Africa, an isolated hill, often formed by denudation of the land around it.

kyle. In Scotland, a channel or strait between two islands or between an island and the mainland, or a narrow inlet into the coast, e.g. Kyles of Bute, Kyle of Tongue.

L

laccolith or **laccolite.** A large mound of *igneous rock* beneath the earth's surface, sometimes attaining the size of a mountain; it is caused by the intrusion of *magma* from below into the crust of the lithosphere without reaching the surface, the surface strata being arched up over the intrusion. It is formed when the magma is viscous, and instead of spreading widely, heaps up at a particular level. Well-formed laccoliths have a flat bottom and a dome-shaped upper surface, but they are often very irregular. See *sill*. (See Fig. below.)

lacustrine. Relating to a *lake*.

ladang (Indonesian). In the Malay Archipelago, the practice of *shifting cultivation*: the *equatorial forest* is cleared, the vegetation burned, the land, fertilized with the ashes, is cultivated, and when the soil approaches exhaustion the plot is abandoned.

lagoon.* A shallow stretch of water which is partly or completely separated from the sea by a narrow strip of land. In the case of a *coral reef*, it is the channel of sea water between the reef and the mainland, or, when an *atoll* has been formed, the sheet of water enclosed by the latter; a fringing reef, close to the shore, has a relatively narrow and shallow lagoon, while a barrier reef, far from the shore, has a much wider and deeper lagoon. A lagoon may also be formed by a spit of land, composed of mud, sand, or shingle, closing or almost closing the entrance to a bay, e.g. off the Nile delta. Again, it may be formed when the sea throws up a bank of shingle at high water mark, and

Section through a laccolith.

encloses a sheet of water between the bank and the cliff; the lagoon then sometimes disappears at low tide. A lagoon may be formed, too, when an arm of the sea is enclosed by sandbanks. See *haff*.

lahar (Indonesian). A flow of volcanic mud formed by the mixing of water with *volcanic ash*, sometimes assuming the destructive power of an avalanche. The water may be supplied by seasonal rainfall or by the overflow from a *crater-lake*.

lake. An extensive sheet of water enclosed by land, occupying a hollow in the earth's surface. The name is sometimes loosely applied, too, to the widened part of a river, or to a sheet of water lying along a coast, even when it is connected with the sea; there are many gradations, in fact, between bays and lagoons which are almost enclosed and coastal lakes.

Usually the amount of water entering a lake exceeds that lost by evaporation, and there is an outflowing stream; the water of the lake is thus fresh. In a region of low rainfall and great evaporation, however, the lake may have no outlet, and forms an inland drainage area. All the salts brought down in solution by the rivers accumulate in such a lake, which thus acquires a very high *salinity*; the Dead Sea and the Great Salt Lake, Utah, USA, are examples of this kind of lake. See *salt lake*. When rainfall is seasonal, the level and area of a lake may fluctuate considerably; Lake Chad, in Africa, for instance, decreases greatly in size during the dry season. A lake may also dry up entirely during a drought or in the dry season, leaving only a salt-covered mud flat; Lake Eyre and other lakes of central Australia disappear in this way. A lake remains permanent provided that the amount of water it receives, as rain and as water draining into its hollow, equals the amount lost. Lakes are sometimes classified according to their origin: more lakes are due to glacial erosion than to any other agency. See also *crater-lake*, *ox-bow lake*, *tarn*.

lake dwelling. A prehistoric human shelter raised on a platform supported by piles above the surface of a lake, believed to have been characteristic of Neolithic times in Switzerland. Excavations of remains in recent years have cast some doubt as to whether some of the pfahlbauten ('pile structures') were in fact 'lake dwellings' in the original sense. Similar dwellings are in use today in various parts of the world, e.g. in New Guinea, Borneo, the estuary of the R Amazon, but in entirely different geographical environments from the Swiss lakes.

lake rampart. A ridge round the margin of a lake, formed in a climate where the winter range of temperature is great. When a thick layer of ice lies on a mass of cold water, the temperature of the under-surface of the ice is kept nearly constant owing to the presence of the water, while the upper surface is exposed to great variation owing to the changes in air temperature. The upper surface expands and contracts, and thus sometimes cracks and sometimes buckles up, according as it

1. Typical **bad lands** scenery, showing hillsides lined with **gullies** in South Dakota, U.S.A.

2. View of Crater Lake, Oregon, the best-known **caldera** in North America. The small island is a volcanic cone formed after the original volcanic summit had sunk.

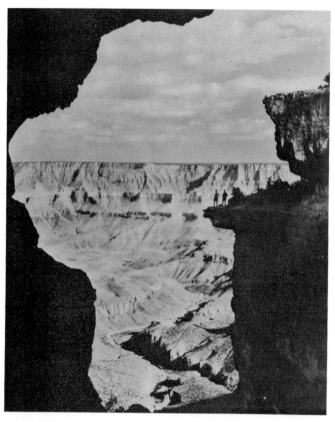

3. Part of the Grand Canyon of the Colorado River, Arizona, U.S.A., the largest **canyon** in the world; the river is just discernible at its foot.

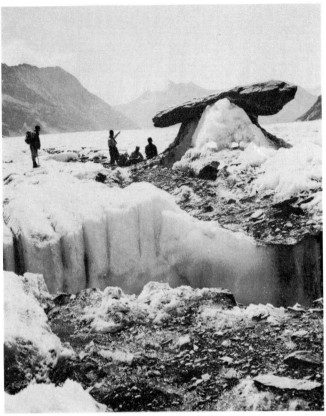

4. On the Great Aletsch Glacier, Switzerland: in the foreground the broken rock material of a **moraine**, with a **crevasse** beyond. Near the climbing party is a **glacier table**.

5. A 'coral garden' at Heron Island, a **cay** in the Great Barrier Reef, the world's largest **coral reef**, off the coast of Queensland, Australia. The coral is composed of the skeletal remains of myriads of **coral polyps**.

6. The famous Old Faithful **geyser**, Yellowstone National Park, Wyoming, U.S.A., in eruption.

7. Part of the Giant's Causeway, Northern Ireland, showing the hexagonal columns of **basalt**.

8. An aerial photograph of Surtsey, off the SW. coast of Iceland, taken in 1964, five months after the volcanic island's first appearance – an example of **fissure eruption**; molten **lava** is escaping from the vent and flowing in incandescent streams to the sea, where its heat raises dense clouds of steam.

9. An aerial view of Meteor Crater, 17 miles (27 km) W. of Winslow, Arizona, U.S.A., caused by a **meteorite**; it is about 4,000ft (1,220 m) in diameter and 600 ft (183 m) deep.

10. The **midnight sun**, seen from within the Arctic Circle in northern Norway.

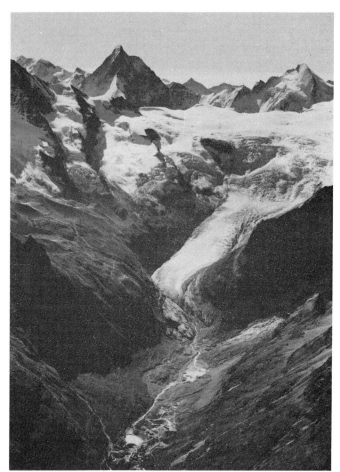

11. The Ferpècle **glacier** in the Pennine Alps, Switzerland, showing the **snowfield** where it originates and the **snout** at which it ends, below which is the **valley train:** it has the typical tongue-like shape of a **valley glacier**. In its upper course is an **icefall**, and on shelves above the valley are **hanging glaciers**. In the middle distance is the Matterhorn (4,477 m).

12. Sand **dunes** near Béchar, Algeria, illustrating their encroachment on an **oasis** of palm trees. Photo: Ofalac, Algiers.

13. In southern Kenya, a section of the African **savanna**, showing characteristic coarse grass and scattered trees. The giraffes are essentially browsing animals, feeding on such trees as the acacia (right).

14. A remarkable **scarp** formation, produced by **erosion** and bounded by numerous **talus** slopes: the Great Organ and Temple, Capitol Reef National Monument, Utah, U.S.A.

15. Devil's Tower, Wyoming, U.S.A., a **volcanic neck**, consisting of solidified **lava**, which is 865 feet (264 m) from base to summit; it was left behind when the remainder of the cone was worn away by **weathering**.

16. A mountain pasture, or **alp** in the Bernese Alps, Switzerland, such as enable farmers to practise **transhumance**, it stands on a ledge above forest – the tops of the trees are visible. The highest peak in the distance is the Schreckhorn (4,078 m).

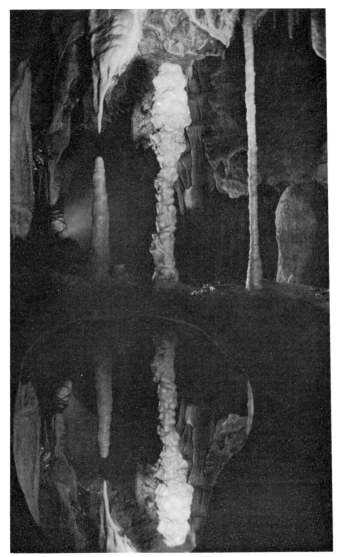

17. The **stalagmite** known as the Speaker's Mace in Cox's Cave, Cheddar, Somerset, England, and other stalagmites and **stalactites**; the formations are also seen reflected in a pool on the floor of the cave.

18. A scene in Java, showing **terrace cultivation** of rice fields.

19. A small section of the great **coniferous forest** region of Canada, showing the **timber line** in the background, and, at a still higher level, the **snowline**. Canadian Pacific Photograph.

20. The **crater** of the Raoeng **volcano**, Java.

21. An aerial view of Niagara Falls, the best-known **waterfall** in the world. Canadian Pacific Photograph.

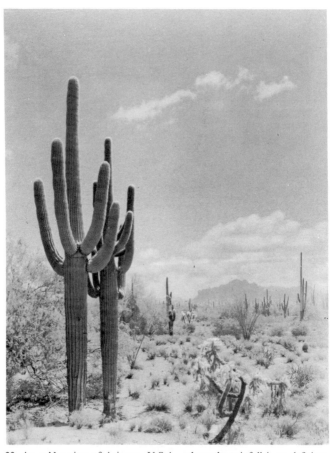

22. An **arid** region of Arizona, U.S.A., where the rainfall is so deficient that the only plants are **xerophytes** such as these cacti.

23. The Matterhorn, Switzerland: the classic example of a **horn** or **pyramidal peak** with **arêtes**. In the foreground is the resort of Zermatt.

24. In a **mangrove swamp** on the coast of Nigeria; the picture shows the long arching roots of the trees. The men are carrying instruments for a seismic oil survey.

25. A clearing in the **equatorial forest**, in the middle Magdalena valley in Colombia.

26. Part of the **incised meanders**, known as the Great Goosenecks, of the San Juan river, in Utah, U.S.A.

27. The entrance to Milford Sound, the best-known **fiord** of the South Island, New Zealand.

28. **Cumulonimbus** cloud, with typical anvil top, over Renfrewshire, Scotland.

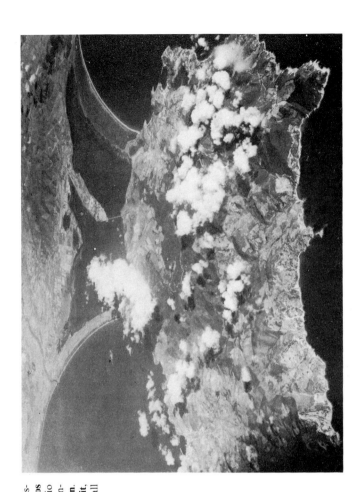

29. On the coast of Tuscany, Italy: two **tombolos** join Monte Argentario (foreground) to the mainland, and enclose a **lagoon**. In the lagoon is a **spit**, on which stands the small town of Orbetello.

30. **Hoar frost** on trees in Essex, England. A **mist** hangs over the fields.

31. A **hot spring** in the Wairakei Valley, in the North Island, New Zealand.

32. Part of the Tarn **gorge** in the **Causses** region of France.

The lakes of Finland, resulting from glaciation.

is contracting or expanding. If the shore on which it is resting is low, the expanding ice is pushed over its margin, and, besides modifying this margin considerably, often pushes over it loose rock material from the shallow water. As it retreats again, the ice leaves this rock material behind, and it ultimately forms the lake rampart.

lalang (Malay). The coarse grass which, mixed with bushes and trees, constitutes the *secondary forest* of the Malay Archipelago: forest which has developed on abandoned clearings where *ladang* agriculture has been practised.

Lambert's azimuthal equal-area or **equivalent azimuthal projection.** An equal-area or homolographic hemispherical *map projection*. The relative sizes of the areas are correctly shown, but except at the equator there is a north-south extension and an east-west compression of the right and left margins as compared with the centre. Besides being a homolographic projection, it is also azimuthal – all points have their true compass directions from the centre of the map. The projection is commonly used in atlases to show the hemispheres.

land breeze. A diurnal wind blowing from the land out to sea, caused by the differential cooling of land and sea: the cooling of the air over the land by radiation during the night causes the air to descend and flow seawards. It is confined to coastal regions and lake sides, and, though most characteristic of tropical lands, may also be observed in the temperate zone during the summer. It is most developed when the general *pressure gradient* is slight and the sky clear; it may then set in about midnight or a few hours later. The land breeze is much influenced by topography, and varies considerably in different parts of a coast. It often alternates with the *sea breeze*, but is usually less developed than the latter.

landes. Low-lying, sandy plains bordered by sand *dunes*, especially applied to the district of this name in S W France.

land hemisphere. That half of the globe, mainly situated north of the equator, in which the great majority of the land surface, about six-sevenths, is contained. Such a high proportion of the land surface may be included by constructing the hemisphere with its centre at London, or Paris, or some neighbouring point in northern Europe.

land-ice. Ice formed inland from fresh water, in contrast to ice formed from sea water.

landslide or **landslip.** The downward movement of a large mass of earth or rocks from a mountain or cliff. It is often caused by rain water soaking into the soil and earthy material on a steep slope; their weight is much increased, and they become more mobile. It may also be caused by an earthquake, or on the sea coast by the undermining action of the sea.

langley. See *solar constant*.

lapiés (French). The surfaces of limestone rocks in a *karst region* which are grooved and fluted owing to solution by rain water containing carbon dioxide, the grooves and flutings being the channels where the latter runs down the rock faces. The ridges and furrows are equivalent to the *clints* and *grikes* of N England. The corresponding German term is karren.

lapilli. Small rock fragments ejected from a volcano; they are smaller than *volcanic bombs*, but larger than *volcanic ash*, being generally considered to vary in size from peas to walnuts. They are also known as cinders.

lapse rate. The rate of change of temperature with height in the atmosphere, being usually expressed in degrees Fahrenheit per thousand feet or degrees Celsius per hundred metres. It is taken as positive when the temperature decreases with height, as it normally does, and negative when the temperature increases with height, as in a temperature inversion. See *inversion, temperature*. The average lapse rate in the atmosphere is about 0.6°C per hundred metres. This is usually known as the environmental lapse rate. When dry or non-saturated air is forced to rise, however, it expands because of reduction of pressure and cools at the dry adiabatic lapse rate of about 1°C per hundred metres (see *adiabatic*). If it continues to rise beyond the condensation level, it will then cool at a lower rate, the saturated adiabatic lapse rate; this rate is very variable, but averages about 0.5°C per hundred metres.

lateral moraine. See *moraine*.

laterite. A reddish rock material produced by *weathering* and occurring near the surface, chiefly in humid tropical regions; it contains the hydrated oxides of iron and aluminium, and may be rich enough in the former to be used as a source of that metal. It is relatively soft when first quarried, but hardens on exposure to the atmosphere, and is used as a building material. It occupies considerable areas of India, Malaysia, Indonesia, and equatorial Africa and South America.

latitude. The angular distance of a point on the earth's surface north or south of the equator, as measured from the centre of the earth. *Parallels of latitude* are lines drawn round the earth parallel to the equator, and may thus be described as approximate circles with the two poles as centres, the circles becoming smaller with increasing proximity to the poles. As one-quarter of the complete circumference of the earth is traversed in moving from the equator to the pole, one right-angle or 90° being covered, the parallels of latitude are marked off in ninety divisions or degrees from the equator to each of the poles; the equator represents 0° latitude, while the N pole is 90° N latitude, and the S pole 90° S latitude. Each degree is sub-divided into 60 minutes, and each minute into 60 seconds. Degrees of latitude are equivalent to approximately the same linear distance, 111 km (69 miles), everywhere on the earth's surface; near the poles, owing to the flattening of the earth, they are slightly longer.

Laurasia. The northerly of the two ancient continents into which the earth's land mass was once divided, the other being *Gondwanaland*. See *Pangea*.

lava.* Molten rock or *magma* which has flowed from the interior of the earth on to its surface, through the crater of a *volcano* or through fissures in the earth's surface. On the surface the molten material solidifies more quickly than in the interior of the earth. Some lavas contain much silica and are said to be 'acid', others have little and are termed 'basic' lavas. The acid lavas have a high melting point, are very viscous, flow slowly, and do not travel far; the basic lavas have a lower melting point, are very fluid, move rapidly, and may flow for several kilometres before solidifying. Acid lavas thus lose their gases

The globe illustrating latitude and longitude.

the less readily, and cause the volcanoes to erupt explosively, the whole mass sometimes bursting into fragments or even dust; basic lavas give comparatively quiet eruptions, with a widespread flow of lava. Most volcanoes, however, are of an intermediate kind. The surface of solidified lava is usually very rough; often in both acid and basic lavas the escaping gases cause the upper layers of the stream to be vesicular. See *scoria, aa, pahoehoe, pillow lava*.

lava fountain. A spout of molten *lava* rising from a volcanic *crater*, of which probably the highest ever observed was a fountain 600 m (1,900 ft) high on Kilauea, Hawaii, during the 1959–60 eruption.

lava plateau. An extensive elevated area consisting of deposits of *lava*, usually formed by a series of *fissure eruptions*. Among the many examples are the *basalt* Antrim plateau (Ireland) and Snake River plateau (USA).

leaching. The process by which soluble substances such as organic and mineral salts are washed out of the upper layer of a soil into a lower layer by percolating rain water.

leap year. A *year* of 366 days, occurring every fourth year, and devised in order to allow for the fact that the duration of the earth's revolution round the sun is about $365\frac{1}{4}$ days; by the addition of a complete day every fourth year, or leap year, the correction necessary to cause the seasons to fall in the same months of every year is approximately made. See *calendar*.

lebensraum (German). A term signifying 'living space', formerly much used in discussions of *geopolitics*, particularly in seeking to justify the country's need for territorial expansion.

leeward. The side or direction which is sheltered from the wind, e.g. by a range of mountains.

lenticular cloud. A lens-shaped type of cloud, most often seen over hills or mountains. It has sharp edges, and the numerous cloudlets of which it is formed are often seen streaming through the cloud. It is frequently associated with a *föhn wind*.

leste. A hot, dry, southerly to easterly wind experienced in Madeira ahead of an advancing depression; it is often dust-laden, and resembles the *leveche*.

levada (Portuguese). In Madeira, an *irrigation* canal which leads down from a high point on the island, where rainfall is most abundant, providing water to the small cultivated, terraced plots on the lower slopes.

levanter. The easterly wind sometimes experienced in the Straits of Gibraltar and in southern Spain, named after the direction from which it blows. It causes dangerous eddies on the lee side of the Rock of Gibraltar. With a moderate wind strength, a *banner-cloud* extends from the summit of the Rock a kilometre or more to leeward; when the wind has gale force, the cloud lifts and disappears. The wind is also known as the *solano*.

leveche. The hot, dry, southerly wind experienced in S E Spain, corresponding to the *sirocco* of North Africa; it blows ahead of an advancing depression, and often carries a great deal of dust.

levee. The natural bank of a river formed during flooding by the deposition of sediment. When the flood subsides, the sediment remains, and the levee is thus the highest portion of the *flood-plain* of a river. The height and length of a levee may be sufficient to divert the course of a tributary. A levee continues to be raised by flooding, and as the river also goes on depositing material in its own channel, and raises the bed, both levee and river bed may finally lie above the adjoining country. This is the case in the middle and lower reaches of the Mississippi. The levees along the lower reaches of the River Po, in northern Italy, too, are so high that the surface of the river is above the roofs of neighbouring villages. Occasionally a flood may be heavy enough to break down levees and inundate large areas of land. A city or town is sometimes built on a levee, New Orleans being an example; there the natural levee was only a few feet above the river level on one side and the swamp on the other side. Artificial levees are constructed so as to supplement the work of the natural levees in keeping the water of such rivers as the Mississippi within its proper channel.

level of saturation. See *water table*.

ley farming. A method of farming in which *arable land* is sown with grass and is then maintained as pasture for a number of years.

125

Section through the flood-plain of a river illustrating the formation of levees.

liana or **liane.** A tropical climbing plant common in the *equatorial forest*. The stem of the liana, which is usually thick and woody, climbs and twists round the trunk and branches of a tree till the summit is reached, and sometimes kills it. Even when the tree has rotted away, however, the liana is still able to hold itself in place by its lateral branches, which extend for long distances through the boughs of other trees.

lido (Italian). Strictly speaking, a *barrier beach* on the coast, named after the Venice Lido, a long curved beach with firm sand which separates the lagoon of the famous city from the Adriatic Sea. Hotels, villas and gardens were constructed here facing the sea, and the Lido became a world-renowned resort. In recent times many lidos have been created far from the sea, using, for instance, the water of a lake or reservoir, and are so called because they are designed to attract people interested in bathing and other aquatic activities.

lightning. See *thunderstorm*.

light-year. A unit of length in astronomy, usually employed to indicate the distances of stars from the earth or the *solar system*: equal to the distance travelled by light waves with a velocity of approximately 300,000 km (186,000 miles) per second in 1 year – about 9.4×10^{12} km (5.9×10^{12} miles).

lignite or **brown coal.** A coal of woody appearance, usually considered to represent the second stage in the transformation of vegetable matter through *peat* into coal. Lignites and brown coals are sometimes classified as separate types.

limestone. A rock consisting essentially (at least 50 per cent) of calcium carbonate. There are many types of limestone, all of which have certain common characteristics owing to their similar chemical composition, and are distinguished by name from one another according to texture (e.g. oolitic limestone), mineral content (e.g. dolomitic limestone), origin (e.g. coral), geological age (e.g. Carboniferous limestone). Most of them are partly or wholly of organic origin and contain the hard parts of various organisms such as the shells of molluscs and the skeletons of corals. The calcium carbonate of limestone is readily soluble in water which contains carbon dioxide, and many limestone areas develop underground drainage and other characteristic features. See *cave, karst region, stalactite*.

limnology. The scientific study of lakes and ponds with respect to their physical, chemical and biological properties.

line squall. A line of *squalls* of considerable length, sometimes several hundred kilometres, occurring simultaneously, its passage usually being marked by a line of low, dark cloud and a sudden rise in wind speed, often with other violent changes in weather conditions. Its position marks the replacement of a warm air current by a much colder air mass, and it is accompanied by the typical *cold front* of a depression; the ascent of the warm air over the cold air produces the cloud, together with heavy rain or hail; and a veer of wind, a rise in pressure, and a fall in temperature occur at the passage of the front.

lingua franca. A common language which is spoken or understood over a wide area by people of various races, although not their native tongue. English is the most important lingua franca, being spoken or understood over more than half the world. Other examples are Mandarin Chinese, Malay, and Swahili. See *pidgin English*.

lithosphere. The rigid part of the earth's *crust*, extending to a depth of about 65 km (40 miles) below the surface, and comprising the *sial*, the *sima*, and the upper *mantle*. Beneath it is the softer, weaker layer known as the *asthenosphere*.

littoral. The seashore, the strip of land along a sea coast, or, more strictly, the land lying between high and low tide levels; pertaining to the seashore. The littoral region of the *ocean* comprises the shallow waters adjacent to the sea coast; this region has the richest vegetation and so supports the most abundant animal life. In the littoral region, sometimes known as the *continental shelf*, in the temperate zone, are situated the world's most important fishing grounds.

llanos (Spanish). A term originally meaning simply 'plains'. To many geographers, however, it has come to mean the vast tropical grasslands or *savanna* of the Orinoco basin and the Guiana highlands, north of the equatorial forests of the Amazon basin in South America.

load, river. The solid matter carried along by a river, including (1) material in solution in the water, (2) material suspended in the water, mainly mud, silt, and sand, and (3) the larger, heavier material carried along the bed of the river. The material in solution is sometimes excluded from the load. The maximum or full load of a river depends on its velocity and its volume, and on the size of the particles constituting the load; when the limit to the possible load has been reached, any further addition involves the dropping of an equivalent portion of the original load.

loam. A rich soil consisting principally of a mixture of sand and clay, together with *silt* and *humus*; it has the good qualities of both sand and clay, but not their bad qualities.

local time. The time at any point on the earth's surface calculated by the position of the sun; noon local time is thus the moment when the sun reaches its highest position in the sky. In view of the rotation of the earth on its axis, places lying on the same *meridian* will thus have the same noon and the same local time. Of two places on different meridians, however, the more easterly will have a local time preceding the other's: i.e. at any given instant its clocks will be 'fast on' or 'in front of' those of the more westerly place. As the earth rotates through 360° once in 24 hours, local time changes by one hour for every 15° longitude, or 4 minutes for every 1° longitude. Local time is synonymous with *apparent time*.

loch. In Scotland, a lake, fiord, or arm of the sea. The most numerous of the Scottish lochs are the small *tarns*, which lie in hollows formed by glaciation or by the damming effect of moraines left behind after the glaciers have retreated. More important are the larger *glen* lochs, which lie in hollows in the glens, and the long, narrow sea lochs, or *fiords*, which are especially common along the western Highland coast.

lochan. In Scotland, a small lake or *loch*, often occupying a *corrie*.

lode. A composite mineral *vein*, consisting of a number of parallel fissures filled with mineral matter which contains *ores*.

loess. A deposit of fine silt or dust which is generally held to have been transported to its present situation by the wind. One characteristic is its ability to maintain vertical walls in the banks of streams, and another is the number of small vertical tubes running through it, probably due to the remains of roots. It covers wide areas round the margins of the arid interior of Asia, having been transported there by winds which have swept along the fine dust from the dry plateaux. In northern China, where it has enormous extent and thickness, the loess is a fine *loam*, rich in lime and yellowish in colour. Its great advantage is its extreme porosity, for rain sinks quickly into it and its surface is normally dry, but when irrigated it is very fertile. Through the loess, streams have cut deep valleys, often with vertical walls. There are also extensive loess deposits in central Europe and the central United States, and, mixed with a high proportion of *humus*, it forms the fertile *black earth* of the USSR.

logan-stone or **rocking-stone.** In England, chiefly in Cornwall, a mass of granite, including the famous Logan Rock, near Land's End, which is so balanced that it can be rocked by hand. It is formed by *weathering* in a similar way to a *tor*.

longitude. The angular distance, measured along the equator, between the *meridian* through a given point and a standard or prime meridian; since 1884, the meridian through the former Royal Astronomical Observatory at Greenwich, in London, has been accepted by international agreement as the prime meridian. Longitude is thus measured in degrees west or east of Greenwich, from 0° to 180°, the Greenwich meridian representing longitude 0°; the meridian 180° W coincides with meridian 180° E. The complete angular distance round the earth round any parallel of *latitude* is 360°, so if 360 meridians are drawn from pole to pole at equal intervals, they will lie 1° of longitude apart. As the parallels of latitude become shorter with increasing nearness to the poles, it follows that a degree of longitude also decreases towards the poles. It is longest at the equator, where it approximates to a degree of latitude, about 111 km (69 miles); at 30° N or S the length of a degree of longitude is about 96 km (60 miles); at 60°N or S 56 km (35 miles); at 80° N or S 19 km (12 miles); and at the poles it is zero. The longitude of a place may be found from the difference between *local time* and *Greenwich Mean Time* or *GMT*, as shown by *chronometers*.

longitudinal coast. See *concordant coast*.

longitudinal valley. A valley which runs parallel to conspicuous mountain chains; more strictly the term should be applied to a valley which is parallel to the *strike* of the rock strata. See *transverse valley*.

longshore drift. The movement of shingle and sand along a seashore, due to the waves advancing obliquely up the beach: the material is driven up the beach obliquely by the *swash*, while some is drawn down again at right-angles to the shore-line by the *backwash*. There is thus a general movement of shingle and sand *along* its shore.

lopolith. A large saucer-shaped mass of *igneous rock*, caused by the intrusion of *magma* into the *lithosphere* without reaching the surface, and differing from a *sill* in that its upper surface forms a shallow basin.

lough. In Ireland, a lake, fiord, *ria*, or arm of the sea.

low. A *depression*, or a region where the atmospheric pressure is lower than that of its surroundings. On a *weather chart*, the centre of a depression is usually indicated by the word 'low'.

lowland. The low-lying land of a region, in contrast with the mountainous areas.

loxodrome. See *rhumb-line*.

lunar day. The duration of one rotation of the earth on its axis with respect to the moon, or the period of time between successive crossings of a meridian by the moon, equal to about 24 hours 50 minutes. It is closely associated with the operation of the *tides*, and is sometimes termed a *tidal day*.

lunar eclipse. See *eclipse, lunar*.

lunar month. The interval of time in which the *moon* makes one complete revolution round the earth, as from new moon to new moon – approximately 29.5 days. It is often popularly taken to be a period of 28 days.

lynchet or **linchet.** A terrace or slope along the face of one of the chalk *downs* of southern England. Being man-made, it was probably due originally to an ancient agricultural practice. See also *terracette*.

M

macchia (Italian). See *maquis*.

mackerel sky. A sky partially covered with *cirrocumulus* or *altocumulus* clouds, i.e. with small, high, rounded and detached cloud masses with blue sky in the gaps, somewhat resembling the markings on the side of a mackerel. It is usually seen in summer, during dry warm weather.

macroclimate. The climate of a major climatic region, e.g. the *tundra* climate, or of a large area such as a continent, as distinct from *microclimate*.

macroclimatology. The science which treats of *macroclimates*.

maelstrom (Dutch). A large *whirlpool*. The term has been applied specifically to the Moskenstrom, a strong current between Mosken and Moskenaes, two of the Lofoten Islands, off the west coast of Norway.

maestrale (Italian). A cold northerly to north-westerly wind, corresponding to the *mistral*, experienced in N Italy.

maestro. A north-westerly wind experienced in the central Mediterranean area, most strongly on the western side of a depression; especially so-called in the Adriatic Sea, the Ionian Sea, and round the coasts of Corsica and Sardinia.

magma. The molten material which exists below the solid rock of the earth's crust, and sometimes reveals itself on its emission from a *volcano*. It does not always reach the surface in a molten state through a volcano, however, but may cool and solidify as it forces its way upwards. See *dyke*, *sill*, *laccolith*, *batholith*. Magmas vary considerably in chemical composition; those which contain more than about 50 per cent silica are commonly called acid, those which contain less than 50 per cent silica are called basic.

magnetic declination. See *declination, magnetic*.

magnetic pole. See *magnetism, terrestrial*.

magnetic storm. A large, irregular variation or disturbance of the earth's magnetic field, of world-wide effect, mainly or completely masking the normal diurnal variations. See *magnetism, terrestrial*. It may last for a few hours or a few days, and may occur at any time of the year. It is associated with *sunspots*, and occurs almost simultaneously with them; the *aurora* is usually observed in low latitudes during a magnetic storm, and at these times there is considerable interference with radio and telegraphic communications.

magnetism, terrestrial. The magnetic properties displayed by the earth, causing it to act like a huge bipolar magnet; the science of the study of these properties. At any point on the earth's surface, a magnetic compass, allowed to swing freely in a horizontal plane, will come to rest pointing approximately in the direction of the North and South Poles; the actual points which the compass needle indicates, known as the North and South Magnetic Poles, lie respectively NNW of Boothia Peninsula, North America, and in Victoria Land, Antarctica. Although a compass is used to find true north, it therefore points somewhat east or west of true north at most places. See *declination, magnetic*.

A number of theories have been evolved to explain the cause of terrestrial magnetism, but none adequately explains all the observed facts. Besides the irregular variations of the earth's magnetic field, known as *magnetic storms*, there is a diurnal variation, in which the compass swings through an angle of several minutes, and a secular variation of several degrees, which occupies a period of many centuries.

maize rains. One of the two heaviest falls of rain experienced during the year in East Africa, occurring between February and May. See *millet rains*.

mallee scrub. The *scrub*, consisting largely of low eucalyptus bushes, which is characteristic of parts of the dry sub-tropical regions of south-east and south-west Australia.

Malthusianism. The teachings of T. R. Malthus (1766–1834), the English economist, whose outstanding work was his 'Essay on Population', in which he declared that the world population was increasing at a substantially faster rate than the means of subsistence.

mandated territory. A territory which was transferred after World War I from either the German or the Turkish Empire to the League of Nations, and was thereafter governed, under Mandate of the League, by one of its member states. Territories such as Iraq, Syria, and Palestine were to be administered by the Mandatory Powers only until they were able to govern themselves, and subsequently achieved independence. Some territories, such as most of the former German colonies in Africa, were to be administered by the Mandatory Power but were to retain their entity; these also have become independent. Others, such as South-West Africa and former German colonies in Australasia, were to be governed by the Mandatory Power as part of its territory. After World War II the remaining mandated territories except South-West Africa (now called Namibia) became *trust territories*.

mango showers. See *blossom showers*.

mangrove swamp. * A swampy area occupied chiefly by mangroves, occurring mainly in the low coastal lands of tropical regions, most extensively near river mouths; from the trunks and branches of the trees descend long arching roots, which anchor the trees and form an almost impenetrable tangle at ground level.

mantle. The layer of rock below the earth's crust or *lithosphere*, consisting of rocks of higher density than those of the latter, and separated from it by the *Moho*; it extends downwards to about 2,900 km (1,800 miles) below the earth's surface. Below the mantle is the *core*.

mantle rock or **regolith.** The layer of loose rock material, subject to *weathering*, the surface part of which is called soil, which covers most of the earth's land area, and varies in thickness from place to place.

map. The representation on a flat surface of all or part of the earth's surface, to show physical, political, or other features, each point on the diagram corresponding to a geographical position according to a definite scale or projection. See *map scale, map projection*. The most accurate maps of Great Britain are the Ordnance Survey maps, prepared by surveyors from actual measurements. In the United States, many official maps are prepared by the Geological Survey (US Department of the Interior); others are produced by the Defense Mapping Agency (US Department of Defense) and the National Ocean Survey (US Department of Commerce).

map projection. A method by which the curved surface of the earth is represented on a flat surface map, so that each point of the latter corresponds to one point only of the former. It involves the construction on the plane surface of a graticule formed by two intersecting systems of lines, corresponding to the parallels of latitude and the meridians of longitude on the earth. Some projections aim at showing directions correctly, others areas or shapes, and for general purposes the most useful projections are those which take all of these factors into consideration. It is impossible, however, to construct a map of a considerable portion of the earth's surface on a flat surface without some distortion of shapes, relative areas, or directions; the only true representation of the earth is a globe. In atlases, *cylindrical projections* and *conical projections* are commonly used.

map scale. The ratio between the distance between two points on a map and the actual distance it represents. It may be expressed by the two lengths, e.g. one inch to one mile; this would be for a large-scale map, for the lengths on the map representing certain actual distances are relatively large. Such a large-scale map shows surface features in great detail, and could be constructed only in a country which had been well surveyed; one series of British OS maps, for instance, is on this scale. A map scale may be expressed, too, as an arithmetic ratio or fraction known as the *representative fraction*, e.g. 1:63,360, which corresponds to the scale of 1 inch to 1 mile. A more recent series of OS maps is on the 1:50,000 scale. Many series of maps in other countries are also on this scale, others are on the 1 cm to 2 km or 1:200,000 scale. A scale such as 1:2,000,000 would be for a small-scale map, such as is used in atlases, any length on the map being small in relation to the actual distance it represents. (1:2,000,000 corresponds to a scale of 1 cm to 20 km or 1 inch to about 32 miles.)

maquis (French) or **macchia** (Italian). The low *scrub* of parts of the Mediterranean region, consisting of small trees or shrubs which are able to withstand drought and are usually growing in siliceous soils; among them are the wild olive and the myrtle. The maquis is of little use to man, for it is difficult to clear for cultivation. It corresponds to the *chaparral* of California. See *garigue*, *Cape maquis*.

marble. A coarse-grained, crystalline *metamorphic rock* derived from *limestone*; the term is applied commercially to any *calcareous* rock that can be polished.

march. A boundary or frontier between two countries or regions: one is said to 'march' with the other. The boundaries between England and Wales are known as the Welsh Marches; those between England and Scotland are the Scottish Marches.

In central Italy the region known as The Marches (Marche) includes the provinces of Pesaro and Urbino, Ancona, Macerata and Ascoli Piceno. After belonging to the Church for some centuries, Marche became part of the kingdom of Italy in 1860.

mares' tails. Popular name for wispy, tufted *cirrus* clouds.

maritime climate. A climate which is mainly influenced by the proximity of the sea, giving a comparatively cool summer and a comparatively warm winter. This is due to the different thermal capacities of land and water; the sea is warmed and cooled less readily than the land, and its influence tends to create an equable climate. See *insular climate*, *continental climate*.

market gardening. The *intensive cultivation* of vegetable crops, and possibly fruit and flowers, for market. See *truck farming*.

marl. A mixture of clay and calcium carbonate – though the term is rather loosely applied to a wide variety of rocks and soils. Some of the marls are marine deposits, while others are of fresh-water origin.

marsh. A tract of soft, wet land, usually low-lying and at times partly or completely under water; the extreme dampness is due to the impermeable nature of the soil and the poor drainage. A well-known example was the Pontine Marshes of Italy, which were drained in the 1930s and mainly cultivated. The term is often popularly used as if synonymous with *swamp*. See *salt-marsh*.

massif (French). A mountainous mass which breaks up into peaks towards the summit, and has relatively uniform characteristics. Probably the best-known example is the Massif Central of France.

meander. A curve in the course of a river which continually swings from side to side in wide loops, as it progresses across flat country: the name being derived from the river Meander of Asia Minor, which in its lower reaches has a particularly twisting course. The meander is

Meander belt (between broken lines) of a river in its valley.

continually being accentuated by the river itself. On the concave side of a curve the bank is worn away by the current, while on the convex side solid material is deposited. As a result the concave (outer) bank is often steep while the convex (inner) bank has a relatively gentle slope. Ultimately the meander may form almost a complete circle, when the river will cut across the narrow strip of land, and this part of its course will become almost straight. See *incised meander*, *ox-bow lake*.

meander belt. In a valley containing a meandering stream, the belt of land along the valley floor which lies between the outermost *meanders* of the stream, i.e. across which the stream swings from side to side.

mean sea level or **msl.** The average level of the sea, as calculated from a large number of observations taken at equal intervals of time. It is the standard level from which all heights are calculated. On the Ordnance Survey Maps of Great Britain, the Ordnance Survey Datum, above which the heights of all places are given, is taken as mean sea level at Newlyn, Cornwall.

mean sphere level. The mean level of the *lithosphere*. It is represented by an imaginary spherical surface in such a position that if all the land projecting above it were sliced off, this land would just fill all the depressions below it.

medial moraine. See *moraine*.

Mediterranean climate. The type of climate experienced by the lands bordering the Mediterranean Sea and also by other regions, in both hemispheres, situated in a similar geographical position: on the western sides of the continents, on the tropical margins of the intermediate or temperate region, and in approximately the latitude of the subtropical high-pressure systems – between 30° and 40° N and S latitude. Owing to the seasonal swing of the world pressure belts, it is dominated by the *westerlies* in winter and the *trade winds* in summer; the moderate rainfall is thus received mainly during the winter, the summer being relatively dry. The vegetation is specially adapted to withstand the summer drought. Other characteristics are the warmth of the summer, the mildness of the winter, and the ample sunshine. It is a climate which has acquired a high reputation for the abundance of fruit and flowers which it produces, and in it many of the world's great holiday resorts, such as those of the Riviera, have been established. Typical fruits are the grape, the olive, and the citrus fruits – orange, lemon, and grapefruit. Considerable areas are covered by small trees and shrubs (see *maquis*). Besides the lands around the Mediterranean Sea, other areas enjoying this type of climate are central California, central Chile, the southern tip of South Africa and parts of S W and southern Australia.

meltemi. The Turkish name for the *etesian winds*.

menhir. A tall, upright stone of Neolithic origin, probably set up for religious purposes, e.g. to mark a burial place.

Mercator's projection. A type of *cylindrical projection*, used for maps of the world, and first published in 1569. All the parallels of latitude have the same length as the equator, whereas on the globe they decrease in length towards the poles; hence there is an east–west stretching on this projection everywhere except at the equator, and this stretching increases with distance from the equator. On the globe, the parallel of latitude at 60° is one-half the length of the equator, so at that latitude the stretching is two-fold; to compensate for this, a two-fold north–south stretching is also made. Thus a small area, say 1° square, at latitude 60° is on the map stretched to twice its length and twice its breadth, or four times its area compared with an area of 1° square at the equator. As the stretching, both east–west and north–south, becomes so much greater towards the poles, maps on this projection are rarely taken beyond 80°, for at this latitude stretching is about six-fold in each direction. The effect may be best observed by comparing Greenland and South America; although the former has actually less than one-twelfth the area of the latter, on Mercator's projection it is depicted as slightly the larger of the two.

There is so great a distortion of distances, areas, and shapes of land masses and oceans on this projection, in fact, that it is unsuitable for general use. One of its advantages is that the 'equal stretching' causes compass bearings to be truly represented, and makes it useful for marine charts; the compass course between any two points is the straight line joining them. This property is due to the facts that (1) the meridians are parallel straight lines, (2) the projection is *orthomorphic*. Mercator's projection is also valuable for certain climatological maps, as, for instance, where the true directions of winds in various regions are to be represented.

Mercator's projection.

mere. (1) A small lake (as in Cheshire, England), pond, estuary, or arm of the sea. In the English Fens, the term is applied to marshland. (2) A boundary or landmark.

meridian. A line of *longitude*, or half of one of the *great circles* which pass through the poles and cut the equator at right-angles; it is not the complete great circle for there is a difference of 180° longitude and twelve hours of time between the two halves of a great circle passing through the poles. The Greenwich meridian is the meridian passing through Greenwich, London, and is taken as the zero or prime meridian from which other meridians are measured. At the equator the distance between any two meridians, or 1° longitude, is about 111 km (69 miles); this distance diminishes with the distance from the equator, and at 50° latitude is rather less than 72 km (45 miles).

mesa (Spanish). A flat, table-like upland, which falls away steeply on all sides; the word in Spanish means 'table'. The harder top layers of rock have resisted denudation, and, being practically horizontal, have maintained a uniform surface parallel to the stratification. Mesas may be formed, as for instance in the Colorado basin of the United States, when a river cuts a deep *canyon* through a region, and later the valley floors widen, and the plateau becomes broken up into large, individual, flat-topped masses. A mesa is related structurally to a *cuesta*. In time a mesa becomes reduced by dissection and erosion to a *butte*.

meseta. The extensive plateau of interior Spain, which covers about three-quarters of the country. It is a much eroded and broken block of the earth's crust, and is crossed by certain higher mountain ridges.

mesophyte. A plant which requires an average amount of moisture.

Most of the common trees, shrubs, and herbs living in intermediate climates of moderate rainfall and temperature are mesophytes. See *hygrophyte, xerophyte.*

mesosphere. The part of the *atmosphere* which lies above the *stratosphere*, extending upwards from about 50 km (30 miles) (the *stratopause*) to about 80 km (50 miles) (the *mesopause*); within the mesosphere the temperature falls with increasing height.

Mesozoic era. The Middle Life era, the second of the three major divisions of the geological scale of time (after pre-Cambrian time): that period of the earth's history between the *Palaeozoic era* and the *Cainozoic era*, extending from about 200 million to 70 million years ago. It is divided into the Triassic, Jurassic, and Cretaceous periods. Throughout the era there was a great deal of terrestrial disturbance, with the formation of mountains and much volcanic activity. It was characterized by the number, variety, and enormous size of its reptiles, both on land and in the sea, and is often known as the Age of Reptiles; in the middle of the era, flowering plants, deciduous trees, and the first birds appeared. It is sometimes known as the Secondary era.

mestizo. Mainly in S America, the offspring of a European, usually Spanish or Portuguese, or a *Creole*, and an American Indian.

metamorphic aureole. The rock immediately surrounding a mass of *intrusive rock*, such as a *boss*, which has undergone metamorphism, or change, by contact with it. See *metamorphic rocks.*

metamorphic rocks. Rocks which were originally *igneous* or *sedimentary rocks*, but have been changed in character and appearance; they form one of the three main types of rocks which comprise the earth's crust. The change in their original state may have been due to the heat, which sometimes causes the minerals to recrystallize, or pressure, which alters the rock structure, or possibly to the action of water, which dissolves some rock material and deposits other material, changing the composition of the rock. Sometimes the metamorphic rocks differ so greatly from the igneous or sedimentary rocks from which they were derived that their origin is practically impossible to determine. Most common igneous and sedimentary rocks have a metamorphic equivalent. *Granite*, for instance, may have its principal crystals separated and arranged in crude layers, to become a *gneiss; limestone* may be recrystallized to *marble; shale* may be transformed by great pressure into *slate.*

meteor or **shooting star.** A fragment of solid matter which enters the upper atmosphere from outer space, and becomes visible through incandescence caused by the resistance of the air to its passage. It travels up to 80 km per second, and usually becomes luminous when it is between 80 and 160 km above the earth's surface, disappearing at a height of about 80 km. Little is known about the origin of meteors. Most of them are very small, and are so much disintegrated during their passage through the atmosphere that they fall to the surface as dust; occasionally, however, a larger body, known as a *meteorite*, falls to the ground.

meteorite.* A large mass of rock or mineral similar to a *meteor*, but so large that it is not disintegrated to dust in the atmosphere, but reaches the earth's surface. Some meteorites are entirely metallic, consisting chiefly of an iron-nickel alloy; others contain silicates as well as metallic materials, others are almost wholly silicates. None of them has been found to contain any chemical element not previously found on the earth. One of the best-known meteorites is one which fell near Winslow, Arizona, USA, probably about 50,000 years ago, and formed a basin over a kilometre in diameter and about 180 m deep. See *crater*.

meteorology. The science which investigates the *atmosphere*, in particular the physical processes which occur therein, and the connected processes of the lithosphere and hydrosphere. The subject therefore includes the study of atmospheric pressure and temperature, the winds, precipitation, cloudiness, sunshine, etc. Knowledge obtained from this study is applied especially to the preparation of weather forecasts, with the help of *weather charts*.

microclimate. The climate of a very limited area, possibly even a small urban environment, dependent largely on extremely localized influences of site, soil, vegetation, etc., often significant in the study of *ecology*: as distinct from *macroclimate*.

microclimatology. The science which treats of *microclimates*.

midnight sun.* A phenomenon of high latitudes observed at and around midsummer, when the sun does not sink below the horizon throughout the 24 hours, and therefore may be seen at midnight; it is due to the inclination of the earth's axis to the plane of the *ecliptic*, and the consequent tilting of each hemisphere towards the sun during its summer. At North Cape, Norway, just north of 73° N latitude, for instance, at least part of the sun's disc is continuously visible, day and night, from 12 May to 29 July.

mid-oceanic ridge. A ridge which rises from the ocean floor, the best-known example being the Mid-Atlantic Ridge, which runs N–S more or less parallel to the continental coastlines on either side, and has linking counterparts in the other oceans. Here and there the ridges reach the surface as *oceanic islands*, e.g. the Azores. Recent investigations (see *continental drift*) suggest that they mark the edges of lithospheric plates that are moving apart, and that a rift running along their crests is the source of *lava* which wells up from below, to spread across the ocean floor at rates of a few centimetres per year.

mile, statute. A unit of linear measurement used in Great Britain and other English-speaking countries, including the USA, equal to 1,760 yards (1,609 m); the name was derived from the Roman measure of 1,000 paces, about 1,618 yards. See *geographical mile, nautical mile*.

millet rains. One of the two maximum falls of rain experienced in East Africa, from October to December. See *maize rains*.

millibar. A unit of pressure equal to one-thousandth of a *bar*. It is the unit of atmospheric pressure usually employed by meteorologists in drawing weather charts, the *isobars* being drawn at intervals of 2 or 4 millibars. A pressure of 1,000 millibars is equivalent to approximately 29.53 inches or 750.1 millimetres of mercury.

millionaire city. A city with a million or more inhabitants.

mineral. A natural inorganic substance which possesses a definite chemical composition (normally a rock does not), and definite physical and chemical properties. There are about 2,000 known minerals, with many different crystal forms, but within a single mineral species little variation occurs. Of the large number of minerals, one to two hundred are abundant, while less than a dozen are common in most *rocks*.

mineralogy. The science of the study of *minerals*.

mineral spring. A *spring* which contains a perceptible quantity of mineral matter in solution – except calcium carbonate or calcium sulphate; a *saline spring*, for instance, contains certain salts in solution (e.g. common salt), a *sulphur spring* contains sulphuretted hydrogen, a *chalybeate spring* contains iron compounds. A mineral spring often has medicinal value, e.g. the *hot springs* of Karlovy Vary, in Bohemia, Czechoslovakia.

minute. (1) A unit of time equal to one-sixtieth of an hour.

(2) A unit of measurement of *latitude* or *longitude* equal to one-sixtieth of a degree.

mirage. An optical illusion in which images of distant objects are seen, caused by the refraction of light through layers of air of different density. In a hot desert, for instance, an observer may have the illusion of a distant sheet of water, shimmering in the sunlight: the air near to the ground, owing to excessive heating, becomes less dense than the layers above; rays of light from the sky, approaching the observer at a slight angle, are refracted towards him, and appear to come from the surface of a sheet of water. Other objects may appear to be floating on the water, their lower parts being invisible. A similar mirage may sometimes be seen over a smooth road surface on a hot day even in temperate regions. Another type of mirage is that in which double images of distant objects can be seen. Sometimes a mirage is formed, too, when light rays are bent downwards from a warm layer of air resting on a cooler, denser layer; this is frequently seen in polar regions, and causes ships or icebergs to appear as if inverted and suspended in the sky, though nothing is visible on the sea. See also *fata morgana*.

mire. A stretch of swampy ground; the term is derived from Old Norse, and the equivalent in modern Swedish is *myr*.

misfit or **underfit river.** A river that appears to be too small to have carved out the valley through which it flows. This may be due to the fact that it has lost its headwaters by *river capture*.

mist.* A mass of water drops present in the lower layers of the atmosphere, caused by the condensation of water vapour in the air, and giving a moderate reduction of visibility. According to British meteorological practice, such a phenomenon is a mist when the visibility is less than 2,000 m and exceeds 1,000 m, but becomes a *fog* when the visibility falls below the latter limit.

mistral. A cold, northerly or north-westerly wind experienced on the shores of the north-west Mediterranean, especially around the Rhône delta. It is most prevalent during the winter, when pressure is relatively high over the western Mediterranean; it reaches great force in the rear of a deep depression situated over the Gulf of Lions which is moving away eastwards or south-eastwards. The air sweeps southwards from the Central Plateau of France, is funnelled through the Rhône valley, and thus reaches the delta as an extremely strong wind, as well as being cold and dry. The wind strength on the surface is often 60 km per hour, but speeds of over 130 km per hour have been recorded, and trains have been overturned; it is of special significance to aviation as it was in the past to the navigation of sailing-ships. When the mistral is blowing, the sky is often cloudless, but the wind frequently brings temperatures well below freezing point. Along the lower reaches of the Rhône, its power is displayed by the permanent set of the trees towards the south-east; gardens and orchards are protected from it by thick hedges of cypress, and many of the smaller houses have doors and windows only on the south-eastern side. See *bora*.

mixed farming. The combination of *agriculture* and *pastoral farming*.

mizzle. See *Scotch mist*.

mock moon. See *paraselene*.

mock sun. See *parhelion*.

mofette. An opening in the ground from which carbon dioxide is emitted, together with some oxygen and nitrogen; it occurs in a region of former volcanic activity, as in the Yellowstone National Park, USA.

mogote (Spanish). In a tropical *karst region*, a conical hill of residual limestone, a *hum*, especially in Cuba and Puerto Rico. See also *pepino hill*.

Moho or **Mohorovičić discontinuity.** The boundary surface between the earth's *crust* and the *mantle*, named after A. Mohorovičić, who discovered it (1909). It lies about 40 km (25 miles) below the continents, about 8 km (5 miles) below the oceans. The velocity of earthquake waves increases considerably after passing through the Moho.

Mohs' scale. The empirical scale devised by Friedrich Mohs (1773–1839) for expressing the hardness of minerals. The scale takes the form of a list of ten minerals, arranged in order of increasing hardness from 1 to

Mollweide's projection.

10; talc is assigned the value 1, diamond 10, while other minerals are given intermediate values. Using the 'scratch' test, the hardness of an unknown mineral may thus be approximately determined and its identity possibly established.

mole. A jetty or *breakwater* of large stones, rubble, or other material, laid in the sea so as to protect a harbour or anchorage from storms.

Mollweide's projection. A type of equal-area or *homolographic projection*, in which the entire earth's surface is depicted in one map. All parallels of latitude and the central meridian (usually the Greenwich meridian) are straight lines, the latter being at right-angles to the former, but other meridians are curved, and curvature increases towards the marginal meridians. Each area bounded by two adjacent parallels and two adjacent meridians is equal to any other area similarly enclosed. There is therefore no distortion of areas (as in Mercator's projection), and the projection is suitable for showing distribution of phenomena, etc., and generally speaking, for a study of world geography, but distorts shapes, directions, and distances, and is therefore useless for navigation.

monadnock. An isolated hill or mass of rock which stands above the surrounding country because its rock has been more resistant to erosion than the rock of the latter: named after Mt Monadnock.

monocline. A *fold* in which the bend is in only one direction; the rock stratum changes its *dip* by increasing its steepness of inclination, and then levels out again or resumes its gentle dip.

monsoon. A term derived from the Arabic word *mawsim* meaning 'season', applied by the Arabs to the seasonal winds of the Arabian Sea, which blow for about six months from the SW and six months from the NE. It is now applied generally to the type of wind system in which there is a complete or almost complete reversal of prevailing direction from season to season. It is especially prominent within the tropics on the eastern sides of the great land masses, but it occurs, too, outside the tropics, for in eastern Asia it reaches as far north as about 60° N. Southeast Asia is pre-eminently a monsoon region. Here the intense heating of the land in the summer causes a low-pressure area to be established over NW India and the inblowing winds of the south-west monsoon, having originated as the SE *trade winds* in the southern Indian Ocean, are warm and saturated with moisture. They advance northwards over the region from spring to midsummer, bringing copious rains to large areas, especially where mountain ranges enhance the effect, e.g. on the slopes of the mountains of western India and Burma, the eastern Himalayas, the Assam Hills, the Ganges and Irrawaddy deltas; the strong winds, heavy seas, overcast skies, and frequent rainfall contrast sharply with winter conditions. The south-west monsoon moves forward with a definite front, and arrives at each place at approximately the same date each year; the first rain is known as the 'burst of the monsoon'. Violent *tropical cyclones* occur in its van and rear and occasionally while it is at its height. The summer monsoon lasts from about April to September, though its duration anywhere depends upon the geographical situation of the place in question. In autumn, as the land cools, higher pressure is established over the Asiatic continent, with lower pressure to the south. The north-east monsoon, which now advances southwards as the south-west monsoon retreats, is thus to most of the region a cold, dry wind, bringing rain only to the limited areas which it reaches by a partial sea-track, e.g. SE India, Sri Lanka. The prevailing direction of this monsoon in N China is NW and in Central China N, and owing to the proximity of the deserts the winds are dusty as well as dry and cold; N India is protected by the Himalayas and the Tibetan plateau, and the winds are much lighter than in China. The relief of the land largely controls the effect of the winter, as well as the summer, monsoon. It lasts approximately from October to March. Other areas which experience similar but less pronounced seasonal changes of wind direction include the south-eastern United States, East Africa, and north Australia, and these are sometimes rather misleadingly termed 'monsoon regions'. In the SE United States there is not a complete reversal of wind; in the southern continents there are damp, inblowing winds on the east coasts during the summer but the extra-tropical land masses are too small to develop winter anticyclones of the Asiatic type, and there is no marked system of outblowing winds.

monsoon forest. The type of tropical forest that is characteristic of regions experiencing the true monsoonal climate (see *monsoon*), where the rainfall is between about 1,000 and 2,000 mm annually, i.e. much of India, Burma, Thailand, and other parts of SE Asia. Its climate differs from that of the *equatorial forest* in that there is a marked dry season, but sufficient rain falls during the 'wet' monsoon to support tree growth through the 'dry' monsoon. The broad-leaved trees are often described as semi-deciduous: they shed their leaves during the dry season, but their new foliage appears when the monsoon rains begin to fall. Monsoon forests are generally more open than equatorial forests, and have fewer species; two of the best-known trees are the teak and the sal, both of which provide valuable hardwood timber.

montaña. The mountainous region on the eastern slopes of the Andes, in South America, particularly in Peru, which has a heavy rainfall and is largely covered with dense forest, though not in such profusion as on the lowlands of the Amazon basin.

month. See *lunar month, calendar*.

moon. The satellite of the earth, the only heavenly body which revolves round the earth; in astronomy the term is also applied, however, to the satellite of any planet. One revolution of the moon round the earth is completed approximately once each lunar month. Its sidereal period of revolution (i.e. with respect to the so-called 'fixed' stars), is about $27\frac{1}{4}$ days; its synodic period of revolution (i.e. the interval from new moon to new moon) is about $29\frac{1}{2}$ days, but varies by about 13 hours because of the eccentricities of the orbits of the moon and the earth. The diameter of the moon is rather more than one-quarter of that of the earth. Unlike the sun and the stars, the moon shines only by reflected light, the light having been emitted by the sun, and only the half which is illuminated by the sun can be seen; as it revolves round the earth, this illuminated portion appears and disappears. As the moon rotates on its axis once in each orbital revolution, the same face of the moon is always turned towards the earth. See *moon, phases of*.

moon, phases of. The various stages or changes of appearance through which the moon passes during its revolution round the earth, known as new moon, full moon, etc., owing to the changes in relative position of the earth, moon, and sun. When the moon is between the earth and the sun, the dark side faces the earth, and no moon is visible; this period is called the *new moon*, for immediately afterwards a 'new' moon begins to appear. When the moon has revolved through about one-eighth of its orbit, its illuminated portion, as seen from the earth, has a crescent-shaped appearance. When about one-quarter of the orbit has been traversed, one-half of the circular disc is seen; this is called the *first quarter*. After another eighth of the orbit, three-quarters of the disc is seen; this is the *gibbous moon*. Then, when the earth is between the moon and the sun, all the moon's illuminated portion is visible; this is the *full moon*. Throughout these phases, from new moon to full moon, the moon is said to have 'waxed'; for the second half of its orbit, when the amount of moon visible from the earth decreases from full moon to new moon, it is said to 'wane'. It will be noted that new moon and full moon occur when earth, moon, and sun are practically in the same straight line, while first quarter and last quarter occur when the line from earth to moon is perpendicular to the line from earth to sun.

moor, moorland. A wild stretch of land, usually elevated, and covered with heather, coarse grass, bracken, or similar vegetation; it sometimes includes patches of pasture grasses, and sometimes marshy hollows.

moraine.* The debris or fragments of rock material brought down with the movements of a *glacier*. When lumps of rock, broken off by frost and other agencies, fall down the valley slopes on to the ice, they form the *lateral moraines*, one on each side of the glacier. When two glaciers meet, two lateral moraines unite to form a *medial moraine*; if other glaciers join them later, several medial moraines may be formed. Fragments which are deposited and lie beneath the ice form a *ground moraine*. At the end of the glacier, where the ice is melting, all the debris which has been transported down is dropped, and forms a *terminal* or *end moraine*, which extends across the valley. Debris which sinks into the *firn* or falls into a *crevasse* and is carried down the valley embedded in its ice is called *englacial moraine*. Debris near the base of the ice which has either sunk through the ice or has been torn up from the valley floor by the ice is called *subglacial moraine*. The material of a moraine differs from that brought down by water, in that large boulders may occur side by side with small fragments; again, the lumps of rock, instead of being rounded, are angular in shape and often scratched, for they are dragged and not rolled along. See also *recessional moraine*. (See Fig. p. 145.)

morass. Popular name for a *bog* or *marsh*.

mortlake. A term sometimes used, mainly in England, for an *ox-bow lake*; Mortlake, a district in SW London, is situated near a drained ox-bow lake of the R Thames.

mother-of-pearl or **nacreous cloud.** A rare type of high cloud formed according to estimates at about 20–30 km (12–18 miles) above the earth's surface and therefore within the *stratosphere*. It has been observed in high latitudes, over Norway and Alaska. It is delicate and usually lenticular, and is so called because of the iridescent colours it exhibits, persisting for some time after sunset.

moulin (French) or **glacier mill.** A vertical shaft or pipe formed in a glacier when streams of water from the melting ice reach a *crevasse* and plunge inside, carrying stones and rock waste with them; the water takes on a rotary movement, and whirls its load of stones round as it rushes through the ice, forming the moulin or glacier mill. The whirlpool of water not only reaches the base of the glacier, but acts upon the bed of rock beneath.

mountain. A mass of land considerably higher than its surroundings and of greater altitude than a hill; in Britain an eminence is often considered a mountain rather than a hill when its elevation from foot to summit

Diagram to illustrate the formation of lateral, medial, and terminal moraines.

is well over 600 m (2,000 ft), but the distinction is arbitrary. The summit area of a mountain is small in proportion to the area of its base; in this respect it differs from a *plateau*, which might be of similar elevation. Although the highest mountains are higher than any plateau, many mountains are less elevated than the highest plateaux – e.g. the Tibetan plateau, about 4,500 m above sea level. Few of the highest mountains occur as single, isolated peaks; most of them are arranged in ranges or groups. See *range, chain*. Mountains may be formed by earth movements. See *folded mountain, block mountain*. They may also be formed by *erosion*, the more resistant rocks being left while the softer rocks surrounding them are worn away. See *relict mountains; monadnock*. Thirdly, mountains may be formed by volcanic action.

mountain climate. The type of climate which is chiefly determined by relief and altitude rather than by latitude and situation with respect to the sea; it may thus occur in any region, and is somewhat outside the

145

scheme of the main *climatic regions*. Compared with the lowlands, mountains show a decrease in atmospheric pressure, temperature, and humidity, an increase in intensity of insolation and radiation, and up to a certain height a greater rainfall. To some extent the various climatic zones up the mountain slopes correspond to those which extend from the equator to the poles, and altitude so tempers heat in low latitudes that a high mountain peak, even on the equator, may be snow-covered throughout the year. But there are fundamental differences: the intensity of sunshine through the thin, clear atmosphere above the *snowline*, for instance, is much greater than that received obliquely through a considerable thickness of atmosphere in the polar regions. There is often diurnal reversal of wind direction, corresponding to land and sea breezes. See *anabatic, katabatic, mountain winds*.

Owing to the establishment of temperature inversions during the colder months and at nights, temperatures may then be relatively high on mountain summits, and diurnal and annual ranges of temperature in middle and higher latitudes may thus be lessened. Ranges of temperature, however, are very considerable in valley bottoms, and are much greater on plateaux than on mountains of the same height. There are great contrasts of temperature, too, between sunny and shaded mountain slopes. See *adret, ubac*.

mountain sickness. A complaint which affects people at high altitudes, and appears to be due to the diminution in the oxygen supply to the lungs. One of the first signs is the increase in the speed of respiration; and headaches, sleeplessness, and sickness may be caused. If the change in altitude is made gradually, no ill effects may be suffered. Muscular exertion may accelerate the mountain sickness, but does not seem to be an essential factor; on the other hand, the expenditure of muscular energy may be severely limited: the average time for which riveters could work on the Oroya Railway in Peru, for instance, was one week. The severity of the complaint varies with individuals, and those in good physical training are the less affected.

mountain wind or **mountain breeze.** The flow of cool air at night down mountain slopes and valleys; it often alternates with the daytime *valley wind*. See *katabatic wind*.

mouth. See *river*.

mud rain. Rain which contains large quantities of dust particles imprisoned in the water drops. The dust enters the atmosphere during a *duststorm*, and may be carried hundreds of kilometres away from the desert where it originated. Thus mud rain sometimes falls at a considerable distance from an arid region, e.g. in England. When it is red in colour it is often known as *blood-rain*.

mud volcano. A mound of mud, sometimes conical in shape with a crater at the top, formed in a volcanic region by hot water issuing from the ground mixed with fine rock material. It is not, therefore, a true volcano, but a type of *hot spring*. There are mud volcanoes in the North Island, New Zealand, in Iceland, and in Sicily. When the mud acquires a colour from its rock material, the feature is often known as a *paint pot*. Mud volcanoes are also found at Baku, USSR, in southern Baluchistan, and in other non-volcanic regions; there the water is ejected by gases of other than volcanic origin – at Baku, for instance, by volatile gases from the petroleum wells.

mulatto. The offspring of a white and a Negro.

mulga scrub. The *scrub*, consisting largely of a species of acacia known as mulga, which covers parts of western and central Australia.

muskeg. A *bog* or *swamp*, largely filled with sphagnum moss, in the *tundra* or the *coniferous forest* region of Canada.

N

nacreous cloud. See *mother-of-pearl cloud.*

nadir. A hypothetical point in the heavens directly opposite, or antipodal, to the *zenith.*

nappe (French). A huge recumbent *fold* with both limbs practically horizontal which has been forced a great distance, i.e. several kilometres, over the underlying formations thus covering them like a cloth: so named after the French word nappe, meaning table-cloth.

national park. A region designated for the preservation of natural features and wild life, largely for public enjoyment but also because of their historic and scientific importance. In the United States, where natural resources were often wastefully exploited in the early days of white settlement, many extensive regions are now administered by the national park service, among them Katmai and Glacier Bay, in Alaska, and Yellowstone, mainly in Wyoming, each covering more than 2 million acres (810,000 hectares). Canada, too, has several great national and provincial parks, the largest Wood Buffalo, Jasper, and Tweedsmuir. In Africa the main purpose of the national parks and reserves is the preservation of wild animals, as in the great Kruger national park, in South Africa. Many countries in other continents, notably the USSR, now maintain national parks and reserves. In Britain the national parks, first established in 1949, cover an area of well over 3 million acres (1,214,000 hectares), and include the Lake District, Snowdonia, and the Yorkshire Dales.

natural bridge. A bridge or arch of natural rock. Sometimes such a bridge is formed when the tough, unjointed rocks of a valley spur are cut through by the stream. It is more common, however, in *limestone* country, where it is probably the remnant of the roof of an underground cave or tunnel. A well-known example is Natural Bridge, a limestone arch 66 m (215 ft) high with a span of 27 m (90 ft), carrying a road, in Virginia, USA.

natural region. An area which possesses within its borders a comparatively high degree of uniformity of relief, climate, and vegetation, and therefore to some extent a uniformity in human activities. In some cases a natural region corresponds closely to a *climatic region*, or to an area in which a certain type of *natural vegetation* prevails.

natural vegetation. The vegetation of a region as it exists or has existed

148

before being modified to a marked extent by man, e.g. through agriculture or urban development.

nautical mile. A unit of distance used in navigation, equal to the length of one minute (1') of arc on a *great circle* drawn on a sphere having the same area as the earth; this is approximately 6,080 ft. For all ordinary purposes the length of one minute of arc along a meridian, the length of a minute of arc on the equator (the *geographical mile*) and the nautical mile may all be considered equal to 6,080 ft.

naze. A promontory or headland: see also *ness*.

neap tides. The *tides* of small amplitude produced when the gravitational pull of the sun opposes, i.e. is at right-angles to, that of the moon; a consideration of the phases of the moon will show that they occur twice a month, about the time of first and last quarters. See *moon, phases of*. At these times the sun tends to produce high water where the moon would produce low water, and vice versa. There is thus an unusually small difference between high water and low water; the high tide is lower and the low tide is higher than usual.

neck. See *volcanic neck*; a neck or narrow strip of land.

nehrung (German). Along the Baltic coast of East Germany and Poland, a *spit* at the mouth of a river which forms a *haff* or lagoon.

nekton. The larger, actively swimming marine creatures, principally fishes, as distinct from the passively drifting *plankton* and the sedentary *benthos*.

nephoscope. An instrument used to measure the speed and direction of motion of the clouds; generally speaking, its use is confined to observations on medium and high clouds. One of the commonest types is the Besson comb nephoscope, which carries a number of pointed rods fixed like the teeth of a comb to the top of a long vertical rod; by rotating the rod till the clouds appear to move along the points, their direction can be determined, and if the height of the clouds be estimated, their speed can also be calculated.

ness. A promontory or headland: see also *naze*.

nevados (Spanish). The cold winds which blow down from the mountains with considerable regularity in the higher valleys of Ecuador; they are caused by the cooling of the air on the mountains, partly by nocturnal radiation, and partly by contact with ice and snow, the cold air flowing down the slopes. See *katabatic wind*.

névé. See *firn*.

new town. In Great Britain, a town planned and developed to relieve overcrowding in London or another large city, the first of such towns having been designated following the New Towns Act of 1946.

nimbostratus. A type of low *cloud*, dark grey in colour and of almost uniform base, which often gives continuous rain or snow; sometimes the precipitation does not reach the ground, and portions of the cloud then appear to trail. A thick mass of nimbostratus cloud is often associated with the *warm front* of a *depression*.

nitrogen. The most abundant gas in the *atmosphere*, occupying approximately 78 per cent by volume of dry air; it is chemically inactive, and serves to dilute the *oxygen*.

nivation. *Erosion* due to the action of snow. An example is the *solifluction* or *soil creep* caused by the thawing of a thin snow cover and the upper parts of the ground, when the latter slides downwards over the frozen mass beneath. Another example is due to the alternate thawing and freezing around the edges of a patch of snow in a hollow: when the snow melts during the day, its water may enter the crevices of rocks, and freeze and break up the rocks at night; the hollow is thus gradually enlarged, and the process may lead to the formation of a *cirque*.

noctilucent cloud. A thin silvery cloud, somewhat like *cirrostratus*, seen in the *stratosphere*, usually in high latitudes, consisting either of dust or of ice crystals.

nomadism. The practice among certain primitive peoples of frequently changing their habitation: especially applied to inhabitants of the *steppes* and deserts, who wander in search of pasture for their livestock, or food such as fruit and roots for themselves, or, possibly, for trade. Such people are known as nomads. When food is scarce, pastoral nomads, such as the Bedouin, may be forced to raid their settled agricultural neighbours.

Norfolk rotation. See *rotation of crops*.

norte (Spanish). The northerly wind experienced in winter in Central America, being a continuation of the United States *norther*, and likewise bringing a sudden and often considerable fall of temperature; the temperature may be reduced by 6° to 9°C for a day or two – a severe change for such latitudes – and the wind may blow with gale force on exposed coasts. On the northern coasts of the Isthmus of Tehuantepec, where the nortes are strong and almost constant throughout the winter, these winds are accompanied by heavy rainfall; when they reach the Pacific side, on the Gulf of Tehuantepec, they are still cold but dry. The name is also applied to the cold, northerly wind experienced in eastern Spain during winter, when the high atmospheric pressure of the interior produces an outblowing current, and to the warm, humid, northerly wind associated with a depression in Argentina.

norther. The *cold wave* sometimes experienced in the southern United States, usually in rear of a depression. The temperature may fall by about 20°C in 24 hours, causing great damage to fruit crops. The norther often blows with great violence, possibly 60 to 100 km per hour, is accompanied by severe thunderstorms and hail, and may give *line squall* conditions. In the Sacramento valley of California, however, this wind is often dry and dusty, having been heated and dried by descent from the mountains.

northern circuit. The general northerly route by which depressions cross the North American continent from west to east, via the Great Lakes and the St Lawrence basin. It is the most frequented track in summer, though the depressions are then fewest in number, weakest, and the least constant. See *southern circuit*.

northern lights. See *aurora borealis*.

north magnetic pole. See *magnetism, terrestrial*.

North Pole. See *Poles*.

nor'-wester. (1) In the South Island, New Zealand, a hot, dry *föhn wind* which descends from the mountains.

(2) On the plains of northern India, a type of *squall*, usually accompanied by violent thunderstorms and heavy rain and hail showers, experienced during the hot season (April to June). At this season the rainfall of Bengal, Assam, and Burma is largely derived from the nor'-westers, and in Assam they are extremely important to the tea crop.

nuée ardente (French) or **peléan cloud.** The blast of hot, highly gas-charged, swiftly moving lava fragments which sometimes sweeps down the slopes of a volcano when upward movement has been obstructed; despite the French term, the cloud surmounting the blast does not always glow. The English term is derived from Mont Pelée (see *volcano*).

nullah. In India, a normally dry watercourse, which only temporarily becomes a stream immediately after heavy rain. See *arroyo, wadi*.

nunatak. An isolated mountain peak or hill projecting, like an island, from the mass of snow and ice near the margin of an *ice sheet*, e.g. in Greenland: the term was borrowed from the Eskimo language. The nunataks become more numerous towards the extreme edge of the ice sheet, for there the ice is thinnest. There are also nunataks in Antarctica.

O

oasis.* An area in the midst of a desert which is made fertile by the presence of water. It sometimes consists merely of a clump of palm-trees, sometimes it is a fertile region several hundred square kilometres in area. In the smaller type the water usually consists of a small isolated spring; alternatively it may be a spot where a stream flows down from a mountain canyon to form an *alluvial fan*. The larger oases, such as those formed by the Nile and the Euphrates, may support a huge agricultural population. In the oases of the hot deserts, the typical tree is the date-palm, the fruit of which forms the main food supply.

obsequent river. A tributary to a *subsequent river*, flowing in the opposite direction to the original *consequent river*.

occlusion. In a *depression*, the closing of the *cold front* on to the *warm front*. The *warm sector* of the depression is lifted by the advancing cold air, and at the earth's surface is reduced to a line – the line of the occlusion; it still exists in the upper air, however, and the cloud and rain of the original fronts remain with it for some time. On European *weather charts*, lines of occlusion appear quite frequently, for most of the depressions passing eastwards across the North Atlantic are occluded by the time they reach Western Europe. If the warm sector is lifted up the surface of the warm front, the occlusion is known as a *warm front occlusion*; if it is lifted up the surface of the cold front, the occlusion is called a *cold front occlusion*. In each case the front is said to be 'occluded'.

ocean. The sheet of salt water which surrounds the great land masses of the earth; it is divided by them into several extensive portions, each known as an ocean, and altogether covers about 71 per cent of the earth's surface. The individual oceans are the Pacific, the largest, flanked by high mountain chains, having a deep, fairly level floor, and remarkable for the number of small islands, largely of volcanic origin; the narrower Atlantic, with few islands; the Indian, still smaller, and enclosed on three sides by continents and islands; the Arctic, surrounding the North Pole; and the Southern Ocean, surrounding Antarctica.

The oceans may be divided into three distinct regions, the *littoral*, the *pelagic*, and the *abyssal*. Alternatively, they may be divided according

Section through a cold front occlusion. Arrows show direction of movement.

to depth into four regions: (1) the *continental shelf*, which adjoins the land, (2) the *continental slope*, immediately outside the continental shelf, (3) the *deep-sea plain*, a wide and almost level area forming most of the ocean floor, and varying in depth from about 4,000 to 6,000 metres, and (4) the *deeps*. The ocean floor, like the land surface, has many ridges and valleys; its area and depth may be represented diagrammatically by a *hypsographic curve*. At the surface, the temperature of the ocean is usually a few degrees higher than that of the air above, and thus varies considerably, from over 25°C near the equator to below freezing point in the polar regions. But ocean temperature decreases rapidly with depth below the surface; below 4,000 metres, temperatures are uniformly low in all oceans, being only a few degrees above freezing point. The *salinity* of the oceans also varies.

ocean current. A movement of the surface water of the ocean. Of the various causes of ocean currents, the most important are the prevailing winds and the differences in density due to variations in temperature or salinity; some deflexion of currents is caused by the rotation of the earth. Those currents caused by prevailing winds are known as drift currents, the best-known being the Gulf Stream. The circulation of the main ocean currents between the equatorial and the temperate regions is clockwise in the northern hemisphere and anti-clockwise in the southern hemisphere. In the Atlantic, for instance, the currents driven by the NE and SE *trade winds* combine near the equator to form the westward-moving equatorial current. This divides off the Brazilian coast, the northward portion forming the Gulf Stream, which moves along the east coast of the United States, meets the cold Labrador current off Newfoundland, persists as the North Atlantic Drift, and in the main continues with the prevailing *westerlies* to Europe; then it divides, the northern branch reaching the coasts of NW Europe as a warm current, passing into the Arctic Ocean, while the southern

153

branch moves to the coast of N W Africa as a cold current. (The terms 'warm' and 'cold' for a current denote their temperature relative to that of the neighbouring atmosphere.) The currents of the South Atlantic are very similar, though the general circulation is anti-clockwise. Those of the Pacific are also similar, the warm-current of the North Pacific corresponding to the Gulf Stream of the North Atlantic being the Kuro Shio. Ocean currents often have a considerable influence on climate; the North Atlantic Drift, for instance, is largely responsible for the mild winters of N W Europe, and the meeting of the Gulf Stream and the cold Labrador current gives the dense fogs off Newfoundland. Currents caused by differences of temperature are known as *convection* currents. Warm water of the equatorial regions flows towards the polar regions, where it is cooled, sinks, and returns along the ocean bed, as a bottom current, towards the equator; it then rises to the surface again. An example of a current due to a difference of salinity is the surface current which enters the Mediterranean Sea from the Atlantic Ocean. Owing to a small rainfall, great evaporation, and the small number of inflowing rivers, the Mediterranean has a higher salinity than the Atlantic; a relatively fresh surface current thus flows from the Atlantic into the Mediterranean while a relatively salt undercurrent flows in the reverse direction.

oceanography. The study of the oceans, including the nature of the water, its movements, its temperature, its depth, the ocean bed, the flora and fauna, etc.

octoroon. The offspring of a *quadroon* and a white, thus having one-eighth Negro blood.

offshore bar. See *bar* (2).

ogive. In *glaciology*, one of several curved bands across the surface of a *glacier*, consisting of alternate light and dark ice; its downstream convexity illustrates how the middle of the glacier moves more quickly than its margins. Glaciologists do not all agree as to the formation of ogives, but it is generally held that a combined light and dark band together represent one year's forward movement of the glacier.

okta. The unit employed in meteorological reports to describe the prevailing *cloudiness*, the proportion of sky covered by cloud, and equal to one-eighth of the whole sky.

onion weathering. See *exfoliation*.

ooze. One of the deposits, mainly liquid mud, which cover the *deep-sea plain* of the *oceans*. They consist largely of the remains of various organisms which exist in the surface waters and on dying settle to the bottom; they also contain volcanic dust, which has been carried by the wind, and has likewise sunk to the ocean bed. Oozes are classified as calcareous or siliceous, and they are named according to the organisms which are most abundant in them. *Pteropod ooze* and *globigerina ooze* are calcareous oozes; *radiolarian ooze* and *diatom ooze* are siliceous oozes. See also *red clay*.

opaco. See *ubac*.

opencast or **strip mining.** The extraction of a mineral, usually coal, lignite or iron ore, on a site where the deposits lie near the surface and are of considerable extent: the *overburden* is first removed by machinery, then the mineral is extracted, and normally when operations are completed the subsoil and topsoil are restored so that the area may be devoted to agriculture, forestry, or some other useful activity. *Strip mining* is the American term for the enterprise.

opisometer. An instrument consisting of a small toothed wheel to which is fitted a recording dial, used for measuring distances on a map. The wheel is run along the line, which may be irregular, e.g. the course of a river, and the length is given in inches or centimetres, which can then be converted into miles or kilometres.

opposition. The direction of two heavenly bodies when they are in the opposite direction to each other as viewed from the earth, i.e. their longitudes differ by 180°. The term is usually applied to the position of a heavenly body when its direction, as viewed from the earth, is opposite to that of the sun.

orbit. The path of a heavenly body through space in relation to some selected point.

orbit, earth's. The path of the earth round the sun. This path is very nearly circular, actually elliptical; the sun is not at the centre, but at one of the foci of this ellipse. The earth is thus nearer to the sun at one season than at the opposite season, when it has reached the farther side of the ellipse. See *aphelion, perihelion*.

ordnance datum. See *mean sea level*.

ordnance survey. An accurate and detailed geographical survey of Great Britain made for the Government, originally by the War Office.

ore. A mineral aggregate which is worth mining on account of the valuable metalliferous *minerals* it contains.

orogenesis. Mountain-building: changes in the level of the earth's crust in which rocks are thrown up into folds or blocks to form ranges of mountains. In course of time the mountains may be considerably denuded, and may thereafter be depressed or elevated by *epeirogenesis*.

orographic rain. Rain which is caused by mountains standing in the path of moisture-laden air; this air is forced to rise, is thereby cooled, and, if sufficient water vapour is present, rain is deposited on the high ground. Substantial amounts of orographic rain are produced by mountain ranges rather than by isolated peaks, especially when they are aligned at right-angles, or nearly so, to the direction of the wind. On account of orographic rain, places in mountainous or hilly regions often receive a consistently higher rainfall than neighbouring places situated on low-lying ground. See *rainfall*.

orography. The branch of physical geography which is concerned with *relief*, more particularly with mountain systems.

orrery. A clockwork model illustrating the relative movements of the planets and other heavenly bodies, including the earth and the moon, about the sun. It was invented about the beginning of the eighteenth century, and a copy was made for Charles Boyle, Earl of Orrery (1676–1731), after whom it was named.

orthographic projection. The type of *map projection* in which the globe is viewed as if from an infinite distance, so that only one hemisphere is depicted; the projecting rays are parallel and perpendicular to the plane of projection. At the margins there is considerable compression, and at the centre expansion, and distances, directions, shapes, and areas are distorted. The projection, which is a kind of *zenithal projection*, is of little geographical value, but is frequently used for charts of the heavens.

orthomorphic projection. A type of *map projection* in which the *shape* of any very small area on the map is the same as the *shape* of the corresponding small area on the earth. It is sometimes known as a *conformal projection*.

os. The anglicized version of the Swedish *ås*.

outcrop. The portion of a rock stratum which projects above the earth's surface, and is thus exposed to view.

outlet glacier. A *glacier* which flows out from an *ice sheet* or *ice cap*, e.g. around the margins of the Greenland ice sheet.

outlier. A mass of comparatively new rocks surrounded by older rocks, having been separated from the main mass to which it belonged, e.g. by erosion. See *inlier*.

outport. A port which is auxiliary to another seaport, but, being situated nearer the sea, is more accessible than the latter to the larger vessels: e.g. Avonmouth is an outport of Bristol, Cuxhaven of Hamburg.

outwash plain or **sandur** (Icelandic). The alluvial plain formed by the streams originating from the melting ice of a glacier, which carry away some of the material of the moraine, and deposit it over a considerable area; the coarser material is deposited near to the ice, the finer material farther away. See also *valley train*.

overburden. The rock material, subsoil and soil which overlie a mineral deposit, e.g. coal, iron ore, and have to be removed before *opencast* or *strip mining* can commence.

overfold. A *fold* in which the axial plane is so far inclined that the strata of the lower limb are overturned, or inverted; the limbs of the overfold dip in the same direction, though at different angles.

overlander. In Australia, a stockman employed in driving cattle or sheep over long distances across country.

ox-bow lake or **cut-off.** A lake formed when a meandering river (see

Arrangement of strata in an overfold.

Diagram of an exaggerated meander and an ox-bow lake.

meander), having bent in almost a complete circle, cuts across the narrow neck of land between the two stretches, and leaves a backwater; silt is gradually deposited by the river at the entrances to this backwater, till the latter is finally separated from the river, and becomes a lake. Such ox-bow lakes are very common beside the banks of the Mississippi, and are often known as *bayous*. See also *mortlake*.

oxygen. The chief gas in the *atmosphere* from the viewpoint of mankind and the animals, being essential to the process of breathing: in the body it unites with carbon to form *carbon dioxide*, which is then exhaled. Oxygen occupies about 21 per cent by volume of dry air. It is also the most abundant element, forming about eight-ninths by weight of water, and nearly one-half by weight of all the rocks of which the earth's crust is comprised.

ozone. A gas which is an allotropic form of *oxygen*, with a rather pungent odour, present in minute amounts in the *atmosphere*. Its concentration varies with altitude, reaching a maximum at about 20–25 km (12–15 miles).

ozone layer. That part of the *atmosphere* extending from about 10 km

157

(6 miles) to about 50 km (30 miles) above the earth's surface which contains ozone, or the layer where the concentration of ozone is greatest, at about 20–25 km (12–15 miles), either being sometimes known as the *ozonosphere*. It shields the earth from ultra-violet radiation.

ozonosphere. See *ozone layer*.

P

Pacific coast. See *concordant coast*.

pack-ice. Large blocks of ice, of greater extent and depth than *ice-floes*, formed on the surface of the sea when the latter or broken pieces of them have been driven together to form an almost continuous mass of ice. They are termed 'close pack' if the blocks are mainly in contact, 'open pack' if they are not. Much of the pack-ice gradually melts and disappears in warm weather.

padang (Malay). In the Malay Archipelago, a term applied rather loosely to a heath-like terrain carrying *scrub* vegetation, as distinct from the denser, more luxuriant *tropical rain forest*.

pahoehoe. The Hawaiian term for *ropy* or *corded lava*, often used in place of its English equivalent.

paint pot. See *mud volcano*.

palaeogeography. The study of the distribution of land and water, etc., during earlier periods of the earth's history.

palaeomagnetism. The study of the magnetism of ancient rocks, based on the retention by these rocks of some of the magnetism bestowed on them at their formation, possibly millions of years ago. It has served to reinforce the modern theory of *continental drift*, and suggests that at times the earth's magnetic field has undergone considerable changes and even complete reversal. See *magnetism, terrestrial*.

palaeontology. The science which deals with extinct organisms, of either animal or plant origin, whose remains are found buried in the rocks; the study of *fossils*. The term is now often applied only to the study of animal fossils (palaeozoology), the study of plant fossils being termed palaeobotany.

Palaeozoic era. The Ancient Life era, the first of the three major divisions of the geological scale of time (after pre-Cambrian time): that period of the earth's history which preceded the *Mesozoic era*, extending from about 600 million to about 200 million years ago. Its rock strata are the oldest in the earth's crust from which definite organic remains have been recorded, though during the era the creatures inhabiting the earth were very different from those of the present day. For long the vertebrates were represented only by fish, but later amphibians appeared, and, at the end of the period, reptiles. The vegetation consisted of cryptogamous plants, such as ferns and mosses. Later in the era, layers of partially decayed vegetation became buried under marine deposits, and by compression and hardening formed coal. See *Carboniferous period*. It is sometimes known as the Primary era.

pampa or **pampas** (Spanish). The mid-latitude *grasslands* or grassy plains lying round the River Plate estuary in South America, from the Andes to the Atlantic Ocean. The western part of the pampas, the so-called 'dry pampa', is largely desert, but the eastern part, the 'humid pampa', with a higher rainfall, has a natural covering of tall, coarse grass known as pampas grass. Vast areas of the pampas are now cultivated, yielding wheat, maize, alfalfa, and flax (for linseed), and enormous numbers of cattle and sheep are reared for the frozen meat industry. In physical characteristics, the pampas are similar to the *prairies* of North America, the *steppes* of the USSR, and the *veld* of South Africa. The term pampa is also applied to other plains in South America.

pampero (Spanish). A violent burst of cold, polar air experienced on the *pampas* of Argentina and Uruguay after a depression has passed. It blows from a southerly to westerly direction, and takes the form of a *line squall*, with the typical roll of cloud; it is sometimes accompanied by rain, thunder, and lightning, and dust is swept up from the pampas. A considerable fall of temperature occurs as the storm passes. The pampero is most frequent in summer, and is comparable with the *southerly burster* of Australia.

pancake ice. The small, thin cakes of ice, roughly circular in shape, which form on the surface of the water when the sea begins to freeze.

Pangaea. The vast continent which, according to Wegener, once constituted the entire land mass of *sial* on the earth's surface and broke up into *Laurasia* and *Gondwanaland*. See *continental drift*.

panhandle. An American term for the long narrow extension of a state or territory between two others or between one other and the sea, e.g. the Alaska panhandle between NW Canada and the Pacific Ocean, the Wakhan panhandle of NE Afghanistan between the USSR and Pakistan. (See Fig. p. 161.)

papagayo (Spanish). The cold, northerly wind sometimes felt on the Mexican plateau, being a continuation of the *norther* of the United States, and comparable with the *norte* of the coastal region.

parallel of latitude. See *latitude*.

paramos (Spanish). The bleak, barren lands extending above the *puna* of the Andes, in South America, as far as the snowline, and invaded in parts by glaciers. Although flowering plants grow in sheltered spots, the vegetation over much of the area is stunted, as on the *tundra*, and consists largely of lichens and mosses.

paraselene or **mock moon.** An image of the moon, similar to the *parhelion* or mock sun; it is formed at the same angular distance from the moon, 22°, as the parhelion is from the sun, when the moon is near the

The Wakhan panhandle of NE Afghanistan, defined 1895 as a buffer between Russia and India.

horizon, and at a greater distance when the moon has a higher elevation. It is similarly due to the refraction of light through the ice crystals of a high cloud; because the light of the moon is so much weaker than that of the sun, the paraselene is less bright than the parhelion.

paraselenic circle. A circular band of light associated with the *paraselene*, passing through the moon and parallel to the horizon. It is caused by the reflection of light from the ice crystals of a high cloud.

parhelic circle. A circular band of light associated with the *parhelion*, passing through the sun and parallel to the horizon. It is caused by the reflection of light from the ice crystals of a high cloud.

parhelion or **mock sun.** An image of the sun, usually coloured, with the red nearest to the sun, and at the same elevation as the sun. When the sun is near the horizon, the angular distance of the mock sun from the sun equals that of the ordinary *halo*, 22°, but when the sun is higher

161

the distance is greater, and the mock sun is outside the halo. It is caused by the refraction of sunlight through the ice crystals of a high cloud.

partial drought. In the British Isles, a period of at least twenty-nine consecutive days, during which the mean daily rainfall does not exceed 0.2 mm. The definition has not been internationally accepted. See *absolute drought*, *dry spell*.

pass. A low and passable gap through a mountain barrier. It is usually caused by erosion, either by glaciers or by two streams which rise close to each other on opposite sides of the mountain barrier. Being approached from both sides of the mountains by a steep valley, and being flanked by mountain peaks, the pass is thus saddle shaped. See *col* (1).

pastoral farming. The practice of breeding and rearing certain herbivorous animals. By its means it is possible for man to satisfy almost all his needs in food, clothing, and shelter; in some regions, in fact, it is essential for him to do so. Some inhabitants of the tundra, for instance, derive most of their necessaries of life from the reindeer, those of desert or semi-desert lands from sheep or goats. The flocks and herds sometimes suffer from drought, cold, or disease, but when large numbers are reared, it is very rare for all the animals to be destroyed. The need for pastures for the animals causes the inhabitants of relatively inhospitable regions to lead a nomadic life; on most of the *grasslands* of the world, however, the pastoral farmers are now following a settled existence.

peak. The more or less pointed top of a mountain, standing above the general level of the range or the surrounding country. It may be formed through the *erosion* of adjacent rocks, those of which the peak is composed being of more resistant material. Sometimes, however, it may be the result of a *fold* or a *fault*, or it may be a volcanic cone.

peat. A brownish or blackish fibrous substance produced by the decay of vegetation and found in *bogs*; it is usually considered to represent the first stage in the transformation of vegetable matter into coal, and contains a high proportion of water. See *lignite*.

pedalfer. One of the two types into which *zonal soils* are sometimes classified; it is roughly equivalent to 'soil of a humid region', and, as the name suggests, is generally rich in iron and clay. The pedalfers are divided into podzolic and lateritic soils (see *podzol*, *laterite*). See *pedocal*.

pediment. In arid and semi-arid regions, the gently sloping plain strewn with boulders that borders the mountains.

pedocal. One of the two types into which *zonal soils* are sometimes classified; it is roughly equivalent to 'soil of an arid region' and, as the name suggests, is generally rich in calcium. The pedocals are divided into pedocals of the temperate zone and of the tropical zone. See *pedalfer*.

pedology. The science of the study of soils.

pelagic. Belonging to the open sea, i.e. to that part of the *ocean* which is deeper than the *littoral* and *bathyal zones*. The *pelagic deposits*, then, are the materials that cover the *deep-sea plains*, and include the *oozes* and *red clay*.

pelagic deposits. The deposits which cover the bed of the *pelagic* zone of the ocean, formed largely of the remains of plants and animals of microscopic size which in life float in the surface waters; they include, however, the products of volcanic eruptions. See *oozes*. There is, in fact, no sharp line of demarcation between pelagic deposits and *terrigenous* deposits.

peléan cloud. See *nuée ardente*.

peneplain. A region which is almost a plain. Its formation is often due to erosion by rivers and rain, which continues until almost all the elevated portions are worn down; the most resistant rocks frequently stand above the general level of the land, though in time they, too, will be brought down to that level. See *monadnock*. When a peneplain is raised, it often becomes a *plateau*, which is then dissected by the rivers as they pass through a fresh cycle from youth to old age.

peninsula. A stretch of land almost surrounded by water.

penumbra. The partly shaded region from which a small amount of light is received, surrounding the *umbra* in an *eclipse*. The term is also applied, for instance, to the similar region surrounding the umbra of a *sunspot*.

pepino hill. Chiefly in Puerto Rico, a term sometimes used for a *mogote*, though applied more strictly to a ridge rather than a hill.

perched block. An *erratic block* that has been left standing in an exposed and precarious position.

percolation. The descent of water through the soil pores and rock crevices. It sometimes leads to *leaching*.

perennial irrigation. See *irrigation*.

perigee. The point in the orbit of the moon or of a planet, or in the apparent orbit of the sun, when it is nearest to the earth.

periglacial. A term applied to areas near an *ice sheet* and to the climatic and other phenomena associated with them.

perihelion. The position of the earth, or of another heavenly body, in its *orbit* when it is at its nearest point to the sun. The earth reaches its perihelion during the northern winter, about 3 January, when it is about 147.2 million km (91.5 million miles) from the sun; although the earth is then nearest to the sun, the northern days are short, and the sun's rays fall very obliquely on the northern hemisphere, and the decreased insolation more than counterbalances the shorter distance. See *aphelion*.

period. A division in the geological scale of time, being part of an *era*, and being itself divided into *epochs*.

permafrost. Ground that is permanently frozen, occurring extensively in polar regions, sometimes, as in N Siberia, to depths as great as 600 m. A shallow layer of soil may thaw during the summer, while the ground below remains frozen; the contraction and expansion caused by the seasonal thawing and freezing there seriously complicate the construction of roads, buildings, etc.

permeable rocks. Rocks which, being porous, allow water, e.g. rain water, to soak into and thus pass through them; sandstone is an example. Some geographers assume the term to be synonymous with *pervious rocks*.

pervious rocks. Rocks which allow water, e.g. rain water, to pass through them, being either porous or fissured. As the water can only pass through the rocks gradually, an exceptionally heavy fall of rain will cause a surface *run-off* even from these rocks. Some geographers use the term *permeable rocks*.

petrology. The study of the composition, structure, and history of the rocks forming the *lithosphere*, or earth's crust, and their mineral structure; it is thus a branch of *geology*.

phacolith or **phacolite.** A long lens-shaped strip of *igneous rock*, placed near the top of an *anticline* or the bottom of a *syncline*. It is formed in a similar way to a *laccolith*, by the intrusion of *magma* from below without reaching the surface, but it is, of course, much shallower than a laccolith. See *saddle-reef*.

phases of the moon. See *moon, phases of*.

phenology. The science which deals with the effects of seasonal changes upon animal and vegetable life. It thus includes such phenomena as the flowering or bursting into leaf of plants, seed-time and harvest, etc., though observations are often limited to the dates at which these phenomena, and, for instance, the first and last appearance of birds and insects, occur. The relations between these dates and the latitude, longitude, and altitude of the various regions are also examined.

photo relief. The process by which a relief model of an area is photographed for reproduction on a map, called a photo relief map; the method merely depicts the salient physical features of the area.

phrygana. In Greece, the type of *scrub* which consists of scattered thorn bushes, with such plants as lavender and cistus, interspersed with extensive patches of bare rock and soil. It corresponds to the *garigue* of the western Mediterranean region.

physical geography. The branch of *geography* which deals with the physical features of the earth, including land, water, and air. It may be regarded, in fact, as the study of man's physical environment, and therefore as complementary to human geography; it is sometimes considered to be synonymous with *physiography*. Books on physical geography almost invariably have sections on the oceans (*oceanography*) and climate (*climatology*) and weather (*meteorology*), as well as on landforms (*geomorphology*); they often also include a treatment of natural vegetation and soils and some mathematical geography and zoogeography.

physiography. The study of the physical features or landforms of the earth, their causes, and their relation to one another. It is sometimes held to be synonymous with the more modern term *geomorphology*, and sometimes, rather loosely, with *physical geography*.

phytogeography. The study of the distribution of plants on the earth in relation to their geographical environment.

pidgin English. A corrupt form of English used as a medium of communication between English-speaking traders and various native races. It was originally the language of business between Englishmen and Chinese, and the words are believed to be a Chinese corruption of 'Business English'. But different forms of pidgin English are current among millions of natives of Africa, south-east Asia, Australia, and the Pacific Islands, particularly Papua New Guinea; each form consists of a few hundred English words and a much smaller number of common native words. See *lingua franca*.

piedmont. Belonging to or related to the foot of a mountain or a range of mountains, e.g. *piedmont glacier*.

piedmont alluvial plain. See *alluvial fan*.

piedmont glacier. An extensive sheet of ice covering low-lying ground at the foot of a mountain range, formed by the union of several *glaciers*. Its width is usually greater than the combined width of the glaciers which form it, and the rate of movement is therefore slow; sometimes, in fact, movement practically ceases. One of the best-known examples of a piedmont glacier is the Malaspina glacier in Alaska, which is 95 to 115 km (60–70 miles) long and 30 to 40 km (20–25 miles) wide.

pike. Chiefly in the Lake District, England, the *peak* of a mountain or hill, e.g. Scafell Pike.

pillow lava. A *lava* which solidified under water, either because it was ejected under water or because it flowed into the water before solidification, assuming shapes that resemble a heap of pillows.

pilot balloon. A small free rubber balloon, filled with hydrogen, which is used to obtain the direction and velocity of the upper winds. Usually the balloon is followed, after release, by means of a single *theodolite*; as the balloon contains a known amount of hydrogen, it has a known rate of ascent, and by determining its position at fixed intervals, normally every minute, its direction and speed – and therefore those of the wind – can be calculated. A pilot balloon may also be used for determining the height of the cloud base: the interval from its release to its disappearance in the cloud is found, and, assuming a known rate of ascent, the height can be calculated.

pingo (Eskimo). In the *tundra*, a dome-shaped hill or mound containing a core of ice, caused by the freezing of ground water, which forces up the overlying layer of earth or gravel. A pingo may exceed 50 m in depth and 500 m in diameter.

pipe. In chalk country, a *sinkhole* that has filled with gravel. These pipes may be seen in section in many chalk pits.

piracy, river. See *river capture*.

pitch or **plunge.** The angle that the axis of a *fold* makes with the horizontal.

piton (French). A *peak* which tapers to a point, e.g. Gros Piton and Petit Piton on St Lucia (West Indies), each of which is an old *volcanic neck*.

plage (French). A beach, usually but not invariably at a seaside resort. Virtually synonymous with the Italian term *lido*, which has largely replaced it (except in France).

plain. An extensive area of level or gently undulating land, usually of low altitude. Plains may be formed in a variety of ways, and are often named accordingly: e.g. *alluvial plain*, *coastal plain*, *flood-plain*. On many of the plains of the temperate zone, the natural vegetation is grass, and the plains have thus come to be known as *grasslands*, and, according to their location, as *prairies*, *pampas*, and *steppes*.

plane of the ecliptic. See *ecliptic*.

plane table. A simple surveying instrument by means of which a map of a small area may be drawn; it consists of a drawing board standing horizontally on a tripod and carrying an *alidade* and a compass. A line representing magnetic north and south is drawn on the paper which covers the plane table, the directions of the various physical features are found by sighting, and distances are obtained from a measured base-line.

planet. One of the roughly spherical bodies, of which there are several hundreds, which revolve round the sun in elliptical paths known as their orbits. There are nine major planets, including the earth, much larger than the rest, and many minor planets or *asteroids*. Those major planets larger than the earth are Neptune, Uranus, Saturn, and Jupiter, those smaller are Venus, Mars, Mercury, and Pluto. Venus and Mercury are nearer the sun than is the earth, the rest are farther away; Pluto, discovered in 1930, is at the greatest distance from the sun. Unlike the sun and stars, and like the moon, the planets shine only by reflected sunlight.

planetary winds. The general distribution of winds throughout the lower atmosphere, which – determined by differences in *insolation* – would be set up similarly in any rotating planet possessing an atmosphere. It consists of the following: the calms and very light winds of the equatorial low-pressure belt – the *doldrums*; the *trade winds*, blowing from the sub-tropical belts of high pressure towards the equator, from the N E in the northern hemisphere and from the S E in the southern hemisphere; the *westerlies*, on the poleward side of the trade winds, being mainly S W in the northern hemisphere and N W in the southern

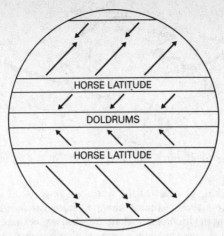

Diagram to show the planetary winds at the earth's surface.

hemisphere; and the outblowing polar winds, from the NE in the northern hemisphere and the SE in the southern hemisphere. The whole system of planetary winds and pressure belts moves north and south with the equatorial belt with which it is primarily associated.

planetesimal or **collision hypothesis.** The hypothesis which proposes that the planets of the solar system were formed by the coalescence of large numbers of minute planets, or planetesimals, owing to collision and gravitational attraction. The idea derives from the fact that there are several spiral nebulae now existing in the universe, each one having a central nucleus about which opposite curved arms revolve; in the arms are dense spots, smaller than the nucleus, about which the planetesimals revolve. Thus the earth was produced from one nucleus, the moon from another. The result of pressure, as more and more material accumulated, was to heat the interiors of the planets, and this heat is now being lost again.

planetoid. See *asteroid*.

planimeter. An instrument for measuring irregular plane areas on charts and maps. The tracing point of the instrument is placed at a certain point on the perimeter of the area to be measured, and is then moved round the perimeter till the point is again reached. An index on the instrument gives the area which corresponds to the distance described by the tracing point. Some instruments have a variable tracer-arm, which permits direct measurement in any unit.

plankton. The minute, floating organisms of plant and animal origin, usually invisible to the naked eye, which inhabit the water of oceans and seas, and form the food of many fishes and other creatures. The

Related landforms – plateau (P), *mesa* (M) *and butte* (B).

principal fishing-grounds of the world are thus found on the continental shelves, where plankton abound. Animal and vegetable plankton also form the food of the whale. See *benthos, nekton*.

plantation. An estate, usually in a tropical or sub-tropical region, which is devoted to the large-scale production of one or more *cash crops*, e.g. coffee, sugar-cane. In the past the owners of plantations often employed slave labour. The term is also applied to an area of planted trees – as distinct from a natural forest or wood.

plateau. An extensive, level or mainly level area of elevated land. Sometimes the plateau is traversed by rivers and mountain ranges, as in the case of the *meseta* of Spain; it may be exceptionally high, as in the case of the Tibetan plateau. If formed of horizontal strata, when young it will be intersected by deep *canyons*; later, the valley floors widen, and it is broken up into *mesas*; later still, most of the surface becomes a plain, dotted with *buttes*. It is usually called a *tableland* when it is bordered by steep, cliff-like faces or *scarps*. Plateaux may be classified as intermontane, piedmont, or continental plateaux (or tablelands). The *intermontane plateaux* are those which have been formed in association with mountains, and are partly or completely enclosed by them; the highest and some of the most extensive plateaux, e.g. the Tibetan plateau, are of this kind. The *piedmont plateaux* lie between the mountains and the plains or the ocean, e.g. the plateau of Patagonia. The *continental plateaux* or *tablelands* rise abruptly from the lowlands or the sea, e.g. the plateau or tableland of South Africa. Many of the plateaux of the world have an arid climate. See also *dissected plateau*.

plate tectonics. See *continental drift*.

playa (Spanish). A tract of land, such as an *alkali flat*, which is temporarily filled with water and becomes a shallow muddy lake after exceptionally heavy rainfall, or the flooding of a river, but dries up again in hot weather. The Great Basin of the western United States, in Nevada and Utah, has many playas.

plucking. The action of a *glacier* when it freezes on to a rock on its valley floor and pulls away a part of the rock as it moves down the valley.

plug. See *volcanic neck* or *plug*.

plum rains or **bai-u.** The early summer rainfall of Japan, caused by depressions of continental origin passing eastwards over central China and across the Yellow Sea. During this period the rain falls very frequently, the sky is overcast, and the atmosphere is extremely humid; the large cloud amounts have the effect of checking the summer rise of temperature. The name is derived from the fact that the rains come at the time of ripening of the plums. This is the period when the rice plants are being transplanted, and the 'plum rains' are therefore extremely important to the rice crop.

plutonic or **abyssal rocks.** The *igneous rocks* which have solidified deep down in the earth, where the cooling has been slow and the various minerals have had time to crystallize; these rocks are thus always completely crystalline and coarse-grained. Granite provides a familiar example.

pluvial. Relating to, due to, or accompanied by rain.

pluviometric coefficient. The mean amount of rainfall at a place for a given period, expressed as a percentage of the 'normal', the 'normal' being the amount that would be precipitated if the rainfall were evenly distributed throughout the year. See *equipluve*.

podzol or **podsol** (Russian). A type of soil which is characteristic of regions having a sub-polar climate, and one which therefore develops mainly under a natural vegetation of *coniferous forests*. It develops, in fact, where the precipitation is only moderate but evaporation is limited. The upper layers are leached of iron compounds and lime, which may form a *hardpan* in the B horizon; the soil thus has a characteristic greyish-white colour near the surface, and is brown below. On the whole, the podzols make poor agricultural soils, but they can be improved by the addition of lime and fertilizers. Huge areas of the coniferous forest regions of northern Canada and the northern USSR are covered with podzols.

point. (1) A cape.

(2) One of the thirty-two directions or dividing lines of the compass.

polar glacier. One of the two categories into which some glaciologists classify *glaciers* according to the temperature of the ice: the type in which the temperature of the ice is always below 0°C, so that no melting takes place at the surface, such as occur in Antarctica and much of Greenland. See *temperate glacier*.

polar winds. The extremely cold winds which blow from the area of high pressure around the poles towards the temperate regions. In the northern hemisphere they blow in general from the north-east, in the southern hemisphere from the south-east.

polder. In the Netherlands, an area of land which has been reclaimed from the sea or from a lake. The land is surrounded by dykes to protect it against encroachment, and is then drained by pumping the water into canals which run along embankments and serve also as means of communication. The polders are usually very fertile, and form valuable agricultural land or pasture land for cattle. The greater part of the former Zuider Zee was thus transformed into polders, or empoldered.

Poles. The two points at the northern and southern extremities of the earth, known as the North Pole and the South Pole, which form the ends of the earth's *axis*, and thus remain stationary while every other point on the earth's surface is rotating about the axis. The term is also used of the North and South Magnetic Poles (see *magnetism, terrestrial*).

Pole Star. The star which is seen virtually in the zenith at the North Pole, and therefore may be used to find true north from any point on the earth's surface where it may be seen, i.e. in the northern hemisphere. At any place, the height of the Pole Star above the horizon is equal to the latitude; at the equator, the Pole Star has no altitude, and is just visible on the horizon. To find the latitude of a place in the northern hemisphere, then, the height of the Pole Star above the northern point of the horizon may be observed. To find the Pole Star, an imaginary line may be drawn through the two stars known as the 'pointers' in the constellation called the Plough, and then produced to about five times its length; this line will very nearly pass through the Pole Star. In the southern hemisphere, although the stars there visible may be used to find directions, there is no single star immediately above the South Pole. See *Southern Cross*.

polje (Serbo-Croat). A closed hollow in a *karst region*, similar to but larger than a *doline*, being flat-bottomed and several kilometres in length. After heavy rain it may temporarily become a lake. It usually has a covering of soil, making cultivation possible (see *terra rossa*). It may be due to erosion, having been formed primarily by solution of limestone, or it may be of tectonic origin, having been initiated by earth movements; the former kind is sometimes known as a *blind valley*.

polster. See '*glacier mouse*'.

polyconic projection. A modified *conical projection*, in which the distances between the meridians along every parallel of latitude are made equal to those distances on the globe. The name is derived from the fact that each parallel is thus constructed as if it were the chosen standard parallel for a simple conical projection. The central meridian is divided truly, each parallel is divided truly, and the meridians are formed by drawing curves through the corresponding points on successive parallels. This type of projection is far from equal-area or orthomorphic, and so is unsuitable for maps covering a large area.

ponente. A westerly wind which blows in the Mediterranean area.

ponor (Serbo-Croat). In a *karst region*, an open vertical shaft enlarged by solution of the limestone, leading downwards from a *sinkhole*.

pororoca. The tidal wave or *bore* of the Amazon River.

port. A town possessing a *harbour*, at which ships call to load and unload goods. One of the simplest types is the fishing *port*, while those which are used by the largest ocean-going vessels are often known as *seaports*. A *river port* is often situated at the highest point on the river which can be reached by vessels large enough to be used for trade. See *outport, treaty port, entrepôt, airport.*

pot-hole. A hole worn in the solid rock, often at the foot of a waterfall, by the revolutions of stones and gravel; the latter have been kept in motion by the eddies of the swiftly-flowing stream. The term is sometimes applied to the type of *sinkhole* or *swallow-hole* commonly found in limestone districts, and also popularly to the caves which are explored by 'pot-holers'.

prairie, prairies. The gently undulating, almost flat, generally treeless, grassy plains – the mid-latitude *grasslands* – of North America, covering the southern regions of Alberta, Saskatchewan, and Manitoba in Canada and the central United States from the foothills of the Rocky Mountains about as far east as the longitude of Lake Michigan. The light summer rains, with local droughts and high summer temperatures, permit a rich growth of natural grasses, but not, in general, trees; these conditions are also suited to the growth of cereals, and the prairies have become one of the most important areas of wheat production in the world. The prairies are sometimes divided into *long grass prairies* (E) and *short grass prairies* (W). They form the North American counterpart of the *pampas* of South America, the *steppes* of Eurasia, and the *veld* of South Africa.

pre-Cambrian. The entire time on the geological scale preceding the Cambrian *period* of the *Palaeozoic era*, and thus ending about 600 million years ago. The pre-Cambrian rocks are now exposed over about one-fifth of the earth's land surface, but our knowledge of the life of the pre-Cambrian world is still very slight. The rocks are of great economic importance, for they contain the world's richest gold mines, including those of the Transvaal.

precession of the equinoxes. The gradual change in the *equinoxes* owing to the fact that the direction of the earth's *axis* in space is very slowly changing: a slight 'wobble' causes the North Pole of the *celestial sphere* to describe a circle once in about 25,800 years.

precipitation. In meteorology, the deposits of water, in either liquid or solid form, which reach the earth from the atmosphere. It therefore includes not only rain, but also sleet, snow, and hail, which fall from the clouds, and dew and hoar frost. The total depth of liquid deposited – the solid forms being melted – is measured at meteorological and climatological stations by means of a *rain gauge*, and expressed in millimetres or inches. *Rainfall* is often used synonymously with precipitation to denote the total amount of water in all forms which is deposited on a given area.

pressure, atmospheric. See *atmospheric pressure*.

pressure gradient. The rate at which the atmospheric pressure changes horizontally in a certain direction on the earth's surface, as indicated by the position of the *isobars* on a *weather chart*; when the isobars are close together, a rapid change of pressure from point to point at right-angles to the isobars is shown, and the gradient is steep, while when they are far apart the gradient is slight. The isobars thus bear a relation to the pressure gradient similar to that of the *contours* on a map to the height gradient.

pressure tendency. The change in atmospheric pressure which has taken place at a given spot during a certain period, usually three hours, preceding a meteorological observation. A number of pressure tendencies from various points in an area is valuable in showing the regions where the pressure is in process of rising or falling. See *isallobar*.

prevailing wind. The wind, indicated by direction, at a certain place or in a certain area which has a considerably higher frequency than any other.

profile, river. The *longitudinal profile* or *long-profile* of a river is a section showing its slope from source to mouth; initially it is irregular, with rapids and waterfalls in the upper reaches, but later it is much smoother. The section then takes the form of a curve, much flattened towards the mouth, with the concavity upwards. (See *thalweg*.) A river is constantly engaged in the processes of *degradation* and *aggradation*, and if these two processes are balanced the river is said to be graded or to have achieved its *profile of equilibrium*, a condition which in practice is seldom if ever attained.

profile, soil. A section through the soil showing the different horizons, or layers, usually designated by the letters, A, B, and C, which extend downwards from the surface to the parent material. (See Fig. p. 173.)

promontory. A headland; a cliff or crag projecting into the sea.

protection. In international trade, the term 'protection' signifies the means by which a country seeks to exclude the foreign products and industries which would compete with its own. A favourite device is to charge import duties on the foreign competitors. For the opposing principle see *free trade*.

protectorate. A term which is used very loosely to denote the relations between two states, one of which exercises some form of control over the other. It varies between suzerainty and a mere agreement on the part of the superior state to protect the safety of the inferior state, but a common feature of all protectorates is the prohibition of foreign relations for the latter, except those permitted by the former. The term is also applied to the protected state itself.

A typical soil profile.

psychrometer. An instrument designed to measure the *humidity* of the atmosphere; a *hygrometer*. One form, Assmann's psychrometer, is very similar to the ordinary hygrometer consisting of wet and dry bulb thermometers, past which a current of air is drawn by means of a small fan operated by clockwork; the temperatures registered by both thermometers are thus given under the same conditions, and the results are more reliable than with the ordinary hygrometer.

pteropod ooze. A calcareous *ooze* which consists chiefly of the shells of the floating molluscs known as pteropods, and covers relatively limited areas of the ocean bed. It occurs mainly on the ridges and plateaux which rise from the *deep-sea plain*. Below about 3,000 m, the shells of the pteropods dissolve in the sea-water, and the ooze is thus limited to depths of about 1,000–3,000 m. At these depths it occurs off certain sub-tropical and tropical islands, mainly in the Atlantic Ocean, e.g. round the Azores, to the west of the Canary Islands, etc.

puddingstone. Popular name for *conglomerate*.

pumice. A type of volcanic rock which was made extremely light and porous owing to the sudden release of steam and gases as it was solidifying, the material swelling up into a froth. Pumice will float on water, and it occurs in all the deposits which lie on the bed of the deepest parts of the oceans especially in *red clay*.

puna. The higher and bleaker parts of the plateaux of the Andes, lying between about 3,000 and 5,000 m above sea level. Here the climatic conditions of the *tierra fria* are exaggerated, and temperatures tend to extremes. Even in summer the nights are bitterly cold; in winter the wind is so cold that it sears the skin, penetrates almost any type of clothing, and causes a number of diseases, especially of the lungs, being known in parts of Bolivia as the 'Harvest of Death'. Although the sunshine may be intensely bright and hot, in the shade the air is frigid, and is avoided by the inhabitants. Heavy shawls and ponchos, or cloaks, are worn to protect the body, and woollen masks to protect the face. Except for the three months when rain occurs, the lakes and rivers mainly consist of shallow *salt pans* and dry watercourses. Only the hardiest of crops, such as barley and potatoes, can be grown, and wool-bearing animals such as the llama and the alpaca are raised on the coarse grass. The Puna Brava of Bolivia, extending from about 4,000 m to the snowline, is an even bleaker and more inhospitable region.

purga (Russian). The cold, north-easterly wind of Siberia, often bearing snow, especially so-called in the *tundra*; it is the same wind as the *buran*.

pusztas (Hungarian). The flat, almost treeless grasslands or *steppes* of the Hungarian Plains.

puy (French). A term used in Auvergne, France, for a hill which is the cone of an extinct volcano, with or without associated lava; there are many examples in that region, of which the largest is the Puy de Dôme (1,460 m), formed when a great blob of viscous lava was ejected on to the earth's surface (it has no crater). Puys also occur in other parts of the world. They may occur as isolated hills or in groups.

pygmies. People of exceptionally small stature, in general those whose average height is below 1.5 m (5 ft). Some of the best-known examples are certain tribes of the *equatorial forests* of Central Africa who live within a few degrees of the equator, and are known as Negrillos; they have an average height of about 1.37 m (4 ft 6 in.), and have a dark, yellowish skin. The Asiatic pygmies, inhabiting parts of Malaya, Sumatra, the Philippines, New Guinea, and other regions of south-east Asia, are known as Negritos.

pyramidal peak.* See *horn*.

pyrheliometer. An instrument for measuring the *radiation* from the sun.

pyroclasts or **pyroclastic rocks.** Fragmental rock materials produced in volcanic eruptions and usually classified according to size, e.g. *volcanic bombs*, *lapilli*, *volcanic ash*.

Q

qanat. See *ganat*.

quadrant. An instrument in the shape of a graduated quarter-circle, formerly used in astronomy and navigation, particularly for measuring angles and altitudes. See *sextant*.

quadrature. The position of a heavenly body when, as viewed from the earth, it makes a right-angle with the direction of the sun; the term is usually applied to the moon, and thus coincides with first quarter and last quarter. See *moon, phases of*.

quadroon. The offspring of a *mulatto* and a white, thus having one-quarter Negro blood.

quagmire. An area of soft, wet ground, which shakes or yields underfoot; a *marsh*; a quaking *bog*.

quaking bog. See *bog*.

quartz. One of the commonest minerals, being present in many rocks and soils in a wide variety of forms, and often filling veins, joints, and cavities; it often contains admixtures of other minerals, including *ores*. It consists of silica, a compound of silicon and oxygen. It forms the major proportion of most sands. In the pure state quartz is glassy in appearance, but it also occurs in translucent and coloured forms; it is so hard that it will scratch glass.

quartzite. An extremely hard, resistant rock consisting mainly of *quartz* (usually 90 per cent or more) and formed from a *sandstone*: unlike the latter, it is non-porous.

Quaternary. The term applied by some geologists to the later of the two sub-divisions or *periods* of the *Cainozoic era* in the geological scale of time, following the *Tertiary* and extending from about 1 million years ago to the present time. Other geologists, however, regard it as the modern *era*, the last of the four major divisions in the geological scale of time following the *pre-Cambrian – Palaeozoic* (Primary), *Mesozoic* (Secondary), and *Cainozoic* (Tertiary).

quicksand. A mass of loose or unstable sand saturated with water, at the mouth of a river, on the sea coast, etc.; it has the nature of a liquid, and quickly engulfs a heavy object placed on its surface.

R

race. A rapid *tidal current*, usually through a narrow channel, often caused by the *tidal range* at one end of the channel being greater than that at the other. A race may also occur near a headland separating two bays.

radial drainage. The type of drainage produced when streams flow outwards from a central dome-shaped upland.

Sketch-map of the Lake District, England, illustrating radial drainage.

radiation. The process by which a body emits radiant energy, e.g. in the form of heat; it causes a loss of heat, and therefore cooling. Radiant energy is constantly emitted in all directions by the sun, some of this reaching the earth and being converted into heat; the earth is constantly losing heat into space by radiation. During the day, the heat received from the sun by *insolation* exceeds the amount lost by radiation, and the temperature rises till a maximum is reached. At night the reverse is the case, and the temperature falls till a minimum is reached. In summer, when the days are long and the sun is high, the ground grows gradually warmer, but in winter, when the days are short and the sun is low, radiation so far exceeds insolation that the ground becomes cold. The land loses heat by radiation more rapidly than water, and high ground more rapidly than low ground.

radiation fog. A type of *fog* chiefly experienced in low-lying areas when *radiation* at night causes considerable cooling, so that the air temperature falls below the *dew point* and leads to condensation. It is most likely to occur, then, when the air is moist, the sky clear, and the wind very light.

radiocarbon dating. A method of dating objects up to about 70,000 years in age, developed in 1949 at the University of Chicago, of great value in *geophysics*, archaeology, etc. The technique is based on the absorption by living matter of the radioactive isotope of carbon known as C^{14} from the atmosphere, and the cessation of this absorption at death; thereafter the content of C^{14} diminishes at a known rate, being reduced by one-half during a period of about 5,600 years.

radiolarian ooze. A type of *ooze*, which is found on the ocean bed only in deep, tropical seas. It is a variety of *red clay*, from which it is distinguished by the presence of many siliceous organic remains, especially the shells of the small, simple animals known as radiolaria; it is therefore named after these. It covers considerable areas of the Pacific Ocean, particularly between 5° and 15° N, and a limited area in the Indian Ocean.

radiosonde. A self-recording instrument used in meteorology, usually for measuring atmospheric pressure, temperature, and humidity in the upper atmosphere, together with a radio transmitter, being attached to a hydrogen-filled balloon. The apparatus is released, and the readings of pressure, temperature, and humidity at heights up to 18 km (11 miles) or more are sent to the ground station by the radio transmitter. It can be used in all weather conditions, and additionally enables wind speeds at various heights to be calculated.

railway gauge. See *gauge, railway*.

rain. Separate water drops which fall to the earth from the clouds, having been formed by the *condensation* of water vapour in the atmosphere. Condensation of this water vapour is brought about by the rise of air to considerable heights above the earth's surface, where *clouds* are formed: many of the small water droplets coalesce, grow in size, and finally fall to the ground. Rain is distinguished from *drizzle* by the fact that its drops have a diameter exceeding 0.5 mm. See *rainfall*.

rainbow. The coloured bow consisting of the colours of the spectrum, seen when sunlight falls on rain, being caused by the reflection and refraction of the light in the water drops. The red is on the outside edge of the bow, the violet on the inside in the *primary bow*. Some of the light falling on to the water drops, however, is twice reflected, and a *secondary* or *outer bow* is formed with the colours in the reverse order of those of the primary bow, and much less distinct. The primary bow has an angular radius of about 42°, the secondary bow one of about 54°.

rain day. In the British Isles, a period of 24 hours from 0900 hours GMT on which at least 0.2 mm of rain is recorded. See *wet day*.

rainfall. The total amount of rain deposited on a given area during a given time, as measured by a *rain gauge*. Melted snow and hail are included with the rain, and this *precipitation* from the clouds constitute most of the rainfall; very small additions are made for dew, hoar frost, and rime. Three different types of rainfall are generally recognized, depending on the process by which the clouds were formed: *orographic*, *cyclonic*, and *convectional*. The comparatively heavy rainfall received on the western slopes of the Sierra Nevada, USA, and the mountains of western Britain, for instance, is largely orographic; cyclonic rainfall, due to depressions, provides much of the rain of the eastern parts of the USA, Britain and continental Europe; conventional rain is typical of the equatorial regions. The rainfall of a place is very largely dependent upon the prevailing winds; it varies seasonally in many regions according to the movement of the sun and the accompanying movement of the rain belts. For climatological purposes, the most valuable rainfall data are the mean deposits for different areas for the different months or seasons, or for the whole year.

rain forest. See *equatorial forest*.

rain gauge. An instrument which is used for measuring *rainfall*. It consists of a funnel fitted into a glass vessel, which holds the rain that has fallen on to the funnel. The water cannot evaporate from this vessel, and when it has been collected for a certain period, it is measured in another vessel graduated according to the area of the mouth of the funnel. The rainfall is thus expressed as a depth, usually in millimetres or inches, and represents the depth to which the ground would have been covered with rain, assuming that none could escape, since the rain gauge was last read. The rain gauge is normally read twice a day. See *hyetograph*.

rain shadow. An area which has a relatively light average rainfall because it is sheltered from the prevailing rain-bearing winds by a range of mountains or hills; it is therefore situated on the lee side of the range. On the windward slopes, by contrast, the rainfall is extremely heavy, owing to the forced ascent of the moisture-laden air. This air is warmed and dried by descent on the lee side, so that little rain is deposited there. One of the best-known examples is provided by the Western Ghats in India: the western slopes, exposed for about five months to the SW monsoon, have a very heavy rainfall, in places exceeding 5,000 mm, but on the eastern slopes – in the rain shadow – the annual rainfall at many places is 600 mm or less.

rain spell. In the British Isles, a period of at least fifteen consecutive days, each of which has had at least 0.2 mm of rain. See also *absolute drought*.

raised beach. A beach which has been raised by earth movement to form a narrow *coastal plain*; it is often bounded by inland cliffs. If more than one rise has taken place, there may be raised beaches at different levels.

rand (Afrikaans). In South Africa, a low ridge of hills, often covered with scrub. The term 'The Rand' is often used specifically for the Witwatersrand, in the southern Transvaal, famous for its rich gold-bearing *reefs*.

range. (1) A line of mountain ridges, with or without peaks, in which the crests are relatively narrow; if the altitude is comparatively low, the ridges may constitute a range of hills rather than of mountains.

(2) In the United States, an extensive area of land over which animals, usually cattle, wander (range) for fodder – often grassland such as the *prairie*.

range of temperature. The difference between the highest and lowest temperatures of a place during a certain period. For climatological comparisons, the value most often used is the *mean annual range* of temperature, the difference between the mean temperatures of the warmest and coldest months. Mean annual ranges are very high in the midst of the great land masses, e.g. in Siberia, but relatively low in the southern hemisphere, owing to the moderating influence of the oceans. At Verkhoyansk, Siberia, for instance, the mean annual range is 66°C; at Quito, Ecuador, practically on the equator, the mean annual range is 0.4°C, though the diurnal range is about 20°C. The *annual extreme range* is the difference between the mean extremes of the warmest and coldest months. The *absolute range* of temperature is the difference between the highest and lowest temperatures ever experienced at a place.

The *mean diurnal range* for any period is the mean difference between the highest and lowest temperatures for each day of that period, a month being usually chosen, over a number of years. Its variation in the different regions is less than that of the mean annual range; both ranges, however, depend very largely on the geographical position of the place. In many regions, especially near the equator, the mean diurnal range is much greater than the mean annual range: for, to obtain the latter, the mean monthly temperatures are first calculated, and this causes the daily maximum and daily minimum temperatures partially to neutralize each other.

rape. In Sussex, England, historically, one of six districts into which the county was divided in the Middle Ages and recorded in Domesday Book. Each rape extended roughly from S to N and was supposed to contain a river, a forest and a castle.

rapids. Part of a river where the current is flowing with more than normal swiftness. They may be caused by a sudden steepening of the slope, or by unequal resistance in the successive rocks traversed by the river. They are often due to *outcrops* of an unusually hard rock. At the outcrops, erosion is less than on the softer rock, and the slope of the river above each outcrop thus decreases, while below it the slope increases; over the hard rocks, then, rapids or *waterfalls* are formed. If the layer of hard rock dips gently downstream, rapids rather than waterfalls are generally produced.

rasputitsa (Russian). In Siberia, the period of several weeks between the winter, when the ground is snow-covered, lakes and rivers are frozen, and transport is largely by sledge, and summer, when the ground is again dry, and transport is by wheeled vehicles over the now usable roads. It is a period of extensive floods and mud, owing to the melting of snow and ice, and transport of any kind is extremely difficult.

rational horizon. See *horizon, rational, true* or *astronomical.*

ravine. A long narrow depression in the earth's surface, rather smaller than a *valley* but larger than a *gully.* Several gullies often lead to a ravine, and several ravines to a valley.

raw materials. Goods which are utilized by certain industries for manufacture into consumable commodities; they include partially manufactured goods, such as wood pulp and wheaten flour, which are afterwards subjected to further manufacturing processes. Some raw materials may become finished products, or vice versa: e.g. coal tar, formerly the finished product of the coal distillation process, is now the raw material of a host of chemical products.

reach. The stretch or section along a river, usually between two bends. Along a canal, which generally has a virtually straight course, it is the section between two locks. On some rivers various reaches have been given specific names: e.g. Long Reach, on the R Thames.

Réaumur scale. The temperature scale, devised by René de Réaumur (1687–1757) and now little used, in which the freezing point of water is $0°$ and the boiling point is $80°$.

recessional moraine. A *moraine* more or less parallel to the terminal moraine, formed in a similar way but during a pause in the recession of the *ice sheet* or *glacier.*

Arrangement of strata in a recumbent fold.

recumbent fold. An *overfold* in which the axial plane is virtually horizontal.

red clay. A type of deposit which covers most of the deeper parts, the *abyssal* region, of the ocean bed, at depths greater than about 4,000 m, and differs from the *oozes* in that it consists mainly of inorganic material. It is composed very largely of minute particles of aluminium silicate, and is thus a true *clay*; it contains volcanic material, especially *pumice*, meteoric dust, and occasionally the teeth of sharks, etc., which resist decay and solution; its uniformly red colour is due to the presence of iron oxide. Red clay covers a very extensive area in the Pacific Ocean, a more restricted area in the Indian Ocean, and several parts of the Atlantic Ocean.

red mud. A marine deposit very similar to *blue mud*, and deriving its reddish colour from the presence of iron oxide. It consists of wind-borne *terrigenous* dust; it occurs off the tropical Atlantic coast of South America, and in the China Sea, where it is due to *loess*.

reef. (1) A ridge of rocks, lying near the surface of the sea, which may be visible at low tide, but is usually covered by the water. The most common type is the *coral reef*.

(2) A mineral vein, especially of gold-bearing quartz.

reforestation. The planting of trees on land where a forest has previously stood, but has been destroyed, e.g. by a forest fire. See *afforestation*.

reg (Arabic). In the Sahara, the extensive areas of flat, desert plain from which the fine sand has been blown away, leaving the surface covered with small stones and gravel. See *hammada*.

regelation. The process by which ice is frozen again, after it has been melted under pressure, or by which pieces of ice are joined together under pressure. The melting is due to the fact that the melting point of ice is lowered by pressure, so that on the release of that pressure the melting point rises, and the water freezes again. Regelation is believed to contribute to the movement of a *glacier*.

181

regolith. See *mantle rock*.

regur or **black cotton-earth.** The dark-coloured volcanic soil of the NW Deccan, in India, where cotton is largely cultivated. It is very retentive of moisture, which it holds long after the rains have ceased, but later in the dry season it has a tendency to crack badly.

rejuvenation. The process by which erosive activity is renewed, applied especially to rivers, which are said to be rejuvenated. The rejuvenation of a river may be brought about by the uplift of the land over which it flows, or by a fall in sea-level, so that it begins to cut into its bed once more, and a new *cycle of erosion* is begun.

relative humidity. The ratio between the actual amount of water vapour in a given volume of the air and the amount which would be present if the air were saturated at the same temperature, usually expressed as a percentage. It thus affords a measure of the relative dampness of the atmosphere, and is determined by means of a *hygrometer*.

relict mountains. A term, now little used, for mountains which owe their present form to denudation, having been worn down, for instance, from a *plateau* or a *horst*, or from a chain of *folded mountains*, or simply from inclined strata. See *monadnock*, *inselberg*.

relief. The differences in elevation of any part of the earth's surface.

relief map. A map which seeks to depict the surface relief of an area. A *contour* map and a *photo relief* map both achieve this object. A relief model shows surface relief in three dimensions, though not necessarily to scale. The vertical scale usually has to be much exaggerated; 1 cm on the vertical scale, for intance, may represent only one-tenth or even one-twentieth of the distance that it represents on the horizontal scale.

rendzina (Polish). A dark-coloured *intrazonal soil* which has developed under grass on limestone or chalk. See also *terra rossa*.

representative fraction. See *map scale*.

reversed fault. See *thrust fault*.

rhumb-line or **loxodrome.** A line on the earth's surface which cuts all meridians at the same angle. A vessel which sails along such a line is said to take a rhumb-line course; if proceeding from one point to another directly to the NE, for example, it will maintain a north-easterly direction throughout the voyage. If the two points are near the equator, or almost on the same meridian, the difference between the rhumb-line route and the *great circle route* is comparatively small, but in high latitudes, when one point lies on a meridian far distant from that of the other, the rhumb-line route is considerably longer than the great circle route. On the map according to *Mercator's projection*, the rhumb-line is depicted as a straight line.

ria. A long narrow bay or inlet into the sea coast, caused by submergence in a region of ridges and furrows where these are not parallel to the coast (see *discordant coast*), the valleys being thus drowned. It often branches at the end, and, unlike the *fiord*, gradually deepens towards

Rias along the coast of SW Ireland.

the sea; rivers which were once tributary to the main river valley often flow separately into the ria, and the latter is enclosed by the walls of the former valley. The most resistant rocks of the valley form islets in the ria. Some of the best-known rias are those of the coasts of SW Ireland and NW Spain.

Richter scale. A scale devised in 1935 by the US seismologist C. F. Richter for measuring the magnitude of an earthquake: it has a range nominally 0–10, but hitherto the largest earthquakes have given values between 8.5 and 9.0.

ridge and valley. A descriptive term for terrain that consists of long, more or less parallel ridges of resistant rocks with intervening valleys where the weaker rocks have been much eroded. The classic example is the 'Ridge and Valley province' of the Appalachian Mountains, USA, between the Cumberland Plateau and the Blue Ridge, where the ridges are largely composed of hard sandstone and the valleys of soft shale and limestone.

ridge of high pressure. An elongated area of high atmospheric pressure, forming an extension to an *anticyclone* or high-pressure area, in the

Diagram illustrating the formation of a rift valley.

same way as a ridge projecting from a mountain. It is the opposite of a *trough of low pressure*.

Riding. One of the three districts into which the county of Yorkshire was historically divided – North, West and East Riding; the divisions were introduced by the Danes and were known as Thridings. Lincolnshire was divided into similar districts: Lindsey (N), which contains the chalky Lincolnshire Wolds; Kesteven (SW), wooded and marshy; and Holland (SE), wholly *fen* country.

rift valley. A valley which has been formed by the sinking of land between two roughly parallel *faults*; such a valley is long in proportion to its width. The best-known example is the rift valley which extends through Syria, Israel and Jordan, and East Africa, over 4,800 km (3,000 miles) in length; it includes the Sea of Galilee, the valley of the River Jordan, and the Dead Sea, the Gulf of Aqaba, and the Red Sea, and runs through Lake Rudolf and several smaller lakes to Lake Malawi, with a branch through Lakes Tanganyika, Edward, and Albert (Mobutu Sese Soko). Examples of smaller rift valleys are the Rhine valley between the Vosges Mountains and the Black Forest, and the Central Lowlands of Scotland. The term *graben* (German) is sometimes regarded as synonymous with rift valley. (See Fig. above.)

rimaye. See *bergschrund*.

rime. A deposit of ice crystals formed when supercooled water drops come into contact with exposed objects and freeze on them. Rime that is formed in this way from the water drops in fog is usually known as *soft rime*; when it is formed by the freezing of water drops in *drizzle*, it is usually known as *hard rime*.

river. A stream of fresh water which for at least part of the year is larger than a brook or creek, and flows by a natural channel, being confined within banks, into the sea, or into a lake, or into another river. In a semi-arid region, however, a river may become no more than a series of pools during the dry season; in an arid region it may disappear in a desert. A river may originate, at the point known as its *source*, in a number of rivulets, a spring, a lake, etc.; the path it follows is known

River capture by the more powerful river (left); the bend at E is the elbow of capture.

as its *course*; it gradually swells as it is joined by *tributaries*, all the rivers together forming a *river system*; it enters the sea or a lake or a larger river by its *mouth*. The *upper* parts of a river are situated near its source, the *lower* parts near its mouth. A river is often described as passing through successive stages of development, from youth to maturity to old age (see *cycle of erosion*).

river basin. See *basin* (2).

river capture, river piracy, or **beheading.** The action of a river in acquiring the headstreams of a second river by enlarging its drainage area at the expense of the other. This process is carried out by the more powerful river, which erodes its valley more deeply and cuts back into the valley of its weaker neighbour. The headstreams of the latter are thus diverted into the former, and the latter is said to have undergone *beheading*, or have been *beheaded*; the bend at which the capture took place is known as the *elbow of capture*. See *misfit river*.

river piracy. See *river capture*.

river port. See *port*.

river profile. See *profile, river*.

river terrace. A platform of land formed beside a river flowing across a plain, when for some reason it has commenced vertical *corrasion* again, possibly because of *rejuvenation*. Its channel is thus deepened, and the *flood-plain* becomes a flat alluvial area well above the level of the river even at flood-time. After vertical corrasion has ceased, lateral corrasion will recommence, and a new flood-plain will be formed below the first one. If vertical corrasion again recommences, the second flood-plain, too, will form a river terrace, and the process may continue till a series of terraces at different levels has been created by the side of the river.

Riviera (Italian). A name originally applied to the narrow coastal strip around the Gulf of Genoa in Italy (Italian Riviera) and the adjoining coastland of France (French Riviera), but since extended to other coastal areas similarly endowed with popular resorts and beaches, e.g. Portuguese Riviera (W of Lisbon), Cornish Riviera.

rivulet. A small river or stream.

roadstead. An open anchorage for ships, which may be sufficiently sheltered to give protection from heavy seas, usually by reefs, sandbanks, or islands.

Roaring Forties. The region between latitudes 40° and 50° S where the prevailing westerly winds, being unobstructed by land, blow over the open oceans with great regularity and strength. See *brave west winds*. It is a region where *depressions* follow one another all through the year, and the weather is stormy, rainy, and comparatively mild. The term is also sometimes applied to the winds themselves.

roches moutonnées (French). The hillocks of rock of a glaciated valley (a valley down which a glacier has flowed) which have been smoothed and marked with *striae* by the glacier on the upstream side and left rough and rugged, with steeper slopes, on the downstream side. The upstream side, against which the glacier has flowed, is ground down by the stones embedded in the ice, but on the downstream side the glacier pulls away any blocks which are sufficiently loosened by the development of joints. Thus the appearance of the valley is often very different according to the direction from which it is viewed: looking down the valley, the rocks appear smooth and convex, while looking up the valley they appear rugged.

rock. One of the solid materials of which the earth's crust is mainly composed, being made up of *minerals*; in some cases, it consists of only a single mineral, but usually of several minerals. A rock, however, does not normally have a definite chemical composition, as a mineral does. The many different kinds of rocks in the earth's crust are divided into three major classes – *sedimentary*, *igneous*, and *metamorphic*. More popularly, a rock is any large mass of the harder portions of the earth's crust.

rock drumlin. A *drumlin* which consists of a core of rock covered by a layer of *till*.

rock flour. The finely-ground solid matter produced by abrasion of the bed of a glacier by the stones and rocks embedded in its base, as they move forward with the glacier down the valley.

rock-glacier. A tongue or 'stream' of rock fragments, resembling a *glacier* in form, and composed of *scree*, which moves gradually downwards through the action of alternate frost and thaw and gravity; such rock-glaciers are especially numerous in Alaska.

ropy or **corded lava.** A mass of *lava* which has solidified so that its surface is smooth and exhibits ropy or corded shapes; the Hawaiian term pahoehoe is sometimes used. The ropy appearance of the pahoehoe is due to the formation of a thin skin on the surface while the molten lava is cooling; the liquid lava underneath continues to flow for a time, and shapes the skin into rope-like lengths, which remain when the lava has completely solidified.

rotation of crops. The system of farming by which different crops are repeatedly grown on the same land in a specific order. For field crops the duration of a complete cycle usually varies between two years and eight years, and depends on the number of crops and their frequency of change. Among the advantages of a rotation are the more effective control of weeds, pests, and diseases, and the more economical utilization of nutrients in the soil. The well-known Norfolk rotation, the first type to be generally adopted in England, is completed in four years: roots (e.g. turnips) are followed by barley, then grass and clover (which replenishes the soil with nitrogen), then wheat (which requires abundant nitrogen), in successive years.

run-off. That portion of the rainfall which ultimately reaches the streams; it consists of the water which flows off the surface, instead of sinking into the ground, together with some of the water which originally sank into the ground and joins it later in the streams. The part of the rainfall which leaves the ground surface at once and enters streams is called the *immediate run-off*. Most of the water that sinks into the ground eventually returns to the surface by seepage and from springs, and is called *delayed run-off*. The run-off is faster and greater (1) during heavy rain than during a protracted drizzle, (2) on clay soils than on sandy soils, (3) on frozen soils than on frostless soils, (4) in treeless areas than in the forests. The ratio between run-off and rainfall varies considerably with climatic conditions.

S

saddle-reef. A lens-shaped strip of rock formed in a similar way to a *phacolith*, but consisting of *quartz*. The term is used principally by miners, and is sometimes wrongly assumed to be synonymous with phacolith.

saeter or **seter** (Norwegian). In Norway, a mountain pasture which lies well above the valley or fiord and is used in summer for grazing livestock; it is the counterpart of the *Alps* of Switzerland. The term is also applied to the entire mountain farm, used only in summer, to which the pasture belongs, including the living quarters, cattle sheds, etc.

sagebrush. A type of vegetation, common in the *semi-desert* regions of the western United States, where the common sagebrush predominates. Nevada, which has considerable areas of such vegetation, is sometimes known as the Sagebrush State.

St Elmo's Fire. A luminous discharge of electricity sometimes seen during stormy weather at the extremities of tall objects, such as the mast-heads and yard-arms of ships and the tops of trees.

St Luke's Summer. A period of fine weather supposed to occur about St Luke's Day, 18 October.

St Martin's Summer. A period of fine weather supposed to occur about St Martin's Day, 11 November.

salina (Spanish) or **saline.** See *salt pan*.

salinity. The degree of saltness of the oceans and seas, lakes and rivers, usually expressed as the number of parts per thousand, or the weight of salt dissolved in 1,000 parts of water. The mean salinity of sea-water, for instance, is 35 per thousand, but the salinity varies from over 40 per thousand in the Red Sea to about 30 per thousand in the polar seas. Near the equator there is a region of relatively low salinity, owing to the heavy rains. Bordering this belt are areas of higher salinity, for here the *trade winds* generally are dry, cause rapid evaporation, and the surface waters thus become salt. Beyond these areas, the salinity decreases polewards, for rainfall is greater and evaporation slighter.

Although river water contains a small quantity of mineral salts in solution, it is comparatively fresh. A partially enclosed sea like the Baltic Sea, which receives many large rivers, and also has heavy falls of rain and snow and small evaporation, thus has a salinity below 12 per thousand. The Black Sea, too, is comparatively fresh, with a salinity of about 17 per thousand. The Red Sea, on the other hand, receives no large rivers, has great evaporation and low rainfall, and thus has a salinity of over 40 per thousand. For similar reasons, the salinity of the Mediterranean Sea is over 37 per thousand. Seas and lakes with no outlet to the ocean have a still higher salinity, for the salts brought down by rivers have accumulated since their formation. The salinity of the Dead Sea is about 250 per thousand. See *salt lake*.

Of the 35 parts of dissolved salt contained on the average in 1,000 parts of sea-water, over 27 parts consist of sodium chloride or common salt, the other main constituents being magnesium chloride, magnesium sulphate and calcium sulphate.

salpausselkä (Finnish). In Finland, ridges of sand and gravel running from east to west, usually interpreted as being a series of terminal (recessional) *moraines* formed in the Quaternary *Ice Age*.

salt dome or **salt plug**. A mass of salt, often roughly circular in shape, which has been forced upwards by subterranean pressures, penetrating rock strata which originally lay above it. Many salt domes have a cap rock of limestone.

salt lake. A lake, situated in an arid region, which has no outlet and so accumulates salts brought down by the rivers that enter it. Loss of water by evaporation at least equals the supply of water by precipitation and inflow, and the lake gradually becomes more salty. The Dead Sea has a *salinity* about 250 per thousand, the Great Salt Lake, Utah, USA, about 220 per thousand, and part of the Caspian Sea about 170 per thousand. If its climate becomes less arid, a salt lake may become a fresh one in time; if the climate of a fresh lake becomes more arid, it may eventually become a salt lake.

salt-marsh. A *marsh* which at times is flooded by the sea, or an inland marsh in an arid region in which the water contains a higher proportion of salt.

salt pan. A hollow, formerly containing water, in which a deposit of salt is left behind owing to evaporation of the water. The terms *salina* and *saline* are sometimes used to denote a salt pan.

salt plug. See *salt dome*.

samoon or **samun** (Persian). In Iran, a hot, dry, *föhn* type of wind which blows from the mountains of Kurdistan (NW).

sand. A mass of minute particles of rock material which is finer than *gravel* but coarser than *silt*. It is also not so fine as *dust*, and is not normally lifted by the winds far above the earth's surface. Its movement is thus controlled by obstacles in its path, and it is often heaped up in mounds called *dunes*. Most of the rock-making minerals of the earth's crust occur in sands, but comparatively few are common; of these, *quartz* is by far the most abundant. When consolidated, sand

SANDBANK

forms a *sandstone*. In pedology, the mineral particles of a soil are defined as coarse sand when their diameter is between 2 mm and 0.2 mm, fine sand when their diameter is between 0.2 mm and 0.02 mm. See *clay* (2), *silt*.

sandbank. A submerged ridge of sand in the sea or a river often exposed at low water.

sand-bar. See *bar* (2).

sandur (Icelandic). See *outwash plain*.

sandstone. A porous sedimentary rock consisting of grains of sand bound together by such substances as calcium carbonate or silica. Sandstones are characterized by the nature of the binding material, e.g. calcareous sandstone, and their colour largely depends upon it. Some sandstones are well cemented, containing considerable *quartz*, and form extremely durable rocks; other sandstones are poorly cemented, and readily disintegrate on exposure.

sandstorm. A storm in which a mass of relatively coarse sand is blown along through the air by a strong wind. The sand particles are rarely raised more than 15 to 30 m above the surface, and are not carried far from their source. A sandstorm should be distinguished from a *dust-storm*.

Sanson-Flamsteed sinusoidal projection. A modified *conical projection*, being a particular case of *Bonne's projection*. The equator is chosen for the standard parallel, and thus is a straight line truly divided. The central meridian is a straight line at right-angles to the equator, and is truly divided; the parallels are horizontal straight lines at equal distances apart, and are truly divided, and the meridians on each side of the central meridian are formed by drawing curves through corresponding points on each parallel. The projection is termed sinusoidal because these meridians are sine curves. It is homolographic or equal-area, but shapes are distorted towards the margins; in atlases it is frequently used for the map of Africa, for the extent of this continent in latitude is divided nearly equally by the equator, and its extent in longitude is only moderate.

Santa Anna or **Santa Ana.** The northerly to easterly wind of southern California which, blowing from the deserts and having been heated by descent from the mountains, is hot, dry, and dusty. Like the *sirocco* of the Mediterranean area, it causes much discomfort to the inhabitants and considerable damage to crops by drying up the vegetation. It is mainly experienced in winter, being due to the passage of depressions, but it causes the worst destruction if it occurs in spring, when the fruit trees are in blossom, or when the young fruit is formed.

saprophyte. A plant which lives on decaying organic matter. Most of the saprophytes are fungi.

sarsen. Term for a block of cemented sandstone several of which have been found on the *downs* of southern England, especially in Wiltshire,

Sanson-Flamsteed sinusoidal projection.

one of the remnants of a much larger mass of sandstone which has been eroded away in course of time. In ancient times the sarsens were erected in rings in various places, e.g. Stonehenge.

sastrugi (Russian). Ridges on the surface of the snow, caused by winds and varying in size according to the strength and duration of the wind and the condition of the snow surface: mainly applied to the USSR, but sometimes to snow-covered areas elsewhere.

satellite. In astronomy, a relatively small body which revolves round a *planet*; the *moon*, for example, is the satellite of the earth.

satellite town. A town which is separated from but associated with a large city. The term has sometimes been used as an alternative to *garden city*.

savanna or **tropical grassland.*** The region which borders the equatorial forest in each hemisphere, and thus lies between the latter and the hot deserts; the natural vegetation is mainly grass with scattered trees, for there are distinct wet and dry seasons, and the lack of rainfall during the latter prevents the growth of forests except in particularly moist places. The rains occur during the hot season, when the belt of equatorial calms moves to the savanna, but in the opposite season the savanna is under the influence of the drying *trade winds*. Thus in the hot season the vegetation freshens and grows vigorously, while in the opposite season the ground is parched and vegetation withers. The *llanos* and *campos* of South America are particular examples of savannas, but the most extensive savanna land is in Africa; the climate, in fact, is often known as the Sudan type. Because of the natural covering of grass, great herds of cattle are reared on the savanna. In some areas, e.g. the West Indies, the term 'savanna' signifies a local grass-covered tract.

191

scar. A crag; a steep, bare rock face: chiefly used in N England of a limestone cliff.

scarp.* See *escarpment*.

schattenseite (German). See *ubac*.

schist. A metamorphic rock which has been rendered cleavable into many thin plates through the effect of intense heat and pressure. Schists are named by their most conspicuous mineral, e.g. mica schist. Nearly all types of *sedimentary* and *igneous rocks* become schists if sufficient heat and pressure are applied.

scirocco. See *sirocco*.

sclerophyll. A tree or shrub with hard, leathery leaves which resist loss of water by *transpiration*, enabling it to withstand the hot, dry summer of the *Mediterranean climate*. Sclerophyll or *sclerophyllous woodland* thus refers to the typical Mediterranean vegetation of 'evergreen trees and shrubs'. See *maquis*.

scoria. A volcanic *lava* which is extremely vesicular owing to the escape of gases while it was still viscous, and somewhat resembles furnace clinker; it is formed during a violent eruption, and may be looked upon as a very coarse type of *pumice*.

Scotch mist. A type of precipitation consisting of a mass of minute water drops, resembling both *mist* and *drizzle*; it occurs usually in hilly or mountainous areas, and is due to the presence of dense clouds near to the ground. The name is derived from the fact that the phenomenon is common in Scotland, owing to the mountainous character of most of the country; elsewhere it is sometimes known as 'mizzle' – a combination of 'mist' and 'drizzle'.

scree. See *talus*.

scrub. A type of vegetation consisting of low-growing shrubs and stunted trees, largely about 1–2 m high, with occasional taller trees. It is found in regions which have insufficient rainfall or too poor a soil for forest growth, e.g. in *semi-arid* areas on the margins of the hot deserts; the inhabitants may be forced to follow a nomadic, pastoral life. Specific examples are the *mallee scrub* and *mulga scrub* of Australia; the *maquis* of the Mediterranean region is also described as scrub.

scud. Ragged fragments of very low cloud driven along by a strong wind, often beneath ordinary rain clouds.

sea. One of the smaller divisions of the oceans, especially if partially enclosed by land, e.g. Mediterranean Sea, North Sea; a large expanse of inland salt water, even if completely land-locked, e.g. Caspian Sea. The name is also loosely applied to the great mass of salt water which covers much of the earth's surface.

sea breeze. The diurnal movement of air from the sea to the land, caused by differential heating. During the day, the greater heating of the land causes the air to ascend, and air from the sea moves in to take its place. The sea breeze, like the *land breeze*, is thus most noticeable and most regular when temperature changes are most regular, i.e. when the *pressure gradient* is slight and the sky is clear; it then commences during the morning, and continues till the early evening, reaching maximum strength in the afternoon. It varies considerably in strength along the same coast, being influenced by topography. In temperate regions it does not usually exceed about 15 km (10 miles) per hour, though in the tropics it may reach 30 to 40 km (20–25 miles) per hour; it normally extends a few kilometres on each side of the coastline. Like the land breeze, it reaches its greatest development in the *doldrums*, where the pressure gradient is slight; here it does not, as elsewhere, merely modify the prevailing winds.

sea level. (1) The level which the surface of the sea would assume if uninfluenced by tides, or waves, or swell.

(2) The mean level between high and low tide at any place. See *mean sea level*.

sea loch. See *loch*.

sea-mile. A *nautical mile*.

seamount or **sea mount.** An isolated volcanic peak which rises from the ocean floor but does not reach the surface. It is distinguished from the *guyot* by the fact that the latter is flat-topped.

seaport. See *port*.

seasons. Those periods of the year which are characterized by special climatic conditions, mainly caused by the inclination of the earth's *axis* to the plane of the *ecliptic* and the revolution of the earth about the sun. In middle latitudes, four seasons, each of three months' duration, are generally recognized: in the northern hemisphere spring includes March, April, and May; summer, June, July, and August; autumn, September, October, and November; and winter, December, January, and February; in the southern hemisphere the seasons are the opposite of these, with spring including September, October, and November, and so on. The seasons are reckoned astronomically from specific dates (see *spring, summer, autumn, winter*). In areas where the oceanic influence is considerable, as in Great Britain, the seasonal variations are not nearly so large as in the interior of the continents, and the change from season to season is much more gradual. In regions outside the temperate zone, the year cannot be divided into four seasons. In much of the tropics, for instance, the seasons depend more on rainfall than on the position of the sun, and the year is usually divided into the wet or rainy season and the dry season; over much of India, and elsewhere in the monsoon regions, the year is divided into cold season, hot season, and rainy season. In the polar regions the changes between winter and summer take place so abruptly that spring and autumn are scarcely recognizable.

seaway. A *ship canal*: applied particularly to the St Lawrence Seaway, opened in 1959.

193

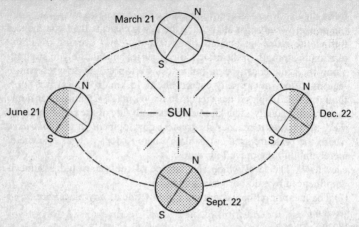

Diagram illustrating how the seasons depend on the position of the earth with respect to the sun. The positions shown are those at the equinoxes and the solstices.

sebkha, sabkha or **sabkhah** (Arabic). Along the low-lying sandy coastal strip of Saudi Arabia in the W and S parts of the Arabian Gulf, salt flats or shallow depressions; where the water evaporates, a deposit of salt mixed with sand is left, drying to a thin crust. If rain falls, the *sabkhah* becomes a morass; on drying again, the crust reappears.

second. (1) A unit of measurement of time equal to one-sixtieth of a minute.

(2) A unit of measurement of latitude or longitude equal to one-sixtieth of a *minute*.

secondary depression. A comparatively small area of low atmospheric pressure associated with a main or primary *depression*. It accompanies the primary depression, frequently revolves round the latter as they both move along their course, and in time may dominate the system and absorb the primary depression.

secular. Extending over a very long period of time.

sedimentary rocks. Rocks which have been deposited as beds, often as sediments (i.e. under water), forming one of the three main types of rocks which make up the earth's crust. They were laid down in distinct layers or strata, separated by *bedding planes*, principally by the sea, but also by lakes, or streams, or glaciers, or even by the wind; they are therefore often known as stratified rocks. Formerly they were sediments similar to the sands, gravels, and muds now being deposited in the seas, lakes, and rivers. The strata, which vary in thickness from a few centimetres to several metres, are sometimes horizontal, sometimes tilted; a considerable tilting of the strata indicates that the materials were disturbed after they had been deposited. Among the common forms of sedimentary rocks are *sandstone*, *shale*, *limestone*, and *conglomerate*, while coal is a sedimentary rock of organic origin. Sedimentary rocks are of extreme importance economically because they contain most of the world's mineral wealth, and historically because they contain the *fossils*. See *igneous rocks*, *metamorphic rocks*.

seepage. The slow oozing out of *ground water* on to the earth's surface, as distinct from the more pronounced flow of a *spring*; also applied to the slow escape of oil on to the earth's surface.

seiche. A variation in the level of the surface of a lake, somewhat resembling a tide, first observed on the Lake of Geneva; the rise and fall of the water may vary between a few centimetres and several metres. The causes of seiches include changes in atmospheric pressure, small earthquakes below the bed of the lake, and the wind. Seiches usually take place in the direction of the longest diameter of a lake but are occasionally transverse.

seif dune. A type of sand *dune*, common in the Sahara, which consists of a long sharp ridge lying parallel to the direction of the prevailing wind. The latter tends to increase the length of the dune, while cross-winds tend to increase its height and width.

seismic focus. The place below the earth's surface where an *earthquake* originates, and from which the vibrations spread in all directions; it is usually several kilometres beneath the surface. It is now held that an earthquake does not originate at a point, but along a line.

seismic sea wave. See *tsunami*.

seismograph. An instrument for recording *earthquake* shocks. The principle of its action consists in the disturbance of a portion of the apparatus by earth tremors, the suitable amplification of the motion thus produced, and then its recording. The vibrations used to be recorded by a pen tracing on a revolving drum, but in more modern instruments a photographic record is obtained on a moving film. Many seismographs are so sensitive that they will record vibrations due to an earthquake thousands of kilometres away, and its distance and also its direction may be approximately calculated. A properly equipped seismological observatory has three different seismographs; two of these will record the horizontal components of the earth's vibrations, one in an east–west and the other in a north–south direction, while the third will record the vertical components.

seismology. The science of the study of *earthquakes*.

seistan (Persian). A strong northerly wind, sometimes exceeding 110 km per hour, experienced throughout the summer in Seistan, a region of eastern Iran. It is known as the 'wind of 120 days'.

selva, selvas (Portuguese). The dense *equatorial forest* of the basin of the River Amazon in South America; the term is also sometimes applied to similar forests in other regions.

semi-arid, semi-desert. Terms applied to the climate and vegetation respectively of regions on the margins of deserts where the annual precipitation is slightly higher and the vegetation a little less sparse than in the latter, e.g. between hot desert and savanna. See *scrub*, *sagebrush*.

send. See *swash*.

sensible horizon. See *horizon, sensible* or *visible*.

séracs (French). Pinnacles or pillars of ice of various shapes into which a glacier is sometimes broken up when it reaches a steep slope, numbers of *crevasses* being formed in all directions and crossing one another. See *icefall*.

sericulture. The culture of silkworms for the production of raw silk.

serir (Arabic). In Libya, a stony, gravel-covered desert, similar to *reg*.

serra (Portuguese). A range of mountains: synonymous with *sierra* (Spanish).

sertão (Portuguese). A term which has been applied to the region of N E Brazil that is largely covered with *caatinga*. To Brazilians, however, it means simply the sparsely populated wilderness beyond the areas of permanent settlement, and may be regarded as equivalent to the American 'backwoods' and the Australian 'outback'.

sextant. An instrument used for measuring the angular distance between two objects. Very similar in design to the *quadrant*, it represents an improved form of the latter. It is most widely used in navigation, for by its means the apparent altitudes of celestial objects may be measured, so that the position of the observer in degrees of latitude and longitude may be calculated.

shake hole. A term used in the limestone districts of the Pennines, in England, for a *sinkhole*; it is usually dry.

shale. A fine-grained *sedimentary rock* produced from *clay*; it may have been formed by compression due to the weight of overlying rocks, or by cementation, e.g. by lime. Shales are rarely pure, and they are characterized by the main foreign substance they contain or by the type of cement. They are usually finely stratified, and thus readily split into thin layers, and they are so soft that they readily disintegrate.

shamal. The extremely constant north-westerly wind, experienced chiefly during the summer in Iraq, which blows across the Tigris–Euphrates plains, being controlled – like the *etesian winds* of the eastern Mediterranean and the *seistan* of eastern Iran – by the seasonal summer low over north-west India and Baluchistan. Being uninterrupted by depressions, it blows with great regularity. It is particularly strong during the day, when it carries clouds of dust, and causes severe duststorms, especially in southern Iraq, but there is normally a marked lull at night. The shamal is also experienced in winter, but with far less regularity.

sheep-tracks. See *terracettes*.

sheet erosion. See *soil erosion*.

shelterbelt. See *windbreak*.

shield volcano. A *volcano* formed from basic *lava* in a quiet eruption, with few explosions (a Hawaiian type of eruption), taking the shape of a gently-sloping dome like an inverted saucer. The best-known example is Mauna Loa, on Hawaii, the world's largest active volcano (height 4,170 m), which slopes gently downwards to an ocean depth of about 4,600 m where its vast base covers an area of about 47,000 sq. km (18,000 sq. miles).

shifting cultivation. A primitive form of *agriculture*, practised chiefly in the tropics, in which a plot of land is cultivated for a few years and then, when the crop declines because of soil exhaustion and the effects of pests and weeds, is deserted for another area. In the *equatorial forest*, for example, *slash-and-burn* methods are often applied: the vegetation is cut down and burned, so that plant nutrients are returned to the soil. Crops can thus be cultivated for a few seasons, and, when the soil shows loss of fertility, a new area is found and the procedure is repeated. See *ladang*.

shingle. A collection of loose pebbles often found on the seashore.

ship canal or **seaway.** A *canal* constructed of more than usual depth and width to permit the passage of ocean-going vessels. Its function is usually to shorten the voyage between two seas by cutting through an *isthmus*. The most important examples of this type are the Suez Canal, joining the Atlantic Ocean through the Mediterranean Sea with the Indian Ocean, and the Panama Canal, joining the Atlantic Ocean to the Pacific Ocean. Sometimes a ship canal is constructed from the sea inland, in order to convert an inland place into a seaport; examples are the Manchester Ship Canal and the St Lawrence Seaway.

shire. In England, in Anglo-Saxon times, a major unit of local government, divided into *hundreds* and *wapentakes*. After the Norman Conquest, the term 'county' was often applied to a shire.

shoal. (1) A ridge of sand or of rocks just below the surface of the sea or of a river, and therefore dangerous to navigation.

(2) A multitude of fish swimming near to the surface of the sea.

shooting star. See *meteor*. Practically the only relation that a shooting star bears to a true star is that, being seen at night against the sky, it *appears* to move among the stars.

shore-line. See *coastline*.

shott or **chott** (French). A shallow, temporary *salt lake* or *salt-marsh* found on the Algerian plateau and in the valleys south of the Atlas Mountains. The shotts extend for about 400 km (250 miles) over the plateau, which is often known as the Plateau of the Shotts. The dry basins left behind when the lakes have disappeared are characterized by deposits of salt and often by the absence of vegetation.

sial. The term used to denote the comparatively light rocks of the *lithosphere*, including granite, lying beneath the continents. The name is derived from the initial letters of silicon and aluminium, the principal elements contained in these rocks. See *sima*.

sidereal day. The period of time during which a star describes a complete circle in its apparent journey round the *Pole Star*, representing the period of rotation of the earth on its axis, with respect to the stars, and equal to 23 hours 56 minutes 4 seconds. It is thus about 4 minutes shorter than the Mean Solar Day. See *solar day, mean*.

sierra (Spanish). An elongated range of mountains with a jagged crest, mainly in Spain and Spanish America.

sill. A sheet of igneous rock, often almost horizontal, formed when *magma* forced its way between two layers of sedimentary rock and there cooled and solidified; its thickness may be a few centimetres or several hundred metres, but its horizontal extent is always great in comparison with its thickness. A sill may give rise to *dykes*; again, it often protects softer rocks beneath, and owing to unequal erosion may lead to the formation of a ridge or a flat-topped mountain. See *laccolith*.

silt. A deposit which is laid down in a river, lake, etc.; it is finer than *sand* but coarser than *clay*. In pedology, therefore, its particles are assumed to have a diameter between 0.02 mm and 0.002 mm.

silver thaw. In the USA, a term commonly used for *glazed frost*.

silviculture or **sylviculture.** The cultivation of trees and thus a branch of forestry.

sima. The term used to denote the comparatively heavy rocks of the *lithosphere*, including basalt, lying at a lower level than the *sial* and believed to lie beneath the ocean basins. The name is derived from the initial letters of silicon and magnesium, the principal elements contained in these rocks.

simoom (Arabic). A hot, dry, suffocating wind or whirlwind experienced chiefly during spring and summer in the Sahara and the Arabian deserts. It usually carries with it dense masses of sand, which reduce visibility to a few metres or almost zero, and sometimes change the shape of the sand dunes along its track.

sinkhole, sink, or **swallow-hole.** A saucer-shaped depression in the earth's surface, usually found in a limestone region, through which water may enter the ground and pass along an underground course. It is caused by the solvent action on the rock of rain water containing carbon dioxide from the atmosphere, and may be enlarged by the collapse of rock above an underground cave. The term *pot-hole* is sometimes popularly applied to a sinkhole. See *karst region*. See also *shakehole*.

sinter. A mineral deposit from a *hot spring* or *geyser*, which sometimes occurs in mounds, cones, or terraces. There are two principal kinds, calcareous sinter and siliceous sinter, depending on composition. The former is often known as *travertine*, the latter as *geyserite*.

sirocco or **scirocco.** The southerly wind experienced in North Africa, Sicily, and southern Italy, which, blowing from the Sahara, is hot, dry, and sometimes dust-laden. Where it descends from a mountain range, as on the Algerian coast, its heat and aridity are increased. It crosses the Mediterranean, picking up moisture, and reaches southern Italy as a hot, humid, and very enervating wind. The sirocco is formed ahead of one of the depressions which pass from west to east along the Mediterranean; it may therefore occur in all seasons, but it is very rare in summer, and is specially important in spring, when the depressions are most vigorous and the desert is already hot. It usually lasts for a day or two, and is then replaced by a much cooler northerly wind behind the depression. The sirocco withers vegetation and often causes much damage to crops, especially if it blows while the vines and olives are in blossom. In Egypt the wind is known as the *khamsin*, in south-eastern Spain as the *leveche*, in Tunis as the *chili*, in Libya as the *gibli*.

skerry. A rocky islet, chiefly applied to Scandinavia and N Scotland. The term is derived from Old Norse, and the equivalent Swedish term is *skär*.

sky cover, state of sky. See *cloudiness*.

slash-and-burn. See *shifting cultivation*.

slate. A dense, fine-grained *metamorphic rock* produced by heat and pressure from a fine clay; it readily splits into thin, smooth plates suitable for roofing purposes. The true slates do not usually split along the bedding, but along planes of *cleavage*.

sleet. In Great Britain, precipitation consisting of a mixture of snow and rain. In North America, the term signifies the ice pellets which consist either of frozen rain drops or of snow which has partly melted and has been re-frozen when falling through a cold layer of air near the earth's surface.

slickensides. Rock surfaces on either side of a *fault plane* which have been polished or marked with *striae* by friction between the moving blocks.

slip-off slope. In the valley of a meandering river, the comparatively gentle slope of the spur, rising from the convex (inner) side of the *meander*, in contrast to the steep bank on the concave (outer) side.

small circle. A circle on the earth's surface which does not bisect the globe: e.g. any parallel of latitude except the equator. See *great circle*.

smog. A *fog* that is heavily laden with smoke or similar atmospheric pollutant, and is therefore commonest in industrial and densely populated urban areas. The term was coined from the two words 'smoke' and 'fog'.

smokes. The heavy morning and evening mists experienced during the dry season along the Guinea coast of Africa, corresponding to the *cacimbo*.

snout.* See *glacier snout*.

snow. *Precipitation* which takes the form of ice crystals of a delicate, feathery structure, having been formed from water vapour in the atmosphere at temperatures below freezing point. The snow may the form of individual crystals, or as large flakes produc amalgamation of a large number of crystals. Often the snc during its descent, and reaches the surface as rain; hence ground rain may be falling, while on neighbouring hilltop the temperature is lower, freshly fallen snow may be observed ren cm or a dm of snow is regarded as equivalent to approximately 1 cm of rain, but the actual ratio varies considerably with the nature of the snow; for meteorological records the snow is melted, and its amount expressed as the equivalent depth of rain.

snowdrift. Snow which has been driven into a bank or heap by the wind, sometimes by accumulation in a sheltered spot, sometimes by transportation of fallen snow.

snowfield.* A region of permanent snow; as temperatures must be low, it is common only in mountainous areas or in high latitudes.

snow-gauge. An instrument used for measuring the depth of snowfall. Most types are merely *rain gauges* which have been adapted to enable them to collect the snow, so that it can then be melted and measured. See *snow*.

snowline.* The line on a mountain or hill slope which represents the lower limit of perpetual snow; below the line, any snow which falls is melted during the summer. It is not a sharply defined line, for towards the margin of perpetual snow the covering becomes patchy and irregular, until finally it disappears altogether. The altitude of the snowline varies considerably in different regions, and in general falls from the tropics to the polar regions. Near the equator it is about 5,000 to 6,000 m above sea level, in the Alps and Pyrenees about 2,500 to 3,000 m, in northern Scandinavia about 1,250 m, while in the higher polar latitudes it is down to sea level. The altitude depends largely on the summer temperatures, which determine the rate of melting of the snow; exposure is an important factor, and the snowline is usually higher on the equatorial than on the polar side of a mountain. On a steep slope much of the snow descends as *avalanches*, so that on a gentle slope, where most of the snow lies till it melts, the snowline is lower. But the most important influence on the snowline, along with summer temperature, is the amount of winter snow; other factors being equal, the snowline is higher in a dry region than in a wet region. In the Himalayas, for instance, the snowline is about 600 m higher on the northern slopes than on the southern slopes, the higher temperatures of the latter being more than counterbalanced by the heavier precipitation due to the SW monsoon.

social geography. A term which is close to the once common term human geography, or *anthropogeography*, but now more accurately related to the term used by many American geographers – cultural geography: a description of the earth's surface after the changes and modifications wrought by man's activities. This includes the distribution of population over the earth, both in cities and towns and in rural communities, and the way of life of the various communities in their different environments.

soffione or **suffione** (Italian). In a volcanic region, a vent in the earth's crust from which steam and such gases as hydrogen sulphide and carbon dioxide are emitted. See *fumarole*.

soft hail or **graupel** (German). White opaque grains of *hail* of diameter between 2 mm and 5 mm, somewhat resembling and often preceding snow. The term *small hail* is applied to grains of similar diameter consisting of soft hail which has been glazed with clear ice; this is usually associated with rain rather than snow.

soil. The loose material or the upper layer of the *mantle rock*, consisting mainly of very small particles. It is penetrated by the roots of plants, which derive from it nutrients and moisture; in fact, from the standpoint of agriculture, soil consists of the top few cm of mantle rock in which cultivated plants are grown. Its depth, however, varies from a fraction of a cm to many m. Over 90 per cent of the dry substance of the average soil is inorganic mineral matter, produced from the original rock material by *weathering*, and it also contains *humus*. In the pore spaces are liquid and gaseous components, chiefly water and air. Soils may be classified into *zonal*, *intrazonal*, and *azonal soils*.

soil colloids. Particles in the soil which are so finely divided as to have colloidal dimensions. They are measurable in microns rather than millimetres (1 micron = 0.001 mm), and include both organic and inorganic particles; it is the colloidal particles of *humus* that impart the dark colour to soil.

soil conservation. Protection of the soil from *soil erosion*, e.g. by *terrace cultivation*, *windbreaks*.

soil creep. The slow, almost imperceptible, but continual movement of the surface soil and rock fragments down slopes. When in dry weather the sun's heat causes the soil to crack, the crack opens downhill; when the soil fills with rain water, the crack is closed, again downhill. There is, then, a downward movement of the soil amounting probably to only a few millimetres. A similar effect is produced by the expansion and contraction due to heat and cold. See *solifluction*.

soil erosion. The wearing away and loss of *topsoil*, mainly by the action of wind and rain. *Sheet erosion* occurs, chiefly on sloping farmland, when the rain washes away a thin layer of topsoil. In *gully erosion* the rain forms small channels down the slope and these develop into gullies. *Wind erosion* is usually experienced in dry regions: the top-soil becomes loose and powdery, and the wind then carries it away.

soil group, great. An extensive group of soils having similar internal characteristics. The great soil groups include tundra soils, desert soils, *podzol* soils, *chernozem* soils.

soil horizon. See *horizon, soil*.

soil profile. See *profile, soil*.

soil series. A group of soils having similar profiles (see *profile, soil*), except for the texture of the surface soil, and developed from a particular type of parent material.

soil texture. The character of a soil with respect to the size of the particles (see *clay*, *sand*, *silt*). A clay soil may thus be described as fine, a sandy soil as coarse, while a silt soil is intermediate. The standard unit for measurement of soil particles is the millimetre, but a smaller unit is the micron (1 micron = 0.001 mm), which is applicable, for instance, to the measurement of *soil colloids*.

soil type. A term used in the classification of soils, signifying the same as *soil series*, except that the texture of the surface soil must only vary within narrow limits. It is the principal unit used in soil mappings as well as other soil studies.

solano. An easterly wind which often brings rain to south-eastern Spain and the Straits of Gibraltar. See *levanter*.

solar constant. The intensity of the sun's radiation in space at the mean distance of the earth from the sun, usually expressed in calories per square centimetre per minute. A wide accepted value is 2.0 calories per sq. cm per minute or 2.0 *langleys* per minute, the langley being the unit of radiation intensity.

solar day, mean. The average length of the solar day, equal to 86,400 seconds – the 24 hours or day of civil time. Owing to the eccentricity of the earth's *orbit* and the inclination of the equator to the *ecliptic*, the solar day varies slightly in length at different times of the year, so that the average length, the mean solar day, is taken. The solar day is the interval of time between successive occasions when the sun is in the meridian of any fixed place; as the earth travels in its orbit round the sun in the same sense of rotation as that of its rotation about its axis, the solar day is slightly longer – nearly four minutes longer – than the *sidereal day*. To view the problem from another angle, the stars are at such a great distance from the earth that their apparent position is little affected by the earth's movement round the sun: the sun is so much nearer to the earth that its apparent position is materially affected, and it appears to lag behind each day. As the earth makes 1/365 of its revolution round the sun each day, the change of position due to one day's apparent annual motion of the sun equals the change of position due to about 1/365 of 24 hours, or nearly 4 minutes, of apparent daily motion.

solar system. The group of celestial bodies consisting of the *sun*, the *planets*, which revolve round it, the planetoids or *asteroids*, *comets*, *meteors*, and *meteorites*, and the satellites which revolve round the planets, e.g. the *moon* round the earth. It does not include the stars, which are other suns at vast distances from the earth.

solfatara (Italian). The vent associated with a *volcano* which no longer ejects molten *lava* or ashes, but continues to give off steam and certain gases; in distinction from the *fumarole*, the exhalations from the solfatara consist principally of hydrogen sulphide and other sulphurous gases. The name is derived from the dormant volcano Solfatara, near Pozzuoli, west of Naples, whose crater is continually giving off these gases.

solifluction. Soil flow: the movement of soil and rock fragments down slopes, being more rapid than *soil creep*; it occurs mainly in the *tundra*, where the top layer of soil remains saturated, and alternate freezing and thawing take place. The term is sometimes regarded as synonymous with soil creep.

solstice. The time during summer or winter when the sun is vertically above the point which represents its farthest distance north or south of the equator, i.e. when the *declination of the sun* reaches its maximum or minimum: at this period the altitude of the sun at noon seems to be practically unchanged for a few days. In the northern hemisphere, the day on which the sun is vertical over the *Tropic of Cancer*, its farthest north, about 21 June, is known as the *summer solstice*, and represents midsummer. The *winter solstice*, about 22 December, is the day when the sun is vertical over the *Tropic of Capricorn*, its farthest south, and represents midwinter of the northern hemisphere. The days are longest and nights are shortest at the summer solstice, while the days are shortest and nights longest at the winter solstice. As the seasons in the southern hemisphere are the opposite of those of the northern hemisphere, the winter solstice is about 21 June, and the summer solstice about 22 December.

sonnenseite (German). See *adret*.

soroche (Spanish). In South America, the type of *mountain sickness* suffered on the *puna* of the Andes, sometimes affecting even the natives when they travel from the coast to the puna.

sotch. A term used in the *Causses* region of France for a *sinkhole* or a *uvala*.

sound. A narrow passage of water but usually wider than a *strait*; sometimes a narrow inlet in the sea coast.

sounding. (1) The procedure by which the depth of the sea is determined.

By the simplest method, a leaden weight known as the sounding-lead is attached to a sounding-line, and is then lowered into the sea until it strikes the bottom; the length of line run out from the ship reveals the depth of the sea. By a more modern method known as *echo-sounding*, a sound wave is transmitted to the ocean bed, where it is reflected back to the surface, and the time interval between transmission of the wave and reception of the echo, combined with the known velocity of sound in water, enable the depth to be calculated.

(2) In meteorology, the practice of investigating various properties of the upper atmosphere: for example, wind speed and direction by *pilot balloon*, or, from the late 1940s, by *radar* tracking of a balloon-borne target; pressure, temperature, and humidity by *radiosonde* carried by a *ballon sonde* (or *sounding balloon*). Since the 1950s other techniques to have been developed include *radar* for the detection and, more recently, the measurement of precipitation; the *rocketsonde*, which carries meteorological instruments and functions in a similar way to the radiosonde; and the *satellite*, which yields, along with other data, information on cloud distribution invaluable to the weather forecaster, and also, for example, facilitates the location and tracking of *tropical cyclones*.

sounding balloon. See *ballon sonde*.

source. See *river*.

southerly burster or **southerly buster.** The *cold wave* from a southerly direction experienced in southern and south-eastern Australia, usually behind a *trough of low pressure* extending from the Antarctic. It is accompanied by typical *line squall* conditions, often being heralded by a long roll of cloud. The wind changes suddenly from a warm northerly, the *brickfielder*, to the violent cold southerly, often laden with dust and generally accompanied by a thunderstorm. The fall of temperature is sudden and considerable, usually amounting to 10°C, often to much more. The southerly burster is most frequent in spring and summer, and is felt most severely along the coast of New South Wales; the mountains probably impede the advance of the following anticyclone, a steep *pressure gradient* is created, and the southerly wind blows with extreme violence. It corresponds to the *pampero* of South America.

southern circuit. The general southerly route by which depressions cross the North American continent from west to east, via the central United States. Towards winter, depressions show an increasing preference for this route over the more northerly routes, and by midwinter may be travelling as far south as the shores of the Gulf of Mexico. See *northern circuit*.

Southern Cross. A constellation of four stars visible in the southern hemisphere, arranged in the form of a cross, the longer axis of which points almost due south; if this axis is extended to $4\frac{1}{2}$ times its length, a point nearly over the South Pole is given. The constellation may thus be used in the southern hemisphere, like the *Pole Star* in the northern hemisphere, for finding directions.

south magnetic pole. See *magnetism, terrestrial.*

South Pole. See *poles.*

spa. A town or resort possessing a mineral spring or springs and functioning as a watering-place, attracting visitors in order to receive medical treatment. Spa, a small town near Liège, Belgium, became known for its springs in the fourteenth century, and other places adopted the name because of their springs. Leamington, in Warwickshire England, became Leamington Spa and later Royal Leamington Spa: saline springs had been known there since the sixteenth century. Droitwich, in Worcestershire, England, also became a spa: the town had long been famous for the salt obtained from its brine springs.

spectre of the brocken. See *brocken, spectre of the.*

speleology. The scientific study of caves.

sphere of influence. A term formerly used to denote a region, usually defined by treaty, in which certain nations agreed that one or more of them should have exclusive liberty of action. It was also used rather loosely to denote any territory in which a foreign power sought to exert exclusive influence without annexation.

spinney or **spinny.** A small wood containing undergrowth.

spit.* A narrow, low-lying tongue of sand and shingle, or small *point*, projecting into the sea or across a coastal inlet, and differing from a *bar* in that it is attached to the land at one end. It is formed by *longshore drift*, and it may extend until it becomes a bar; sometimes it curves in towards the coast (see *hook*). See also *nehrung, tombolo.*

spot height. The accurately determined height of a particular point, as indicated on a large-scale map by a dot and beside it the actual height in metres (or feet) above mean sea level, but not shown on the ground. Such spot heights are especially useful in relatively flat areas, where *contours* are widely spaced.

spring. (1) A continuous or intermittent flow of water from the ground; it is formed when rain water sinks through the ground to a certain point, where it accumulates and finally gushes out. Its site thus depends on the position of the *water table*, the shape of the land surface, and the types of rock. A spring may be formed, for instance, when water percolates through a layer of porous rock till it reaches an impermeable layer, along which it runs till it gushes out at the surface; it may be formed when the land surface, e.g. in a valley, is below the level of the adjacent water table; it may be formed, too, when water, sinking through fissures in the ground, is led by them to the surface at some distant point below the level of intake. The water of a spring may be cold or warm, soft or hard. See *geyser, hot spring, mineral spring, vauclusian spring.* (See Fig. p. 206.)

Diagram illustrating the formation of a spring (S) *when a layer of porous rock overlies an impermeable layer.*

(2) For middle latitudes, the season following the *winter*, reckoned astronomically to last in the northern hemisphere from the spring *equinox* (about 21 March) to the summer *solstice* (about 21 June); in the southern hemisphere the dates correspond to the northern autumn. See *seasons*.

spring equinox. See *equinox*.

spring tides. The *tides* of great amplitude when the earth, the sun, and the moon are practically in the same straight line; the gravitational pull of the sun acts in the same direction as that of the moon, and thus reinforces it. The high tide is higher and the low tide lower than usual. A consideration of the phases of the moon will show that they occur twice a month, about the time of new moon and full moon. See *moon, phases of*.

squall. A violent wind which rises suddenly, has a brief duration (normally some minutes), and dies away suddenly; a temporary change of direction is often associated with it. A more precise meteorological definition describes it as a sudden rise in wind speed by at least 8 m per second, increasing to 11 m per second or more and lasting for at least one minute. See *line squall*.

stack. A rocky islet or pillar, near to a coastline, which has been isolated by the erosive action of the waves.

stalactite.* A column of mineral matter hanging from an elevated point, in appearance much resembling an icicle; the commonest example is the column of calcium carbonate often found hanging from the roof of a limestone cave. This is produced from rain water which, with the help of carbon dioxide from the atmosphere, has dissolved the calcium carbonate in percolating through a bed of limestone or chalk, and then trickles down through cracks in the cave roof. As a drop of this water hangs, it partially evaporates, and leaves behind a small quantity of calcium carbonate; then the next drop leaves a further small quantity, and the deposit grows downwards, the water

Diagram illustrating the formation of a cave, with stalactites and stalagmites, by solution of the limestone.

tending to trickle down its side and hang in drops at the lower end. See *stalagmite*.

stalagmite.* A column of calcium carbonate formed on the floor of a cave by water which contains calcium carbonate in solution falling from the roof. Some of the water evaporates, leaving behind a solid deposit of calcium carbonate in the same way as with a *stalactite*, and the stalagmite grows upwards. It is usually shorter and thicker than the stalactite. A stalagmite is often produced by the water dripping from a stalactite, and sometimes stalactite and stalagmite meet, forming a complete pillar from floor to roof of the cave. The deposit of calcium carbonate formed on the walls and floor of the cave from water trickling down is also often known as a stalagmite.

standard time or **zone time.** Time which is referred to the mean time of a certain meridian, and is fixed for use over an extensive area. In general, the standard meridians are chosen to differ from the Greenwich meridian by multiples of 15° or 7½°, i.e. by an exact number of hours or half-hours, and the world is thus divided into a number of time zones. Each zone extends in a west-to-east direction over about 15° longitude, or approximately 7½° on each side of the standard meridian, and all places within the zone follow the same standard time. In western Europe the standard meridian is the Greenwich meridian; for convenience, however, *Greenwich Mean Time* was replaced over most of the area by Central European Time – which is *British Summer Time*. In countries which cover a considerable extent of longitude, several zones have to be utilized; in Canada and the United States, for example, there are Atlantic, Eastern, Central Mountain, Pacific, Alaska–Hawaii, and Bering Times, all differing from one another and from GMT by multiples of one hour. The standard time system eliminates the confusion of having a different *local time* for all places situated on the different meridians round the globe, or a national civil time based on the local mean time of the principal national observatory.

statute mile. See *mile, statute*.

steppes. The mid-latitude *grasslands*, consisting of level, generally treeless plains, of Eurasia, extending over the lower regions of the Danube, and in a broad belt over southern European USSR and south-west Siberia. The term is sometimes applied to the corresponding mid-latitude grasslands in other continents; in North America, however, the commoner term is *prairies*, in South America *pampas*. The term is sometimes applied, too, to the semi-arid regions on the fringe of the hot deserts.

stereographic projection. A *zenithal* orthomorphic projection, in which the projection on to the tangent plane is made from the extremity of the diameter drawn at right-angles to the plane. Areas at a great distance from the centre are exaggerated, though much less so than in the *gnomonic projection*, and the shapes of large areas are somewhat distorted.

Stevenson screen. The standard shelter for thermometers on British meteorological and climatological stations, to enable the true temperature of the air to be taken by protecting the thermometer from solar and terrestrial radiation, wind, etc. It consists of a wooden box, painted white and raised about 1.2 m above the ground on legs; the roof is double, with an intervening air space, the sides are louvred, one of them being hinged so as to serve as a door, and the air is thus permitted to enter freely, and the thermometers give a close approximation of the true air temperature. Such a structure elsewhere is usually known as a *thermometer screen* or *shelter*. The ordinary pattern holds dry bulb and wet bulb thermometers and maximum and minimum thermometers, all of which are supported on a frame inside the screen as far as possible from roof, floor, and sides. A larger pattern also holds a *thermograph* and a *hygrograph*.

stock. A term sometimes applied to a *batholith* of relatively small size. See *boss*.

Stone Age. The period when men used implements and weapons made of stone, preceding the period when they first extracted metals from their ores. See *Bronze Age*. It does not necessarily denote a fixed chronological period in history, for some peoples progressed beyond the Stone Age earlier than others. It is divided into the Palaeolithic or Old Stone Age, the Mesolithic or Middle Stone Age, and the Neolithic or New Stone Age; the last-named ended in NW Europe nearly 4,000 years ago.

stone-river. A 'stream' of boulders formed of *scree* which gradually moves down a valley, being similar in form to a *rock-glacier*; such stone-rivers are well known in the Falkland Islands.

storm surge. An abnormal rise in sea level, far above that of the predicted high tide, caused mainly by winds of excessive strength and possibly resulting in destructive flooding along coasts. The effects are similar to those due to a *tropical cyclone*, to which the term may be applied, and the phenomenon is sometimes popularly called a *tidal wave*. Early in 1953, for example, a deep depression over the North Sea produced northerly gales along the coasts of the Netherlands, Belgium and eastern England, and led to a storm surge which caused immense damage and the loss of hundreds of lives.

stowed winds. Winds which are impeded by mountains, and are thus concentrated in gaps and on high plateaux, their normal velocity being thereby greatly increased.

strait. A narrow stretch of sea connecting two extensive areas of sea. It may have been formed by fracture across an *isthmus*, or by the sea overflowing land which had subsided, or by erosion.

strath. In Scotland, a broad river valley, in contrast to a *glen*.

stratigraphical geology or **stratigraphy.** That section of *geology* which deals with the chronological succession of rock formations. The term is also sometimes used to signify the entire study of historical geology.

stratocumulus. A type of low *cloud* consisting of a layer arranged in globular masses or rolls which are often so close together that their edges join; the layer is usually extensive.

stratosphere. That part of the *atmosphere* which lies above the *troposphere*, extending upwards to a height of about 50 km from a height of about 11 km above the earth's surface in the temperate zone; the height at which it commences, however, is very variable, and is greatest at the equator (about 16 km). The base of the stratosphere also represents the layer at which the normal fall of air temperature with increasing height abruptly ceases. Formerly the stratosphere was sometimes termed the 'isothermal layer' but this was misleading. The temperature probably increases with height to about 50 km, and also changes in a horizontal direction, i.e. with latitude. There are virtually no clouds and practically no dust or water vapour, and no convection currents, in the stratosphere. Above the stratosphere is the *mesosphere*.

stratovolcano. See *composite volcano*.

stratum. A more or less distinct layer of rock, occurring as one of a series of strata in the earth's crust; usually applied only to *sedimentary rocks*. Rock strata vary in thickness from less than 1 cm to several metres, and normally are horizontal, or nearly so.

stratus. A type of low *cloud* consisting of a uniform layer, resembling fog which has been lifted from the ground. When it is broken up into irregular patches it is termed *fractostratus*.

stream. A course of running water; a rivulet, brook, or river.

striae or **striations.** Scratches or narrow grooves which have been worn on the surfaces of rocks when rock fragments have been dragged over them by a *glacier*.

strike. The direction of a horizontal line along a rock stratum perpendicular to the direction of *dip*. The relationship between strike and dip is thus the same as that between the contour and the slope of the ground. (See Fig. p. 60.)

strip mining. See *opencast mining*.

subglacial. A term meaning 'beneath the ice', applied, for example, to a *moraine* which consists of rock fragments torn from the valley floor and then carried along in the ice at the bottom of the *glacier*, or to a stream flowing beneath the glacier.

submarine canyon. A canyon in the sea bed which crosses the *continental shelf*, sometimes continuing across the *continental slope*. Some of the submarine canyons appear to be extensions of river courses of the present day, and were doubtless formed when the sea level was considerably lower than it is now. A well-known example is the submarine canyon at the mouth of the Hudson River, USA, which extends about 320 km (200 miles) into the sea.

submarine ridge. See *mid-oceanic ridge*.

submerged forest. The remains of a forest now covered by the sea, except possibly at very low tide, having been submerged by the sinking of the coast or a rise of sea level. There are several examples round the coasts of the British Isles.

subpolar region. The region which is bordered on the poleward side by the tundra and on the equatorial side by the cool temperate or cool intermediate region or in some cases by the mid-latitude steppes and deserts. It is sometimes known as the *subarctic* or *subantarctic* region, and in the northern hemisphere it practically coincides with the *coniferous forests* of high latitudes. Winters are long and extremely cold, summers are very short; precipitation is relatively scanty, but on account of the slight evaporation is sufficient to promote forest growth.

subsequent river. A tributary to a *consequent river*, flowing approximately in the direction of the *strike*; it usually carves out a broad, deep valley because it flows over weak rocks, and becomes a powerful stream. It is so named because its formation is subsequent to that of the original *consequent river*. See *obsequent river*.

subsidence. (1) The sinking of a portion of the earth's crust relatively to the surrounding parts.

(2) The slow descent of large masses of air towards the earth's surface, characteristic of anticyclones and of a quickly rising atmospheric pressure; the air is dynamically warmed and dried as it descends, so that subsidence is frequently associated with fine, dry weather.

subsistence crops. See *subsistence farming*.

subsistence farming or **subsistence agriculture.** The type of farming in which the produce is consumed mainly by the farmer and his family and is not sold or traded. Crops so produced are known as *subsistence crops*. See *cash crops*.

subsoil. The layer of material lying below the true soil or *topsoil*; it has less organic matter than the latter, and is apt to differ somewhat in its mineral content, being less exposed to oxidizing and hydrating agencies. It is less fertile than the true soil, but is penetrated to some depth by the roots of trees and other vegetation. The term is often regarded as synonymous with C horizon (see *profile, soil*).

subtropical region. The region lying between the tropics and the temperate or intermediate region. Unlike the tropics, it has a distinct seasonal rhythm, with a well-marked winter and summer, but the climate is generally warmer than in the temperate region. It is divided into the areas having a dry subtropical or *Mediterranean climate* and those having a wet or humid subtropical climate – sometimes known as the *cotton belt climate*; the former is experienced mainly on the western sides of continents, and is characterized by long, dry summers and mild, moderately rainy winters, while the latter is found on the eastern sides of continents, and has a higher rainfall, most of the precipitation falling, in general, during the summer.

sudd (Arabic). A floating mass of vegetable matter, applied particularly to that which collects on the White Nile, and at times has seriously impeded navigation; it consists principally of plants from the adjoining swamps. It sometimes forms a dam over 30 km long and up to 5 m deep, and becomes so compact that it will support an elephant.

sumatra. A type of *squall* experienced in the Malacca Strait, mainly at night and most frequently during the south-west monsoon. With the squall there is a sudden change of wind direction from southerly to westerly, and an abrupt fall of temperature; it is accompanied by a heavy bank of *cumulonimbus* cloud, and generally by a violent thunderstorm and torrential rain.

summer. For middle latitudes, the season following the *spring*, reckoned astronomically to last in the northern hemisphere from the summer *solstice* (about 21 June) to the autumnal *equinox* (about 22 September); in the southern hemisphere the dates correspond to the northern *winter*. See *seasons*.

sun. The central body of the *solar system*, a luminous sphere approximately 1,391,000 km (865,000 miles) in diameter; it is believed to consist of a liquid inner portion with a gaseous outer covering. The average distance of the earth from the sun is about 150,000,000 km (93,000,000 miles). All forms of life on the earth and on other members

211

of the solar system are dependent upon the radiation from the sun for their existence.

sunrise, sunset. The times at which the sun appears to rise above and set below the horizon, owing to the rotation of the earth on its axis. As the sun has a substantial apparent diameter, some time elapses between its first and last contacts with the horizon, and sunrise and sunset are therefore usually taken to be the times when its centre is on the horizon. Sunrise and sunset vary with latitude and with the *declination of the sun*.

sunshine. The light received directly from the sun, which renders objects on the earth's surface visible. It consists of that part of the solar radiation with wave-lengths between those of red and violet light. In climatology and meteorology the duration of sunshine is used to indicate how sunny a place is; it is expressed in hours, often as the mean daily duration for a certain period. With sunshine are associated the ultra-violet rays, which are invisible and are of great therapeutic value. See *isohel, sunshine recorder*.

sunshine recorder. An instrument used for measuring the duration of sunshine each day. It usually consists of a spherical glass lens mounted at the centre of a framework in which a strip of graduated card is placed. The image of the sun produced by the spherical lens burns through the card, and the length of the burned track on the card, made as the sun travels across the sky, thus gives the number of hours of sunshine for the day.

sunspot. A spot on the surface of the sun, sometimes so large that it may be observed, through a thin layer of cloud or dark glass, with the naked eye. Its origin is obscure, but it is believed to consist of a whirling mass of gas just within the sun's atmosphere. Some connexion between the number of sunspots and the occurrence of certain terrestrial phenomena has often been sought, but the only certain correlation is that between the number of sunspots and electrical and magnetic disturbances on the earth; when the former is a maximum, the displays of *aurora* and *magnetic storms* also reach a maximum. There is a rough periodicity in the number of sunspots observed annually on the surface of the sun, the mean interval between maxima in the sunspot cycle being about eleven years.

superimposed drainage. A system of drainage which developed on rocks that have since been removed by denudation, and was superimposed on the underlying rocks which are now exposed. The *radial drainage* of the Lake District, in N W England, for example, was superimposed on the existing surface rocks.

surf. Waves breaking into foamy water on the shore or around rocks.

swallow-hole. See *sinkhole*.

swamp. A tract of low-lying land which is permanently saturated with moisture (not, like a *marsh*, temporarily so), and is usually overgrown

Folding of rock strata in a syncline (trough) and an anticline (arch).

with vegetation; it is thus between an entirely aquatic environment and a marsh. It may adjoin a marsh or a *bog*, and there is sometimes confusion between the terms. A swamp (or marsh) is often formed when a lake basin fills up, for the surface is so flat that the *run-off* of rain water is very slow, and in the damp soil vegetation grows and helps to maintain the swampy conditions. In the United States the term is sometimes applied to areas which are partly forest-covered, e.g. the Everglades of Florida, and the Dismal Swamp of Virginia and North Carolina. By the drainage of swamps, e.g. in the Everglades of Florida, fertile agricultural land has been produced, for the soil has a high *humus* content.

swash or **send.** The advance of sea water up a beach after the breaking of a wave. See *backwash*.

swell. The regular, undulating movement of the surface of the sea, which does not break into waves.

syncline. The trough or inverted arch of a *fold* in rock strata. See *anticline*. (See Fig. above.)

synclinorium. A huge trough, in form resembling a *syncline*, each limb of which consists of a number of small *folds*.

synoptic chart. See *weather chart*.

syzygy. The point at which two heavenly bodies are in *conjunction* or *opposition*; the term is usually applied to the moon, when it is in line with earth and sun, and thus coincides with new moon and full moon. See *moon, phases of*.

T

tableland. A *plateau* bounded by steep, cliff-like faces which lead abruptly down to the sea or the adjoining lowlands; South Africa provides the best-known example of a tableland. This terminates in the Great *escarpment* a major part of which is the mountain *range* known as the Drakensberg.

table mountain or **tafelberg** (Afrikaans). A term applied, chiefly in South Africa, to a flat-topped mountain or *mesa*, the best-known example being Table Mountain, near Cape Town.

taiga (Russian). The *coniferous forest* land of Siberia, bordered on the north by the treeless, inhospitable *tundra* and on the south by the *steppes*. The principal species of trees are pine, fir, spruce, and larch. It contains many swampy areas, and during the spring much of the land is flooded by water from the upper reaches of northward-flowing rivers whose lower stretches are still frozen. The name is often applied, too, to other coniferous forests of the northern hemisphere, e.g. in North America.

talus* or **scree.** A mass of boulders and broken rocks of all sizes which accumulates at the foot of a cliff or mountain slope, having been broken from the main rocks by weathering and rolled down under the action of gravity. The talus slope is often so steep that a slight disturbance will send the whole mass sliding downwards.

talus creep. The gentle movement of rock fragments down a *talus* slope.

talweg. See *thalweg*.

tank. In the drier parts of peninsular India and Sri Lanka, a pond or lake formed by building a mud wall across the valley of a stream, so that water collects there during the rainy season and can be used for *irrigation*. The tank may be used when the rainy season is over, but during the hot season it often dries up completely; in some years it does not fill even during the rains.

tarbert, tarbet (Gaelic). In Scotland, a term for *isthmus*, sometimes used (both spellings) in a place name: e.g. Tarbert, at the head of East Loch Tarbert, occupying the narrow isthmus between East Loch Tarbert and West Loch Tarbert; also Tarbet, on Loch Lomond.

tarn. A small mountain lake, usually occupying a *cirque*.

tear fault. A *fault* in which the movement of the rocks is mainly horizontal rather than vertical. Terms regarded as synonymous with tear fault are *wrench fault*, *lateral fault*, *transcurrent fault*, and *strike-slip fault*.

tectonic. Relating to the processes which tend to build up the various features of the earth's crust. The tectonic forces involved in moulding the earth's surface, for example, include those which break, bend, and warp the earth's crust, and create depressions and elevations; they are distinct from the forces of gradation, which tend to wear down the surface to a common level.

temperate glacier. One of the two categories into which some glaciologists classify *glaciers* according to the temperature of the ice: the type in which the temperature of the ice is about 0°C (32°F), at least in summer, so that some melting takes place at the surface, as in the lower parts of many glaciers in the Alps.

temperate zone. The middle latitudes, the zone between the *torrid zone* and the *frigid zone*: in the northern hemisphere between the *Tropic of Cancer* and the *Arctic Circle*, in the southern hemisphere between the *Tropic of Capricorn* and the *Antarctic Circle*. The sun is never overhead in this zone, but its rays vary considerably in directness, and there are therefore well-marked warm and cool seasons, or summer and winter. The term 'temperate' is appropriate to the middle latitudes of the southern hemisphere and to the oceans and the western coastal regions of the northern hemisphere but not to the interiors and eastern regions of North America and Asia, where the climate is often far from temperate and in the interiors may be characterized by extremes of temperature, and here the term 'mid-latitude' is more appropriate.

temperature. The degree of heat of a body, usually expressed in degrees on the *centigrade (Celsius) scale* or the *Fahrenheit scale*, and measured by a *thermometer*. A temperature on the Kelvin or absolute scale is obtained by adding 273° to the temperature on the centigrade scale: $K = 273° + C$. On the earth, temperatures decrease in general from the equator towards the poles, though the temperatures of any particular place depend also upon other factors besides latitude – on altitude, proximity to the sea, prevailing winds, etc. Temperature also decreases with altitude. See *lapse rate, range of temperature, isotherm*.

temperature anomaly. The difference between the mean temperature of a place and the mean temperature along its parallel of latitude, both temperatures being reduced to sea level; the anomaly is positive if the place is warmer than the mean temperature along its parallel, and negative if it is cooler. The greatest temperature anomaly on the earth exists over the north-east Atlantic Ocean, including the British Isles, in January, when a considerable area has a positive temperature anomaly of over 10°C. See *isanomalous line*.

temperature inversion. See *inversion, temperature*.

temporales. The strong SW winds of *monsoon* type blowing in summer on the Pacific coast of Central America.

tephra. A term applied to all the finer solid materials (ash, cinders, etc.) ejected from a *volcano* during an *eruption*.

tephrochronology. The study of past changes in climate, etc., in terms of the geological time-scale, as revealed by examination of successive layers of *tephra* in volcanic regions: devised by Sigurdur Thorarinsson, the Icelandic vulcanologist.

terai. The strip of marshy jungle, largely covered with tall coarse grass, extending along the foothills of the Himalayas, chiefly in Uttar Pradesh (India) and Nepal. It is crossed by many streams flowing down from the Himalayas to the Indo-Gangetic plain, and has been partly drained and cleared for agriculture.

terminal or **end moraine.** See *moraine*.

terrace cultivation.* An agricultural system by which mountain and hill slopes are cultivated: terraces are cut into the slopes, and walls or mud banks are built round the small level patches obtained, so that irrigation water and soil can be retained. Such terrace cultivation is common in mountainous areas where land is scarce or rainfall uncertain, e.g. in the Andes, China, Java, Mediterranean countries.

terrace, river. See *river terrace*.

terracettes or **sheep-tracks.** The small terraces often seen on steep grass slopes, probably due to miniature landslips, and frequently used as paths by grazing animals.

terra firme (Portuguese). In the Amazon basin of Brazil, the higher, well-drained areas which stand above the *flood-plain* and are covered with more open forest than the *várzea*.

terral. The *land breeze* experienced on the west coasts of Peru and Chile. See *virazon*.

terra rossa (Italian). A reddish clay soil found in limestone regions where the *Mediterranean climate* prevails, as in S Italy and Yugoslavia, e.g. on the bottom of a *doline* or *polje* or in a cave, being the insoluble residue – red in colour owing to the accumulation of iron oxides – left behind after solution of the limestone. The term is also sometimes applied to other reddish soils.

terra roxa (Portuguese). A reddish-purple soil with a high *humus* content which is found on the plateau of eastern Brazil; the land where it occurs has been extensively cleared for coffee plantations, e.g. in the state of São Paulo.

terrestrial magnetism, geomagnetism. See *magnetism, terrestrial*.

terrigenous. Derived from the land; for example, those marine deposits, derived from the land, which border the land masses, and include the sand, gravel, pebbles, etc., around the coasts, the sands, silts, and clays of the shallow waters, and the clays of the deeper waters on the fringe of the *pelagic* zone, are known as terrigenous deposits.

territorial waters. The belt of sea adjoining the coast, which is regarded as being under the territorial jurisdiction of the nation occupying the coast; a peaceful passage through the belt is normally permitted to the vessels of all nations. Some nations (e.g. UK, USA) recognize the

3 miles' limit of territorial waters, but in recent years several countries have considerably extended this limit, often to 12 miles (e.g. France, Mexico), sometimes to 200 miles (e.g. Ecuador, Brazil). See *fisheries zone*.

Tertiary. The term applied by some geologists to the earlier of the two sub-divisions or *periods* of the *Cainozoic era* in the geological scale of time, preceding the *Quaternary* and extending from about 70 million years to about one million years ago. Other geologists, however, regard it as an *era* synonymous with the Cainozoic era, following the Mesozoic (Secondary) and preceding the Quaternary.

Tethys. In *palaeogeography*, the name given to the ocean and to the *geosyncline* that the latter occupied, separating *Laurasia* from *Gondwanaland*.

tetrahedral theory. A theory which seeks to explain the apparent symmetry in the distribution of the great land masses and the oceans, and suggests that as the earth cools its outer crust is warping towards a tetrahedral shape. In the western hemisphere, for instance, there is a large triangle of land, base to the north and apex to the south; in the eastern hemisphere, two triangular land masses unite at their bases to the north, and have separate apices in the south; there is a fourth land mass around the South Pole. These four triangular land masses represent the four points of the tetrahedron, projecting above the sea. Between them are three triangular masses of sea, bases in the south, where they unite, apices in the north. The theory, first enunciated by Lowthian Green in 1875, is now generally discredited.

texture, soil. See *soil texture*.

thalweg, talweg (German), or **valley line.** The line joining the lowest points along a valley from the source of a river to its mouth: the concave curve thus produced marks the general slope of the river throughout its course. Despite the literal meaning, 'valley-way', it is usually regarded as synonymous with the longitudinal profile of a river (see *profile, river*).

thaw. The end of a *frost*, when the temperature has risen above freezing point, and ice and snow melt to water. In high latitudes the thaw is an annual event of great significance, taking place each spring, and leading to the melting of the snow and the liberation of ice-bound seas and rivers.

theodolite. An instrument used for measuring angular distances in the vertical plane (elevation) and in the horizontal plane (azimuth); this is done by means of a telescope, whose motion can be accurately controlled. The instrument is used in surveying and also, for instance, in following a *pilot balloon*, when the direction and speed of the upper winds are determined.

thermal belt. A zone in some of the valleys of the Appalachian Mountains, USA, about 100 m above the valley bottom, which is not affected by frost. The green colour of the vegetation is retained throughout the winter, and is separated by a distinct line from the frosted and blackened vegetation of the valley bottom, where temperatures have been much lower.

thermal equator. The term for a rising current of air produced by the relatively intense heating of a small land area by the sun, and utilized in gliding. See *convection*.

thermal or **heat equator.** The imaginary line drawn round the globe through places which have the highest mean temperature for any particular period. Its position varies with the season, moving north in the northern summer and south in the southern summer, but it does not migrate so far north and south of the geographical equator as the sun itself. Being also influenced by the distribution of land and sea and the effects of ocean currents, its mean position does not coincide with the geographical equator, but lies to the north of it.

thermal spring. See *hot spring*.

thermogram. The continuous record of the air temperature, as measured by the *thermograph*, usually to cover a period of a week.

thermograph. A self-recording type of thermometer, in which a continuous trace of the air temperature is made on a *thermogram* fixed to a rotating drum actuated by clockwork. One of the commonest forms uses a bi-metallic spiral, the expansion and contraction of which is transferred to a lever carrying a pen, and the latter then records the temperatures on the rotating thermogram. It is chiefly of value in recording variations in temperature rather than actual temperatures.

thermometer. An instrument used for measuring temperature, usually by means of the change in volume of mercury or alcohol contained in a glass tube with a bulb at one end. In some English-speaking countries thermometers are constructed to the *Fahrenheit scale*, elsewhere mainly to the *centigrade* or *Celsius scale*.

thermometer screen or **shelter.** See *Stevenson screen*.

thermosphere. That part of the *atmosphere* which lies above the *mesosphere*, extending upwards from about 80 km (50 miles) to the outer fringe of the atmosphere (see *exosphere*). Within the thermosphere the temperature increases with height, rapidly to about 200 km (120 miles) and then more slowly.

thicket. A small wood, or group of closely set trees, especially one with dense undergrowth.

thorn forest or **thornbush.** A forest of small, thorny trees in a tropical or subtropical region, where the rainfall, about 250–500 mm annually, is too scanty to permit the growth of normal forests; during the long droughts the trees are leafless. See *caatinga*.

three-field system. A part of the open-field system, a system of agriculture whereby three open arable fields were successively used for, say, wheat in one year; then, say, peas or beans in the next year; then allowed to lie fallow for the following year, and so on in rotation. The system was widely used in Europe and was introduced into Britain in Anglo-Saxon times. Such agriculture became inadequate after the fields were enclosed and farming became more complex.

throw. See *fault*.

thrust fault or **reversed fault.** A *fault* in which the upper rock strata have been pushed forward over the lower strata, the upthrow being on the dip side of the *fault plane*. It may be formed by the breaking of an overturned fold, or *overfold*, at the sharply bent crest of the *anticline*.

Thule. The Greek and Roman name for what was supposed to be the most northerly land in the world. The Greek explorer Pytheas in the fourth century B.C. may have reached it after six days' sail from Britain; he may have discovered the Shetlands, or Iceland, or even a point on the coast of Norway. Ultima Thule came to designate a place or land at an unimaginable distance away. In modern times, Thule has been the name of an actual settlement on the coast of NW Greenland.

thunderstorm. A storm in which there are strong upward currents of air, forming well-developed *cumulonimbus* clouds; from the latter violent showers of rain, possibly with hail, descend, while the development of static electricity causes flashes of lightning, and the thunder is produced by the expansion of air due to the tremendous heat of the lightning flashes. The first condition necessary for the development of a thunderstorm is a sufficient supply of moisture, in order that cumulonimbus clouds should form; the second condition is a high *lapse rate* of temperature, in order that there shall be a strong upward current of air for a depth of at least 3,000 m above the cloud base. (See *instability*.) Thunderstorms are much more numerous and more severe in the equatorial regions than in the middle and higher latitudes, for in those regions there is, firstly, a greater supply of moisture; secondly, the more intense heat gives a high lapse rate, and causes the violent convection currents which, together with adequate moisture, produce the thundery cumulonimbus clouds.

tidal current. The movement of tidal water into a bay, estuary, harbour, etc., at the *flood-tide*, or out of it at the *ebb-tide*, or through a strait. Such currents are of great significance to a seaport like London, situated on a tidal estuary. In an estuary narrowing quickly inland, the tidal current may assume the proportions of a *bore*.

tidal day. See *lunar day*.

tidal or **tide-water glacier.** A *glacier* which reaches the sea, where portions of it may break off as *icebergs* and *ice-floes*.

tidal range. The difference in water level between high tide and low tide at a place. It varies very considerably, from about 0.6 m (2 ft) around the Mediterranean, even less in the open sea, to 15 m (50 ft) or more at the head of the Bay of Fundy (Canada).

tidal wave. See *storm surge*.

tides. The alternate rise and fall of the surface of the sea, approximately twice a day, caused by the gravitational pull of the moon and to a lesser degree of the sun. In the open ocean, the difference between the levels of high and low tides is less than 1 m, but in the shallow seas bordering the continents it may be over 6 m, and in narrow tidal estuaries it may be 15 m or more. The *tidal range* at a place increases to a maximum, then decreases to a minimum, increases to a maximum again, and so on: see *spring tides*, *neap tides*. As the moon travels in its orbit in the same direction as the earth's rotation, a period of rather more than one day – 24 hours 50 minutes – elapses between successive occasions when the moon is vertically over a certain meridian; thus the interval between successive high tides or successive low tides is equal to half this period, i.e. about 12½ hours. The tides may be regarded as two great waves, with their crests, 180° apart, lying along places where the moon is at the zenith or at the nadir, their troughs along places where the moon is on the horizon; the waves sweep round the earth as the latter rotates on its axis, and thus the crest, representing high tide, passes through any particular place twice every 24 hours 50 minutes. These movements are very much modified locally by irregularities in the coastline, e.g. by bays and gulfs.

tierra caliente. In tropical Central and South America, the lowest of the three regions into which the land is sometimes divided according to altitude; it includes the hot, steamy, coastal plains and the slopes of the mountains to a height of about 1,000 m. There is a luxuriant tropical vegetation, in the wetter areas dense forests; banana, sugar, and cacao plantations have been established and on the mountain slopes maize, tobacco, and coffee are grown.

tierra fria. The highest and coolest of the three regions into which tropical Central and South America is sometimes divided according to altitude: the land between about 2,000 m and 3,000 m above sea level. It contains *coniferous forests*, which with decreased rainfall and lower temperatures gradually pass into *scrub* and grassland. The crops are those of the temperate lands, such as wheat, and there are considerable pastures. The mean annual temperature is about 10°C below that of the *tierra caliente*; conditions are thus much more favourable to settlement, especially for Europeans, and the density of population in the tierra fria of Mexico is about four times that of the tierra caliente.

tierra templada. In tropical Central and South America, the middle of the three zones into which the land is sometimes divided according to altitude: the area between about 1,000 m and 2,000 m above sea level. In general, temperatures are very uniform, and the annual range of temperature is often as low as 2° or 3°C. Maize, coffee, tobacco, etc., are cultivated, but owing to the light rainfall much of the area is valueless, even for pastures.

Sketch-map of part of the coast of Dorset, England, showing Chesil Beach, a typical tombolo.

till. See *boulder clay*.

timber line or **tree line.*** The boundary line above which trees do not grow. It is usually clearly marked on high ground in low and middle latitudes, but is not uniform in any region, for its height depends on local as well as general conditions of climate and soil. It is lower in the temperate zone than in the tropical zone, lower on the shady side than on the sunny side of mountains, and is highest on those slopes which provide the best protection from winds and the longest exposure to the sun.

time. See *apparent time, local time, standard time, Greenwich Mean Time*.

tombolo (Italian).*** A *bar* which joins an island to the mainland or joins two islands. An example is the well-known Chesil Beach (or Chesil Bank) on the coast of Dorset, England, a ridge of shingle which joins the Isle of Portland to the mainland. (See Fig. above.)

topographic map. A map on a sufficiently large scale to show the detailed surface features of an area, including its *relief*, usually by means of *contours*, and such physical features as forests, rivers, and lakes, and such artificial features as roads, railways, and canals. Examples are the familiar Ordnance Survey maps of the United Kingdom on the scale 1:50,000.

topography. A detailed description or representation of the features, both natural and artificial, of an area, such as are required for a *topographic map*.

topsoil or **top soil.** Soil that is cultivated; the uppermost layer of true soil, as distinct from the *subsoil*.

tor. An isolated mass of rock, usually of granite, which has been subject to considerable weathering, particularly along *joints*, and often assumes peculiar shapes; the granite rocks of Devon and Cornwall, England, provide good examples.

tornado. (1) In the Guinea lands of West Africa, a violent storm, often known as an 'African tornado'. It consists of a *squall* blowing from a severe thunderstorm, often starting very suddenly and lasting only a short time, but it may cause considerable destruction on land and sea; it is usually accompanied by torrential rain. It is more liable to take place during the day, when the surface air is strongly heated, and is most frequent during the transition periods between the wet and dry seasons. The 'African tornado' is caused by the meeting of warm, damp, monsoonal air from the south-west with dry north-easterly or *harmattan* air from the Sahara; it has a *front* several kilometres in length, sometimes extending to as much as 300 km.

(2) An extremely violent *whirlwind* covering a relatively small area, its diameter being usually less than 500 m. It is most frequent in the United States, east of the Rocky Mountains, especially on the central plains of the Mississippi basin, where hot, damp air from the Gulf of Mexico meets cool, dry air from the north. It is a local phenomenon, travelling in an approximately straight line at 30 to 60 km per hour, and often dying out after about 30 km. While it lasts, however, it causes great destruction along its narrow track; wind velocities near the centre are estimated to exceed 300 km per hour, and trees are uprooted, buildings completely destroyed. The tornado is usually accompanied by heavy rain and thunder. It occurs most frequently during spring and early summer, almost always in the afternoon, when surface heating reaches a maximum. In a suitable meteorological situation, when an extensive area of low atmospheric pressure exists, several tornadoes may develop on the same day. In the United States it is sometimes known as a *twister*, on account of the twisting motion of the funnel-shaped cloud at its top.

torrid zone. See *tropics* (2).

trace element. An element which is required by plants in only minute quantities but nevertheless must be present in the soil if the plants are to grow successfully. Six such elements are generally recognized: iron, manganese, boron, copper, zinc, and molybdenum.

trade route. A route, via land, sea, or air, by which trade is conducted. Overland the most important trade routes lie along the railways, roads, rivers, and canals; over the oceans they are those of the great cargo vessels, often following the *great circle routes*; air routes, for the carriage of light freight, mail, and passengers, are the most modern trade routes.

trade winds. The winds which blow from the sub-tropical belts of high pressure towards the equatorial region of low pressure, from the north-east in the northern hemisphere and from the south-east in the southern hemisphere. In many areas they blow with extreme regularity throughout the year, especially over the oceans, and derive their name from the nautical expression 'to blow trade', meaning 'to blow along a regular track'. In continental interiors they blow much less steadily than over the oceans, but are fairly regular over the hot deserts. Topography may cause local variations in direction, and even over the oceans there are variations; in the North Atlantic, for instance, the direction changes from north-east on the eastern margin to easterly on the western margin. With the seasonal changes in the *declination of the sun*, the trade winds also move northwards and southwards, their range averaging about 5° latitude. Although weather in the trade wind regions is normally fine and quiet, *tropical cyclones* are often experienced there.

tramontana (Italian). In the Mediterranean region, chiefly in central Italy, a cool, dry northerly wind blowing from beyond the mountains (the Alps).

transhumance.* The practice among pastoral farmers of moving their herds and flocks between two regions of different climate. In mountainous regions the animals are transferred from mountain pastures to valley pastures for the winter and back again to the mountain pastures for the summer; they are accompanied by herdsmen, and a feature of the practice is that the latter occupy permanent dwellings in the mountains as well as in the valleys. See *Alps, saeter* or *seter*.

transpiration. The process by which plants, having taken in moisture through their roots, return it to the atmosphere through the stomata of their leaves in the form of water vapour. Transpiration thus represents a considerable loss of soil moisture. See *evapotranspiration*.

transport. (1) The carriage of goods from one place to another. In some ill-developed regions, e.g. China and Central Africa, it is still effected by human porters; various animals, including the horse, mule, donkey, ox, camel, elephant, reindeer, are also used. In more advanced countries, overland transport is chiefly by railway and road, with the locomotive and the motor vehicle respectively supplying the power, and rivers and canals are also utilized. Over the oceans the steamship and the motor vessel, and to a very small extent nowadays the sailing-ship, are employed, while air transport for light freight and mail is widely used.

(2) See *transportation* (2).

transportation. (1) A term sometimes used, chiefly by American geographers, for the carriage of goods. See *transport* (1).

(2) The process by which loose material from the earth's crust is conveyed from one region to another. Some of the agents which wear away the land also carry the material with them. See *denudation*. Rivers are the chief agents of transportation, carrying material for immense distances, mud and sand being held in suspension and stones being rolled along the bed. Glaciers also bring material down from the mountains. See *moraine*. The sea moves material from the coast into deeper water, and carries sand and pebbles laterally along the coast. The wind carries dust, and to a lesser degree sand, for great distances. Sometimes the transported material remains temporarily where it is deposited, either on land or in the sea.

transverse coast. See *discordant coast*.

transverse valley. A valley which, instead of being parallel to the mountain range, cuts across it. See *longitudinal valley*.

travertine or **calcareous tufa.** A deposit of calcium carbonate produced by a spring rich in lime; the calcium carbonate was originally dissolved by the water of the spring, with the help of carbon dioxide from the atmosphere. Travertine is commonly deposited from a *hot spring*, e.g. at Mammoth Hot Springs, Yellowstone National Park, USA. It is sometimes known as calcareous *sinter*.

treaty port. First in China (1842) and later in Japan, a seaport, river port or inland city which was opened to foreign trade by treaty; foreign ships were permitted to load and unload, and foreign merchants to live there and own property. The most important of the treaty ports in China was Shanghai; Canton (Guangzhou) was another, and the remainder were situated mainly on the south-east coast. Extra-territorial rights in the treaty ports were surrendered in 1943.

trellis or **trellised drainage.** The type of drainage produced by *consequent rivers* (parallel to the *dip*) and *subsequent rivers* (parallel to the *strike*), forming a rectangular or trellised pattern.

trench. An elongated *deep* or trough in the floor of the ocean; e.g. the Marianas Trench in the W Pacific, the Tonga Trench in the SW Pacific. The term is also sometimes applied to a long deep valley.

triangulation. A method of surveying by constructing a network of triangles, enabling a large-scale *topographic map* to be drawn. A base-line is accurately measured, a landmark is viewed by *theodolite* from each end, and angular measurements permit the entire triangle to be constructed; the procedure is then repeated for further triangles. On British OS maps a triangulation station or pillar is indicated by a small triangle enclosing a point.

tributary. A river or stream which contributes its water to a main river by discharging it into the latter, from either side, and at any point along its course. Each tributary does not necessarily increase the width of the main river, for often the additional supply of water is carried off by increased rapidity of flow.

Patterns of streams illustrating trellised drainage.

troglodyte. The inhabitant of a cave or rock shelter.

tropical cyclone or **tropical revolving storm.** A region of low atmospheric pressure, relatively small in area but accompanied by violent storm conditions, which originates in tropical regions; it is similar, in fact, to a *depression*, but smaller and much more intense. Winds of hurricane strength circulate round the centre or *'eye' of the storm*, their direction, as in the normal depression, following *Buys Ballot's Law*: in the northern hemisphere they circulate in an anti-clockwise, in the southern hemisphere in a clockwise direction. The 'eye' of the storm covers a restricted area, being often about 30 km in diameter; here the atmospheric pressure is excessively low, and the air is sometimes calm and the sky clear. The whole cyclone has a diameter of 150 to 300 km. The storm is accompanied by dense black clouds, torrential rain, and often thunder and lightning. The winds become less violent with increasing distance from the centre, but there is no abrupt transition to light winds. The cyclones follow fairly well-defined tracks, moving at an average speed of 15 to 25 km per hour, travelling first westwards, then polewards, and finally turning eastwards. They originate near the western flanks of the oceans, where warm tropical currents supply an abundance of water vapour, especially in waters studded with islands; differential heating over land and sea probably causes a small area of low atmospheric pressure to develop. Most of them originate in the equatorial belt of calms, the *doldrums*, when this belt is at its farthest limit from the equator; the necessary rotational movement can then form. They are thus most frequent in late summer and autumn. The necessary local conditions for development of a cyclone include a slack *pressure gradient* and very light winds, sultry weather, and an extensive area of falling atmospheric pressure. The tropical cyclone reaches its highest frequency in the China Seas, where it is known as a *typhoon*. The other areas in which it is known are the Bay of Bengal, the southern Indian Ocean (Madagascar–Mauritius region), West Indies – where it is called a *hurricane* – the SW Pacific (Fiji–Queensland region), the Arabian Sea, and off NW Australia – where it is called a *willy-willy*.

Losses at sea due to tropical cyclones are much smaller now than in the days of sailing ships. On land the storms tend to die out, but in passing from sea to land they often cause immense damage to coastal areas: buildings are destroyed; roads and railways are carried away; trees are uprooted and plantations ruined; moreover, thousands of lives have been lost, e.g. in China, Burma, India, and Pakistan. In recent years their destructiveness has been reduced, since they can be located and tracked by radar or satellite.

tropical grassland. See *savanna*.

tropical rain forest. See *equatorial forest*.

tropical revolving storm. See *tropical cyclone*.

Tropic of Cancer. The parallel of latitude, roughly $23\frac{1}{2}°$ N, indicating the extreme northern positions at which the sun appears directly overhead at noon. The sun's rays shine vertically on the Tropic of Cancer at the summer *solstice* of the N hemisphere.

Tropic of Capricorn. The parallel of latitude, roughly $23\frac{1}{2}°$ S, indicating the extreme southern positions at which the sun appears directly overhead at noon. The sun's rays shine vertically on the Tropic of Capricorn at the winter *solstice* of the N hemisphere, which is the summer solstice of the S hemisphere.

tropics. (1) The *Tropic of Cancer* and *Tropic of Capricorn*.
(2) The region lying between the *Tropic of Cancer* and the *Tropic of Capricorn*, sometimes known as the torrid zone. Within the zone, the sun is directly overhead twice a year, its rays are never very oblique, and the weather in general, then, is always hot. The term is also often extended to include adjacent areas of rather higher latitude, i.e. as far as about 30° N and 30° S, where tropical conditions with respect to climate, etc., are to be found.

tropopause. In the atmosphere, the boundary between the *troposphere* and the *stratosphere*, where the *lapse rate* in the former abruptly changes. Its height varies from about 16 km above the earth's surface at the equator to about 8 km at the poles.

tropophyte. A plant which acts as a *hygrophyte* in one season, and a *xerophyte* in the other. Trees in the *savanna*, for instance, shed their leaves during the drought, temporarily becoming xerophytes, and

A glaciated valley, showing truncated spurs (T), *hanging valleys* (H) *and waterfalls* (W).

produce them again with the onset of the rains, becoming hygro-phytes.

troposphere. The lower layers of the *atmosphere*, i.e. those below the *stratosphere*, from which it is separated by the *tropopause*, extending from a height of about 11 km to the earth's surface in the temperate zone. Its depth, however, is very variable, being greatest at the equator (about 16 km), least at the poles (rather less than 8 km). Within the troposphere the air temperature normally falls with increasing height (see *lapse rate*); unlike the stratosphere, it is a turbulent, dusty zone, containing much water vapour and clouds.

trough. A *deep* or *trench* in the ocean floor, e.g. the Puerto Rico Trough in the N Atlantic. The term is also sometimes applied to a long deep valley.

trough of low pressure. An elongated area of low atmospheric pressure, normally forming an extension to a *depression* or low pressure area, like a valley running upwards from a deep basin; a *front* often lies along the middle of the trough. It is the opposite of the *ridge of high pressure*.

truck farming. The term used in the United States to denote the *intensive cultivation* of vegetables for market, thus corresponding to the term *market gardening* which is usually employed in Great Britain. Truck farming, however, appears to be more specialized, and truck farms are often situated farther from the markets than are market gardens; the name may be due to the extensive use of trucks (lorries) for transporting the produce to market, or is possibly derived from the French *troquer* (to truck or barter).

true horizon. See *horizon, rational, true* or *astronomical*.

truncated spur. In a glaciated valley, a former spur which was partly shaved off by the glacier when the latter moved down the valley.

trust territory. A territory administered for the United Nations by a member state after the end of World War II. Many trust territories were former *mandated territories*.

tsunami (Japanese) or **seismic sea wave.** A large sea wave occasionally experienced along the coasts of Japan and in other regions, especially in the Pacific Ocean, caused by an *earthquake* taking place on the ocean bed; it rises to greater and greater heights as it approaches the coastline, and on a single occasion has been known to cause the deaths by drowning of thousands of people. It is sometimes wrongly called a tidal wave.

tufa, calcareous. See *travertine*.

tuff. A rock formed from *volcanic ash* and *volcanic dust* which have been thrown out of a volcano during eruption and have been consolidated. If the ejected fragments are larger than volcanic ash, i.e. *lapilli*, the resulting rock may be termed *lapilli tuff*.

tumulus. See *barrow*.

tundra. The treeless plains of northern North America and northern Eurasia, lying principally along the Arctic Circle, and on the northern side of the *coniferous forests*. There is no corresponding major region in the southern hemisphere. For most of the year the mean monthly temperature is below freezing point, and winters are long and severe, the ground being covered with snow. The summers are short and warm, but even in July the mean monthly temperature does not rise above 10°C; relatively high temperatures may be reached during the daytime, but the subsoil, i.e. the ground a few centimetres below the surface, may be permanently frozen (see *permafrost*). This, and the strong, intensely cold winds of winter, make normal tree growth impossible, though there may be stunted willows, birches, etc. In summer, mosses and lichens appear in abundance and some flowering plants; much of the flat ground, where drainage is poor, then becomes swampy. *Glei soils* are characteristic of the tundra.

turbulence. The irregular movement of air in the lower layers of the atmosphere, i.e. to a height of about 600 m, where the wind blows in a series of gusts interspersed with lulls, with simultaneous changes of direction. Considerable mixing takes place, and the cooling of water vapour in the air may lead to the formation of cloud, which is usually of the low stratiform or 'layer' type (see *cloud*), e.g. *stratocumulus*. The term is also applied to the movements of air in the ascending and descending currents of an unstable atmosphere, due to uneven heating of the earth's surface or to irregularities in the relief, giving rise to 'bumpy' conditions in flying.

twilight. The faint light which illuminates the various regions of the earth before sunrise and after sunset; the interval during which the atmosphere is illuminated before sunrise (often known as the dawn) and after sunset. It is due primarily to the reflection of the sun's light from the upper layers of the atmosphere on the earth, while the sun itself is below the horizon. Morning twilight commences when the sun is 18° below the horizon, while evening twilight ends when the sun is also 18° below the horizon; each of these is termed the *astronomical twilight*. *Civil twilight* is recognized as beginning or ending when the sun is about 6° below the horizon, and is determined by the amount of light necessary to permit outdoor work. *Nautical twilight* begins or ends when the sun is 12° below the horizon, the illumination being then so poor that only the vague outlines of objects can be distinguished. The duration of twilight depends on the date and on the latitude of the observer; it is plainly much shorter in tropical regions than in higher latitudes. At midsummer there is a zone between the $48\frac{1}{2}$° parallel and the Arctic Circle (or Antarctic Circle) where twilight extends throughout the night for a certain period. The number of nights of continuous twilight increases polewards.

twister. See *tornado* (2).

typhoon. The *tropical cyclone* of the China Seas. It is experienced most frequently during the late summer and early autumn. The Philippine Islands lie in the direct track of many of the typhoons, and the coastal areas of southern China are also seriously affected. Like all tropical cyclones, the typhoons bring winds of tremendous strength and torrential rain, and destruction is often widespread, though the storms weaken as they cross the coastline and move inland. During the Swatow typhoon of August 1922, for instance, the sudden change of wind direction as the centre passed caused a huge wave to sweep over the town, and 50,000 lives were estimated to have been lost.

U

ubac (French). A mountain slope which is shaded from the sun's rays owing to the fact that it faces more or less polewards; the contrast in light and warmth with a sunny slope is thus considerable. See *adret*. The term is principally used in the Alps. The corresponding Italian term is opaco, the German schattenseite.

umbra. The central complete shadow of the earth or the moon in an *eclipse*; the term is also applied to other phenomena, e.g. to the central dark region of a *sunspot*.

underfit river. See *misfit river*.

undertow. The returning undercurrent from a wave breaking on the seashore.

upland. The higher land of a region, in contrast with the valleys and plains.

urstromtal (German). A term meaning literally 'ancient stream valley', applied to shallow valleys now occupied by sections of certain rivers crossing the North European Plain, such as the Elbe and the Oder. The Urstromtäler were created by streams of melt water flowing from the retreating ice sheet of the *Quaternary* period (see *Ice Age*), and explain the partial E–W courses and the right-angle bends of the generally NW-flowing rivers.

U-shaped valley. A *valley* which is U-shaped in cross-section, with a relatively level floor and steep sides, generally regarded as the product of glacial erosion: its characteristic shape is due to the gouging action of a *glacier* as it moved down a former river valley, sometimes straightening the valley and planing off projecting spurs (see *truncated spur*).

uvala (Serbo-Croat). In a *karst region*, a depression larger than a *sinkhole* or a *doline*, and often formed by the coalescence of several dolines, extending in diameter to a kilometre or more; it is, however, smaller than a *polje*.

V

vadose water. Water that lies between the *water table* and the earth's surface.

val (French). A term used, chiefly in the Jura Mountains, for a *longitudinal valley*. See *cluse*.

vale. A valley, usually of a broad, level type.

valley. A long, narrow depression in the earth's surface, usually with a fairly regular downward slope. A river or stream usually flows through it, having carved it out from the surface rocks, and it is then known as a *river valley*: except in arid regions, the valley and the watercourse normally end together in the ocean, a lake, or another river. When a valley is young, it is narrow and its sides are steep; if the land is high, it has a steep gradient, unless it is very far from the sea, and it becomes deep. At this stage it is somewhat V-shaped in cross-section, and its tributaries are short. When a valley is mature, it is wider, its sides are often gentler, and its tributaries are longer. An old valley is very wide, has a broad *flood-plain* and a slight gradient: in fact, its surface is reduced almost to a plain, or to a *peneplain*. A valley carved out by a glacier is U-shaped in cross-section. See *U-shaped valley*, *V-shaped valley*, *longitudinal valley*, *transverse valley*, *rift valley*, *dry valley*, *hanging valley*.

valley glacier. * A *glacier* which originates at high altitude and flows down a valley; most glaciers are of this kind. It is also known as an Alpine glacier, probably because this type of glacier was first studied in the Alps.

valley line. See *thalweg*.

valley train. * The deposit of rock material carried down by a stream originating from the melting ice of a glacier, and thus formed in a similar way to an *outwash plain*; unlike the latter, however, it is not spread over a wide area, but is confined within the walls of a valley.

valley wind. The flow of air up a valley during the day, normally in quiet weather and with clear skies: the slopes are heated by the sun, so that the air immediately above is warmed and rises and flows up the valley. The valley wind frequently alternates with the nocturnal *mountain wind*. See *anabatic wind*.

vapour trail. See *condensation trail*.

vardarac. A cold wind that blows from the mountains down the valleys of Macedonia, including that of the R Vardar, from which the name is derived. It is a similar type of wind to the *mistral*.

variation, magnetic. See *declination, magnetic*.

varve. A pair of sediments, consisting of a lower coarse layer, usually silt, and an upper finer layer, usually clay, deposited in a lake, or the sea, from inflowing streams. By counting the varves, it has been possible to estimate the number of years since the end of the last *Ice Age*, for the coarser layer was the deposit of spring and summer, when the ice of the marginal lakes thawed, and the finer layer that of autumn and winter, when suspended material slowly sank, the lake surface above being frozen; each varve thus represents the deposit of exactly one year. The sediments are known as varved clays or varved sediments.

várzea (Portuguese). In the Amazon basin of Brazil, the low-lying areas of the *flood-plain* of the river and its tributaries, covered with denser, more varied forest than that on the *terra firme* with which they are interspersed.

vauclusian spring. In a *karst region*, a spring composed of water which has flowed through the limestone as an underground stream and issues at a point where the limestone overlies a layer of impervious rock: so named after the Fontaine de Vaucluse, in southern France.

veering. The clockwise change of direction of a wind, e.g. from E through S E to S. It is the opposite change of direction to *backing*.

vega (Spanish). In Spain, irrigated land from which only one crop per year is obtained, in contrast to the *huerta*.

vegetation, natural. See *natural vegetation*.

vein. A crack or fissure in a rock which contains mineral matter deposited from solution. Metallic ores often occur in veins, and mines are located round them; much of the world's gold, silver, lead, etc., is found in such situations. The ores of these metals do not usually fill the cracks, but are often associated with a much larger amount of valueless mineral matter, which must be worked over to extract the ores which are valuable. The term is also applied to any layer of rock which has some economic value, e.g. a vein of ironstone. See *lode*.

veld (Afrikaans). Elevated, open country in South Africa, especially in the Transvaal, which might be considered suitable for grazing, forming part of the great *tableland*. It is often divided into the High Veld, standing about 1,500 to 2,000 m above sea level, the Middle Veld, and the Low Veld, standing about 300 to 900 m above sea level. The High Veld consists of rolling, treeless *grasslands*, broken here and there by *kopjes*, and corresponds to the *steppes*, *prairies*, and *pampas*. The Middle Veld is marked by *rands* as well as kopjes, and these are often covered with scrub. Rands and kopjes also occur in the Low Veld, though the region is generally uniform and is covered with scrub. Besides being divided according to altitude, as above, certain sections of the veld are sometimes classified according to soil, e.g. sand veld, or natural vegetation, e.g. bush veld.

vendavales. Strong, squally, south-westerly winds experienced in the

Straits of Gibraltar and off the east coast of Spain. Being associated with depressions, they blow chiefly in winter, and bring considerable rain.

ventifact. A stone or pebble which has been shaped by wind-blown sand, usually in a desert, so that its surface consists of flat facets with sharp edges. The term dreikanter is sometimes used for ventifacts, but it wrongly suggests that the pebbles always have three facets.

veranillo (Spanish). In tropical America (e.g. Colombia), a short, dry season which breaks the rainy season. See *verano*.

verano (Spanish). In tropical America (e.g. Colombia), the long dry season. See *veranillo*.

vernal equinox. See *equinox*.

virazon. The *sea breeze* experienced on the west coasts of Peru and Chile. See *terral*.

visibility. In meteorology, the greatest distance at which an object can be seen with the 'naked eye' by an observer, expressed in metres (yards) or kilometres (miles); in the regular reports used on the *weather chart* the visibility is normally estimated by the observer. Visibility is impaired by the presence in the air of minute water drops (see *mist*) or dust and smoke particles (see *haze*), and varies markedly from one *air mass* to another.

visible horizon. See *horizon, sensible* or *visible*.

viticulture. The culture of the grape vine.

voe (Gaelic). A narrow bay or inlet into the sea coast, chiefly in the Shetlands: e.g. Sullom Voe, in recent times the site of an important oil terminal; Dury Voe, etc.

volcanic ash. Fine particles of *lava* which have been ejected from a *volcano* in eruption. The particles are rather coarser than those of *volcanic dust*, but the two terms are sometimes used interchangeably.

volcanic bomb. A lump of *lava*, usually rounded in shape, which has been thrown out of a *volcano* in the liquid state, solidifying as it fell. It varies in diameter from a few centimetres to several decimetres.

volcanic cinders. See *lapilli*.

volcanic dust. Fine particles of *lava* which have been thrown out by a *volcano* in eruption, having been blown into small particles by the force of the explosion. Sometimes the dust is shot high into the air, and is then carried immense distances by the wind. After the great eruption of Krakatoa in 1883, for example, volcanic dust was carried over a large proportion of the earth's surface, and gave sunsets of exceptional vividness for several days.

volcanic neck or **plug.*** A mass of solidified *lava* filling the central vent of a *volcano*. It is sometimes left isolated after the remainder of the cone has been removed by *denudation*.

volcano.* A vent in the earth's crust caused by *magma* forcing its way to the surface; molten rock, or *lava*, is finally ejected, sometimes with

Section through a volcano, showing volcanic neck, sill, and dyke.

explosive force, rock fragments and ashes being thrown into the air. The emissions of lava, or *eruptions*, often cause the volcano to take the form of a conical hill or mountain; the latter is gradually built up of ejected material, which is deposited most thickly round the outlet. Eruptions take place from the top or sides of the cone. They may be due to the production of steam, formed when water percolating through the ground meets the hot magma: dense clouds of steam generally accompany a volcanic eruption, and most volcanoes are situated near to the sea. They may be due, too, to the forces set up by earth movements. A volcano is regarded as *active*, *dormant*, or *extinct*. When it is not in action, the pipe leading down from its *crater* is usually plugged with solidified lava (see *volcanic neck* or *plug*). Of the solid, liquid, and gaseous substances ejected from a volcano during an eruption, the liquid materials are of greatest significance, forming the streams of lava which flow out of its crater or out of openings in its side. With some volcanoes the overflow of lava takes place quietly, and generally covers a wide area; Mauna Loa, on Hawaii, is of this type, and is termed a *shield volcano*. Others erupt with explosive violence; Mont Pelée, on the island of Martinique, was of this kind: in 1902 it destroyed the entire city of St Pierre and almost all the 28,000 inhabitants. Others are of an intermediate type, liable at times to erupt explosively; Vesuvius, in Italy, provides an example. Volcanoes are sometimes classified, in fact, according to the type of eruption to which they are subject: e.g. (in order of increasing explosiveness) Hawaiian, Strombolian (after Stromboli), Vulcanian (after Vulcano), Vesuvian, Peléan. Volcanoes are situated along the lines of weakness in the earth's crust, one of which runs right round the Pacific Ocean; there is thus a chain of active and recently extinct volcanoes along the eastern rim of Australasia and Asia, continued down the western rim of North and South America. See *mud volcano*, *composite volcano*.

volcanology. See *vulcanology*.

V-shaped depression. A term formerly applied to a *trough of low pressure*, in which the isobars take the shape of a letter V.

V-shaped valley. A *valley* which is V-shaped in cross-section, usually the product of down-cutting by a river. Vertical *corrasion* is rapid when the river is young, so that the valley is narrow and steep-sided. At a later stage the vertical corrasion becomes slower, and the V is widened owing to erosion of the valley walls. With old age the V is widened still more and the valley becomes broad, open, and almost flat.

vulcanicity, vulcanism or **volcanism.** The range of processes by which *magma*, together with associated solid and gaseous materials, rises into the earth's crust or is ejected on to its surface; thus it is more comprehensive than the mere activities of volcanoes. See *intrusive rocks*, *extrusive rocks*.

vulcanology or **volcanology.** The scientific study of volcanoes.

W

wadi (Arabic). A desert watercourse which is usually dry, and contains water only occasionally, after heavy rainfall. The wadis generally lose themselves in the desert; they may originate in the desert itself, or in the melting snows of distant mountains. The term is mainly used of the Sahara and the Arab countries of south-west Asia. See *arroyo*, *nullah*.

Wallace's line. A line, first described by the British naturalist A. R. Wallace (1823–1913), which divides the islands of Borneo and Bali on one side from Celebes and Lombok (Indonesia) on the other side; the native fauna on the two sides are so different that the line is held to separate two distinct regions, the Oriental and the Australian, in *zoo-geography*.

wapentake. In England, historically (from about the tenth century), a part of a county – especially in Yorkshire, Derbyshire and elsewhere in the Midlands – equivalent to the *hundred* in other districts. Derived from a Scandinavian term, it was common in regions where the Danes held considerable influence.

warm front. The boundary line at the earth's surface between a mass of advancing warm air and the cooler air over which it rises. The frontal surface between warm and cold air rises at a slighter angle than in the case of the *cold front*, the average slope being about 1 in 140. The movement of the warm air over the cooler air leads to the formation of considerable cloud and usually precipitation ahead of the front, and after it has passed there is generally either slight rain or drizzle or no precipitation at all. The passage of a warm front through a place is thus normally marked by a rise in temperature, a slackening or cessation of precipitation, and a veer of wind. Warm fronts occur mainly in the middle and higher latitudes, especially during winter, when the *depressions* with which they are usually associated are most prevalent.

warm sector. The region of warm air lying between the *cold front* and the *warm front* of a typical *depression*; low cloud and drizzle are often associated with it. As the depression moves along, the cold front gradually overtakes the warm front, amalgamating with it to form an *occlusion*, and the warm sector thus often disappears at the earth's surface, though still existing in the upper air.

warm wave. An abnormal rise in temperature experienced in temperate

Upward movement of warm air at a warm front (broken arrow) and direction of movement of the front.

regions when warm air is introduced from lower latitudes, either ahead of a *depression* moving eastwards towards the area or to the west of an *anticyclone*. The term is principally used in the United States, where such warm waves occur during the summer in the central and eastern states.

water cycle or **hydrologic cycle.** The circulation of water from the oceans to the atmosphere, thence to the land, and so back to the oceans: *evaporation* takes place from the oceans (also from lakes, rivers, etc. – see *evapotranspiration*); *condensation* of the water vapour in the atmosphere leads to the formation of clouds and thus to *precipitation* as rain or snow; most of the water which has fallen on the land then returns to the oceans – so completing the cycle.

waterfall.* A sudden fall of water, usually caused by a bed of hard rock in a river course, either horizontal or dipping gently upstream, overlying softer rocks. The softer rocks beneath are worn away by the river, so that the hard rock overhangs, and thus produces the waterfall. The layer of hard rock is undermined by the falling water, and from time to time blocks of it are broken away; the waterfall thus slowly recedes upstream, its crest always remaining on the edge of the layer of hard rock. The best-known example of this retreat of a waterfall is provided by Niagara Falls. A waterfall is also formed when a vertical mass of resistant rock extends across the bed of the stream; in this case the fall does not recede, but is gradually lowered as the surface of the hard rock is worn down. A waterfall is formed, too, when a stream descends from a *hanging valley*, or plunges over the edge of a *plateau*. Waterfalls impede navigation, but are of great value in providing *water power*. See *rapids*.

water gap. A narrow gorge cut by a river or stream through a ridge. One of the best-known is the Delaware Water Gap, USA, where the Delaware River has cut through the sandstone of the Kittatinny

The watershed (broken line) between two river basins.

Mountain ridge; another is the Goring Gap, England, where the Thames cuts through the chalk between the Chilterns and the Berkshire Downs.

water hemisphere. That half of the globe which consists principally of ocean, lying mainly south of the equator; it is the opposite hemisphere to the *land hemisphere*, has its centre near New Zealand and contains only about one-seventh of the total land surface of the globe.

water-parting. See *watershed*.

water power. Energy obtained from natural or artificial waterfalls, and used either directly by turning a water wheel or a turbine, or indirectly by the generation of electricity in dynamos driven by turbines. See *hydro-electric power*.

watershed, water-parting, or **divide.** The elevated boundary line separating the headstreams which are tributary to different river systems or basins. It often has an extremely irregular course, and does not necessarily follow the ridge of a range of hills or mountains. As rivers encroach upon each other's territory (see *river capture*), any watershed should·be regarded as temporary. American geographers use the term watershed as synonymous with *river basin*, employing water-parting or divide to denote the boundary line between river systems. A *continental divide* is a line which separates the rivers flowing towards opposite sides of a continent. (See Fig. p. 238.)

waterspout. A funnel-shaped mass of cloud and water, similar to a *tornado* but occurring at sea, more often observed in tropical and subtropical waters than in those of higher latitudes. A portion of cloud shaped like an inverted cone appears to descend from a heavy *cumulonimbus* cloud till it meets a cone of spray raised from the sea, and a column or spout of water is formed between sea and cloud. The waterspout may be several hundred metres high, and may last up to half an hour. Strong winds circulate round it in its immediate neighbourhood. Its top often travels at a different speed from its base, it becomes oblique or bent, and finally breaks and disappears.

water table or **level of saturation.** The surface of the *ground water*, or the surface below which the pores of a rock are saturated with water; this surface is uneven, and it is also variable. When rainfall is protracted, the pores of the rock become filled with water, some of which emerges at the junction of the permeable or porous rock and the underlying impermeable rock in the form of springs. As the water at the base of the porous rock runs out, the water table falls. During wet weather the water table rises, during dry weather it falls, but there are usually limits above which it never rises and below which it never falls. The lowest level to which the water table sinks in a certain locality is known as the *permanent water table*.

weather. The condition of the atmosphere at a certain time or over a certain short period, as described by various meteorological phenomena, including atmospheric pressure, temperature, humidity, rainfall, cloudiness, and wind speed and direction. Near to the equator, the weather changes so little that it is almost synonymous with *climate*.

weather chart or **synoptic chart.** A chart or map on which are plotted details relating to the weather over the area represented; these details refer to a definite instant of time, e.g. 1200 hours GMT (12 o'clock GMT), and are collected at meteorological stations in the form of coded weather reports from a large number of observation posts. A continuous series of charts is plotted relating to certain recognized times during the day, usually at six-hourly or three-hourly intervals. When all the available observations for the area have been plotted, the isobars are drawn, usually at intervals of 2 millibars, and the main meteorological features inserted – *depressions, anticyclones, fronts*, etc. Such a weather chart is often known as a synoptic chart, for it presents a synopsis of the meteorological situation at a certain time. Weather forecasts are prepared from the study of a sequence of such charts.

weathering.* The decay and disintegration of the rocks of the earth's crust by exposure to the atmosphere; it is one of the main processes of *denudation* and may be classified as either *mechanical* or *chemical weathering*. Solution is one form of weathering, e.g. the solution of rock salt in water. One of the most effective agents of disintegration is rain water containing carbon dioxide from the atmosphere; this dilute solution of carbonic acid readily dissolves the calcium carbonate of *limestone*, forming soluble calcium bicarbonate, a process known as *carbonation*. This is an example of chemical weathering. Oxidation, followed by disintegration, is carried out by rain water containing oxygen from the air, particularly on ferriferous minerals. Hydration, whereby a mineral combines with water to form a new compound, may lead to disintegration or solution. Both oxidation and hydration are further examples of chemical weathering.

The heat of the sun causes rocks to expand, and the subsequent cooling causes them to contract, the alternate expansion and contraction leading to the cracking and breaking of the rocks near the surface. This effect is most noteworthy in the hot deserts, where the temperature changes are usually rapid. In higher latitudes frost is a more powerful agent. Rain water fills the cracks and pores of the rocks, and expands on freezing, exerting a great pressure on the rocks; the alternate thawing and freezing in time break up the rocks. Otherwise, the work of the rain and also the wind is usually excluded from weathering, for, involving transportation, it belongs more strictly to *erosion*.

wedge of high pressure. A *ridge of high pressure*, in which the isobars are V-shaped.

well. An underground source of water which has been rendered accessible by the drilling or digging of a hole from ground level to the *water table*; the water may then be raised or pumped to the surface. If a well is sunk to the water table of the wet season, but not as far as the lowest or permanent water table, it will contain water during the wet season but not during the dry season; if it reaches the permanent water table, however, it will always contain water. See *artesian well*. The term is also used in connection with oil deposits, i.e. oil well.

westerlies. The westerly winds which blow with great frequency in regions lying on the poleward sides of the sub-tropical high pressure areas or *horse latitudes*; the areas in which they blow are often known as the 'regions of the westerlies'. In winter they move southwards in the northern hemisphere, affecting the Mediterranean regions and much of the horse latitudes, bringing winter rain to those areas; in summer they move northwards again. From about 40° N to the Arctic Circle, and from about 35° S to the Antarctic Circle, however, they blow throughout the year. The winds derive their name from the prevailing direction; in the northern hemisphere this is mainly south-westerly, in the southern hemisphere north-westerly. Unlike the *trade winds*, they are very variable in force and direction, especially in the northern hemisphere, where the winds may be easterly for a considerable period.

The weather in this area is marked by an almost constant procession of *depressions* and *anticyclones* moving eastwards, and is made more complex in the northern hemisphere by the alternation of oceans and continents; on the eastern side of Asia, for instance, the effect of the westerlies is broken by the *monsoons*. In winter the North Atlantic Ocean is probably the stormiest region of the globe, at any season, but in summer the winds and weather are much less violent. In the southern hemisphere, on the other hand, the westerlies blow with great strength and regularity throughout the year over the almost unbroken expanse of ocean, and have given the name *roaring forties* to the region.

wet bulb temperature. The temperature registered by a wet bulb thermometer, an ordinary thermometer whose bulb is enclosed by a small piece of muslin which is kept constantly moist by a wick dipping into a small water-bottle. The thermometer thus registers the atmospheric temperature reduced by evaporation from a moist surface, the degree of cooling depending upon the rate of evaporation. The difference between the readings of the dry bulb thermometer and the wet bulb thermometer in relation to the air temperature gives a measure of the *relative humidity*, and tables have been prepared for interpreting the readings; a very slight difference indicates the extreme dampness or high relative humidity of the air, for there is then very little evaporation from the surface of the wet bulb thermometer, and a considerable difference indicates the comparative dryness or low relative humidity of the air. See *hygrometer*.

wet day. In the British Isles, a period of 24 hours from 0900 hours GMT on which 1.0 mm or more of rain is recorded. See *rain day*.

wet spell. In the British Isles, a period of at least fifteen consecutive days each of which has had 1.0 mm of rain or more; the definition has not been internationally accepted. See *dry spell*.

wheat belt. That part of the *prairies* of North America on which wheat is extensively cultivated; it lies east of the Rocky Mountains, and stretches from northern Alberta in Canada to northern Texas in the USA, and is one of the most important wheat-growing areas in the world. In recent years the United States has been second and Canada about fifth in world production (the USSR being first).

wheat crescent. The crescent-shaped area extending round the drier, western margin of the South American *pampas*, on which wheat is widely cultivated; it has enabled Argentina to become one of the leading world exporters of wheat.

whirlpool. A circular eddy in the sea or in a river produced by the configuration of the channel, or by the meeting of two currents, or from similar causes. See *maelstrom*.

whirlwind. A small column of air rotating rapidly round a vertical or slightly inclined axis, having an area of low atmospheric pressure at its centre. It sometimes extends to a considerable height, and in a desert may cause a *duststorm*, or, on a smaller scale, a *dust devil*.

'white horses' or **whitecaps.** The broken white crests of sea waves, produced by the wind.

white man's grave. The name formerly applied to the lands along the Guinea coast, West Africa, more especially to the district around Freetown, capital of Sierra Leone. The atmosphere is almost perpetually hot and humid, the winds being mainly from the Gulf of Guinea; the drier and healthier *harmattan* from the north-east rarely reaches this coastal area. In view of the progress made in recent years in combating tropical diseases, the name is no longer applicable.

williwaw. A violent *squall* experienced in the Strait of Magellan where the winds are almost constantly strong and westerly.

willy-willy. The *tropical cyclone* experienced over north-west Australia, mainly in late summer. It originates in the hot Timor Sea, and moves first south-westwards, often causing severe losses to the pearl fishing industry; then it recurves to the south-east, crosses the coast, where it causes more damage and brings heavy rain, and moves overland towards the Great Australian Bight. In the interior the willy-willy soon loses its violence, and it is generally welcomed there for the rain that it brings. The term is also applied to *whirlwinds* that occur over the Australian deserts – including the relatively small *dust devils*.

wind. A current of air, moving with speed in any direction, but generally assumed to be parallel to the earth's surface. The direction of a wind is indicated by the point of the compass from which it blows: e.g. a south wind is one which blows from the south. The speed of a wind is usually given in kilometres or miles per hour, at sea in *knots*. Winds may be classified according to speed, e.g. on the *Beaufort scale*, and the actual velocities are measured by the *anemometer*.

windbreak or **shelterbelt.** A screen erected to afford protection from the wind, usually in the form of rows of trees – hence the term *shelterbelt*. The windbreak may be designed to shelter a farmhouse, for example, the trees being planted around the sides facing the prevailing wind, as a protection against duststorms in summer and snowstorms in winter. It may also be used to protect crops from a violent, cold wind, e.g. the *mistral*, or a hot wind, e.g. the *sirocco*, or to prevent *soil erosion* by the wind.

wind gap, dry gap or **air gap.** A narrow notch in a ridge, originally a *water gap*, from which the water that formerly flowed through has disappeared.

wind rose. A diagram illustrating the proportion of winds which blow from each of the main points of the compass at a certain place, taken over a considerable period; it thus shows the *prevailing wind* at a glance. In a simple form of wind rose, the proportion of winds blowing from the eight principal points of the compass is indicated by straight lines of varying length and true direction converging to a small circle; a number in the circle gives the percentage of cases in which the air

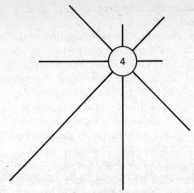

Simple type of wind rose.

was calm. In some forms of wind rose, the different forces of wind are also indicated, e.g. by varying the thickness of the lines.

wind vane. An instrument used to indicate the direction of the wind. It usually consists of a freely moving horizontal arm with a pointer at one end, and below this a fixed framework indicating the four *cardinal points* of the compass.

windward. The side or direction which faces the wind.

winter. For middle latitudes, the season following the *autumn* or *fall*, reckoned astronomically to last in the northern hemispheres from the winter *solstice* (about 22 December) to the spring *equinox* (about 21 March); in the southern hemisphere the dates correspond to the northern *summer*. See *seasons*.

winterbourne. In the chalk regions of southern England, a *bourne* or intermittent stream which flows only in the wetter part of the year, i.e. in winter.

wold. In England, a term which was derived from the Old English *weald* (forest), but later signified open hilly country, and in recent times has referred specifically to certain uplands of chalk, e.g. Lincolnshire Wolds, or limestone, e.g. Cotswolds.

wood. An extensive group of trees, or a small *forest*.

X

xerophyte.* A plant which is adapted to living in a region where little moisture is available, i.e. where *drought* conditions normally prevail. Its structure is modified in various ways in order that the maximum amount of water shall be obtained and conserved: roots are long or enlarged, leaves are small and thick, or even absent altogether, as in many cactus plants, being sometimes replaced by thorns; the stems are sometimes fleshy, enabling the plants to store water for extremely long periods; a thick bark or a coating of wax may protect the plant against transpiration.

Y

yardangs. In the deserts of Central Asia, the steep-sided, undercut, over-hanging ridges of rock, separated by long corridors which have been cut out by wind-borne sand, exemplifying wind *abrasion*; they are roughly parallel, and lie in the direction of the dominant wind. They may be as much as 6 m in height or over 30 m in width.

yazoo river. A *tributary* which is prevented from joining the main river because the latter has built up high natural *levees*; it therefore runs parallel to the main river for some considerable distance, eventually joining it much further downstream. The name is derived from the Yazoo River, tributary of the Mississippi, the classic example of this type of stream.

year. The period of time taken for the earth to complete one revolution in its orbit round the sun, or the period taken to complete the cycle of the *seasons*. Measured from one vernal *equinox* to the next, it equals 365 days, 5 hours, 48 minutes, 46 seconds; for ordinary purposes it is taken to be 365 days in length, and a *leap year* of 366 days is intro-duced every fourth year. See *calendar*.

Z

zenith. That point in the heavens, i.e. the *celestial sphere*, which is vertically above the observer. The *astronomical zenith* is defined as the point at which a plumb-line, extended upwards from the earth's surface, would intersect the celestial sphere; the *geographical zenith* is defined as the point at which the line perpendicular to the earth's surface intersects the celestial sphere. The two points do not always coincide.

zenithal or **azimuthal projection.** The type of *map projection* in which a portion of the globe is projected upon a plane tangent to it; it may thus be regarded as a special case of the *conical projection*, in which the cone is so flattened that it finally becomes a plane. As the name 'azimuthal' indicates, on this projection all points have their true compass directions from the centre of the map. The tangent plane on which the projection is made is not always tangent at the pole; in fact, it is usually tangent at some other point, which is to be the centre of the map. See *zenithal equal-area*, *zenithal equidistant*, *stereographic*, *gnomonic*, *orthographic projections*.

zenithal equal-area projection. A *zenithal projection* in which any area on the map truly represents the corresponding area on the globe. See *homolographic projection*.

zenithal equidistant projection. A *zenithal projection* in which distances from the centre of the map truly represent the corresponding distances on the globe.

zeugen (German). In deserts, the tabular masses of rock each of which consists of a pedestal of relatively soft rock capped by a layer of more resistant rock, resulting from differential erosion by windborne sand. They may rise to a height of more than 30 m.

zodiac. The zone of the heavens in which lie the paths of the sun, the moon, and the chief planets. It is divided into 12 signs (the signs of the zodiac), each sign being 30 degrees in extent counting from the position of the sun at the spring *equinox*, and is marked by 12 constellations. Each of the 12 months of the year is thus associated with one of the zodiacal constellations. The 12 signs of the zodiac are Aries, Taurus, Gemini, Cancer, Leo, Virgo, Libra, Scorpio, Sagittarius, Capricornus, Aquarius, and Pisces.

zonal soil. A soil which owes its well-developed characteristics largely to the influence of climate and vegetation. Zonal soils are divided into *pedalfers* and *pedocals*.

zonda. In Argentina and Uruguay, a hot, sultry wind bringing tropical air from the north, analogous to the Australian *brickfielder*, and usually preceding the *pampero*. It has a very enervating effect on the inhabitants. The name is also used for a warm, dry wind of the *föhn* type which blows from the Andes, similar to the *chinook* of North America.

zones. The five regions or belts into which the earth has sometimes been divided. They are the areas within the *Arctic Circle* and the *Antarctic Circle*, called respectively the North and South *frigid zones*; the area between the Arctic Circle and the *Tropic of Cancer*, and the area between the Antarctic Circle and the *Tropic of Capricorn*, known respectively as the North and South *temperate zones*; and the area on both sides of the equator between the Tropics of Cancer and Capricorn, known as the *torrid zone*. This division is geographically inexact for it takes no account of variations due to altitude, proximity to the oceans, etc., and a much more useful division is that into *climatic regions* or *natural regions*. The term is also widely used in the sense of 'regions' of various types, e.g. *abyssal* zone, *time* zone.

zone time. See *standard time*.

zoogeography. The study of the distribution of animals on the earth's surface.

zoophyte. An animal which resembles a plant, e.g. a *coral polyp*, a sponge.